Critical
Perspectives
on
Democracy

Critical
Perspectives
on
Democracy

Edited by

Lyman H. Legters,
John P. Burke,
and
Arthur DiQuattro

Rowman & Littlefield Publishers, Inc.

ROWMAN & LITTLEFIELD PUBLISHERS, INC.

Published in the United States of America
by Rowman & Littlefield Publishers, Inc.
4720 Boston Way, Lanham, Maryland 20706

3 Henrietta Street, London WC2E 8LU, England

British Cataloging in Publication Information Available

Library of Congress Cataloging-in-Publication Data

Critical perspectives on democracy / edited by Lyman H. Legters,
John P. Burke, Arthur DiQuattro.
p.   cm.
Includes bibliographical references and index.
1. Democracy.   I. Legters, Lyman Harold, 1928–   .
II. Burke, John P.   III. DiQuattro, arthur.
JC423.C747   1994   821.8—dc20   94-8612 CIP

ISBN 0–8476–7888–1 (cloth : alk. paper)
ISBN 0–8476–7889–X (pbk. : alk. paper)

Printed in the United States of America

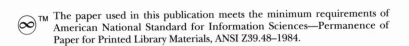 The paper used in this publication meets the minimum requirements of
American National Standard for Information Sciences—Permanence of
Paper for Printed Library Materials, ANSI Z39.48–1984.

Contents

Acknowledgments

It is not through the work of authors and editors alone that a book is published, but by the combined efforts of many different people. The editors gratefully acknowledge the assistance of Lila Abel, Marcia Bastian, and Kim Henderlite, whose contributions were indispensable in preparation of the manuscript for publication. Throughout the final stages of production, Kim Henderlite maintained her customary enthusiasm, patience, and cheerful good nature, thereby enabling us to bring this project to completion. Julie Kirsch and her editorial staff at Rowman & Littlefield were also generous in their assistance, encouragement, and support and deserve mention here.

Introduction

Lyman H. Legters
John P. Burke
Arthur DiQuattro

As the title of this book suggests, there are ways of looking at democracy that go beyond the registration of preference among the existing, available options for the governance of a society. These all begin by taking seriously the defining property of democracy, self-governance, and the rules and institutional forms required to effectuate democracy. Proceeding in this way, it is possible to conclude that other values should override the claims of democratic self-governance. Henry David Thoreau's essay *On Civil Disobedience* strikes out in this direction, as do most other varieties of radical individualism. What is not possible within this framework, however, is an unconditional endorsement of any existing system as satisfactorily democratic. If democracy is a value or norm—the highest or one among several—it always stakes out a critical vantage point for the contemplation of actual practice and may even, in certain circumstances, count as a revolutionary demand. Indeed, the experience of Eastern Europe since 1917 suggests that, as between socialism and democracy, the latter may be at least the prior if not also more fundamental requirement for and index of social transformation.

If this way of looking at democracy seems arcane, out of step with the actualities of our political life, it is because our vocabulary of public discussion is typically uncritical. We apply the term "democracy" to what we already have and to the condition that we generously recommend to others, seldom asking what standard or principle justifies our implied claim. Rhetoric thus displaces critical, rational discourse.

Public discourse is always subject to two opposed tendencies. One favors greater accuracy and clarity: its proponents labor to refine the concepts and vocabulary of politics in the interest of a more rational style of conducting public business. The other prefers the murkiness of slogans and meaningless locution: its agents engage, whether through laziness, ideological commitment, or ignorance, in constant debasement of the language in which public concerns must be expressed.

At first glance it might seem that we are speaking here of scholars and intellectuals on the one hand, politicians and advertisers on the other. But such a conclusion would be much too facile. We are all familiar with instances in which scholars and intellectuals, whether wittingly or not, defend positions in which they have a vested interest in defiance of corrective evidence. And we should be familiar with one of the landmark cases from our own history, *The Federalist Papers*, in which clarification and precision were greatly furthered by politicians. The fact is that neither the urge to debase nor the impulse to clarify is the exclusive possession of any one social group or stratum.

It might also seem that these comments pertain only to a limited range of social orders—those that make explicit provision for and give some encouragement to discussion of public concerns and options. But that too would oversimplify. Hitler's Germany and Stalin's Soviet Union together probably represent the apogee of governing systems that have sought to suppress public discourse by imposing ideological straitjackets on symbolic observance and public utterance. Yet even that most passive style of resistance in the Third Reich, "inner migration" so-called, contained within itself a public discourse in embryo, mostly clandestine to be sure, devoted to the unmasking of official lies. Minimal as such discourse was, it formed a bridgehead on the basis of which accuracy and precision could be reintroduced once the suppression was lifted. A better example, from the Soviet Union, would be the phenomenon known as *samizdat*, the surreptitious circulation of opinion and argument not sanctioned by the regime. It had the twin functions of keeping a precise public discourse alive and of reclaiming from state monopoly a small fraction of the publishing enterprise, and in effect it permitted rational public discourse to survive until such time as it could be practiced openly. The struggle to preserve rational public discussion in the face of ideological dictates is, thus, indissolubly joined to movements of resistance to the regime that enforces them. And it becomes more readily understandable that the effort to correct the historical record should loom so large in oppositional movements such as Solidarity in Poland. The reinterment of Imre Nagy in Hungary and the acknowledgment in public of responsibility for the Katyn Forest massacre figure symbolically as belated or retrospective restorations of rational public discourse.

This characterization of the survival of public discourse under extreme conditions of ideological repression, and of the revival of a reinforced commitment to rational discussion when repression is relaxed, entails a risk. It could induce complacency about the prospect for a genuine and unfettered public discourse in the much less extreme circumstances of relatively open societies.

Such complacency would of course be misplaced, for, if it is an uphill struggle to preserve a semblance of public discussion in systems such as the Third Reich and a Stalinist Soviet political order, it may also be a struggle, albeit one of a different sort, to maintain public discourse where repression is either absent or covert. Indeed, the very point of noting the extreme cases of repression has been to underscore the rapidity with which honest discourse is reinstated once the machinery of repression is dismantled.

In societies that think of themselves as free, it is precisely complacency that allows a debased vocabulary of public discussion to prevail. Whereas repression at least invites challenge (even as it penalizes it), a mindless reliance on slogans tends to induce civic somnolence, the obverse of rational disputation. When a political culture allows or even encourages this debasement of public discourse, the effort to reinstate serious discussion is as difficult—and as important—as it is to do so in the face of a repressive official ideology.

As must be evident by now, we are proposing a distinction more central to our subject than the one between free speech and repression. The difference between rational, truth-seeking public discussion and mere expression of sentiment (whether the latter is an enforced ideology or simply an evasion or perversion of genuine civic concerns) operates in open and closed societies and is equally vital in both. In a closed society the struggle for authentic public discourse is a means for overcoming repression; in an open society it is a means for preserving the free exercise of citizenship.

Another way of phrasing the distinction is to speak of the normative versus the uncritically descriptive elements of public discourse. In the heyday of the Soviet model, as it prevailed at home and in the Soviet client states, the usual way of characterizing (defining) socialism was to describe what actually existed; and the accepted route to socialism was the path actually taken to reach that state. Absent a normative theory of what socialism should be, the authorities proclaimed (and enforced) the existent, substituting description for norm or principle. It was this perversion of legitimate discourse that gave rise, especially among domestic socialist critics of the prevailing order, to the ironic locution, "already existing socialism." (When the authorities used that phrase, it was an attempt to depict normative conceptions as utopian; the critics, on the other hand, could rely on their fellow citizens to understand the sarcasm in their usage.)

In the case of our own society and, more broadly, of all the Western societies that are conventionally labeled democracies, it might be appropriate to speak of "already existing democracy." Although the deviations from democratic norms are substantially different, the relevance of a normative test is the same. Unless we are content with a merely descriptive approach to democracy, the claims and professions of American and West European polities require scrutiny, the more so as public life in all those societies becomes more and more blatantly image-ridden, more and more flagrantly conducted in the terms of slogan and sound-bite. The realization of a healthy public discourse seems even more remote here than it is in the newly independent states of Eastern Europe.

In both places there are of course numbers of convinced democrats, people of critical disposition who understand how drastically political actuality deviates from democratic norms. But there is also, in both places, much promiscuous talk of democracy, incantation rather than analysis, that fosters complacency instead of encouraging efforts to achieve genuine self-governance. In our own public discourse, the fallacy is double-edged. We misunderstand the situation in Eastern Europe, imagining that because a hated, undemocratic system has been overthrown and because our own system seems to have become attractive there, democracy has been achieved—when in reality there is as yet very little real democracy and the prospect of attaining it is at best uncertain. And such wishful thinking in turn reinforces complacency about our own practices and preserves the debased currency of discourse about democracy.

This collection of essays aspires to make a contribution to the other tendency in public discourse, that of clarifying and making more precise the way in which we discuss public concerns. Ron Perrin initiates this discussion in "Rehabilitating Democratic Theory: The Prospects and the Need," with criticism of "realistic" approaches to the study of democracy. Most of these focus on the procedural aspects of democratic practice: competing political parties, constitutional checks, and technical problems attached to the aggregation of majority preferences into public policy. But what, Perrin asks, are the justifying values of the procedures and how do we know that voting outcomes have identified the general interest without some sense of what we are looking for? In a unique application of the critical theorizing of Jürgen Habermas and Hans-Georg Gadamer to American political thought, Perrin seeks a revitalization of normative democratic theory that provides a cognitive foundation for the justification of democratic values. He hopes to find such a grounding in the American political community, but immediately runs up against the results of studies (Robert Bellah et al.) that document the eclipse of community in America. It is hardly a coincidence, Perrin notes, that the rise of "realism" in American political science has proceeded alongside the breakdown of social cohesion: "Bellah's subjects are living out the rationality of the new realism." What, then, are the prospects for working up a normative democratic theory?

Because Perrin rejects normative theory as a "process of speculating upon transcendent values" and instead sees it as "a discussion democracy is having with itself," the task is to get the right kind of discussion going; and that involves drawing out the latent values embedded in American political practice, values that Perrin traces to the Jeffersonian mix of civic republicanism and liberalism and their coming together in local political communities, neighborhoods, and voluntary associations. It is Jefferson's pursuit of intimations of community within liberalism that provides Americans with an indigenous resource to tackle the theoretical and practical crisis of the "new realism."

Timothy Kaufman-Osborn brings to bear postmodernist themes on the turning point of democratic theory and, although unhappy with the politics of the Enlightenment (and presumably with appeals to thinkers such as Thomas Jefferson), he concurs nonetheless with Perrin that decentralization and a healthy ("prephilosophical" and pragmatic) attitude toward modern bureaucracy and its instrumentalist bias is what we need to realize "the power of actions" and "the promise of democratic politics." In "The Politics of the Enlightenment: A Pragmatist Reconstruction," Kaufman-Osborn relies heavily on John Dewey's pragmatism to escape from a bureaucratic domination that runs so deep that it extends to the epistemological and ontological realms. "Pragmatism holds that the capacity of ordinary actors to craft rich qualitative sense from the everyday situations in which they find themselves is the ultimate test of knowledge's value." "Truth" and action within particular communities are inextricably tied, and democratic communities, if they are properly organized, give citizens the opportunity to register their versions of the real and valuable. This kind of democratic activity renders a bit less stubborn "the bars of Weber's iron cage," and so recovers "the integrity of civil society whose knowledge, expressed in the common sense of its members, remains embedded in the ground that nurtures it."

The classical question of whether an ideal society must be a democratic society appears unconventional within contemporary circles, which uncritically assume that it must. John P. Burke poses this question again in "Democracy and Citizenship," seeking to explore the value of democracy in both democratic theory and democratic practice. As he interprets them, neither Jean-Jacques Rousseau nor John Stuart Mill is a democrat without careful qualification, yet Mill can be taken to represent an "individualist" aspect in democratic theory whereas Rousseau represents a "communitarian" tendency. A notion of citizenship may be needed to mediate between these two tendencies in democratic theory. Unfortunately, at the level of one kind of democratic practice in the United States, citizenship seems to be in a sorry state, judging by the quality of a representative public discourse about public education in a nominally democratic society. Citizenship, Burke concludes, may be a value above democracy: providing a surrogate for community, a grounding value for democracy, and a measure for evaluating good societies. We should ask about the quality of citizenship, perhaps, instead of asking how democratic that society is.

The defining features of democracy—most notably, popular rule, the majority principle, and the most inclusive definition of citizenship—are simultaneously descriptive and normative. In "Democracy, Equality, and Racism," Lyman H. Legters elaborates on these procedural characteristics of democracy. Taking inspiration from Gunnar Myrdal's classic work on racism in America, Legters locates the substance of the democratic way of life in the value of equality. The "liberal" aspect of liberal democracy has historically stressed the primacy of property rights and stability. But it is the "democratic" aspect, tied conceptually and practically to the value of equal respect and concern for persons, that provides the deepest justification for democracy and the most valuable asset in combating racist institutions. Although Myrdal expresses the same insight from a different direction, Legters develops it by noting the combined power of moral suasion and participatory versions of popular rule in overcoming racial discrimination.

Majority rule is one of the most traditional ideas associated with democracy, but Iring Fetscher finds reason to question the sufficiency of the majority principle for democracy in "Democracy and the Majority Principle." He begins his critical analysis of the majority principle by invoking Rousseau's well-known distinction between the will of all and the general will. Fetscher reminds us that classical theories of democracy operated with class-restricted conceptions of the citizenry and thus of "the majority," and unrealistically assumed a homogenous society oriented toward common interests. In the contemporary period, we also find heterogeneous populations divided not solely because of wealth differentials but also because of regional differences and local conflicts with federal authorities. "Decisions of the central government intrude ever more deeply into the affairs of communities and provinces."

It is one thing for the majoritarian to stipulate that a majority should be a "qualified" (competent, informed, educated) majority and another thing to decide between such qualified majorities. In a conflict between a local affected majority and a general social "formal majority" or a "majority of federal officials," which majority should prevail if the issue is that of building a potentially hazardous nuclear plant? Should local affected majorities in such cases have "veto rights" even if a formal majority aiming for the general will has observed procedural, constitutional correctness? Perhaps being affected by decisions made by a more remote majority ("at the center") counts as an additional "qualification" in the voting or perhaps an "additional authorization" should be sought from the "locally affected majority" just because it will have to absorb the impact of a decision by a "society-wide majority."

One of the more suggestive and disturbing points raised by Fetscher, with implications for democracy, concerns the "right" and the means by which a minority may become a majority. Part of the moral acceptability of minority acceptance of majority decisions rests on corrigibility: today's minority may become tomorrow's majority and thus reverse the "mistaken" majority decision. But if some decisions are not reversible, easily or at all, this calls into question the morality of the minority's acceding to majority decisions and the majority principle. Without pretending to solve the problem or proposing to abandon majoritarian commitment altogether, Fetscher suggests that agreement "between qualified majorities" should perhaps be required on "high-impact" issues.

Joseph M. Schwartz integrates the moral insights of liberal and communitarian critiques of the welfare state and, by side-stepping the metaphysical and ontological debates that divide them, develops an explanation and defense of welfare provision based on democratic solidarity. As he shows in "Democratic Solidarity and the Crisis of the Welfare State," the U.S. welfare state is not a deduction from abstract philosophical principles but rather the result of the interaction—highlighted in the 1930s and 1960s—of policy makers, mass social movements, and corporate interests. Because the nature of the welfare state is the consequence of political struggle, economic development, and state policy, its resuscitation requires an accommodation of its historical origins to new developments, especially the decline of social solidarity and citizenship in the face of the advance of the politics of difference and the racial, sexual, and ethnic distinctions upon which this politics is based.

The communitarian and liberal emphases on solidarity and individual rights, respectively, can be brought together in the peculiarly American form of pluralism. The Rawlsian idea of overlapping consensus, so intuitively appealing on the *moral* plane, needs as a practical vehicle a strong *political* programme that recognizes diversity but does not yield to it. A unity among men and women, whites, blacks, ethnic groups, and low- and middle-income workers, is the requisite for forging alliances on the national and local levels. "Although diversity is a central value of a pluralist democracy, so too is the social solidarity derived from a sense of common citizenship. If human beings and the particular communities they belong to are to be accorded equal respect, they need to live in a society that guarantees those social rights necessary for each member to fulfill his or her human potential." Especially provocative in his concluding programmatic recommendations is Schwartz's argument that welfare entitlement must be tied to concurrent social obligations, so long as the latter do not take a form that violates the integrity of welfare recipients. Short of these obligations, Schwartz doubts that enough social solidarity can be generated in the democratic process to invigorate the welfare state.

Resnick and Marković are concerned about the prospects for democracy in capitalist liberal democracies and the former "actually existing socialisms" of Eastern Europe. Both speculate about the kind of institutions that might be necessary to facilitate participatory forms of democratic rule, reflecting on past experience and proposing strategies for change based on normative models consistent with that reflection.

In "Trade Unions, Workers' Control, and Democracy," Philip Resnick sounds the call for popular participation in decision-making in the economic realm by focusing on the economically and culturally developed capitalist societies. His model is a form of market socialism in which the state engages in indicative planning aided by fiscal and monetary policies. State policy is to be steered by political parties representing social and economic forces committed to democratization and based on an implicit social contract including groups in addition to, and on equal footing with, the traditional working class and its trade unions. The way to get to the good society is through a strategy that combines the interests of the industrial workers, the numerically dominant white-collar workers, and the middle-income class. And once the system is set in place, although trade unions will continue to defend and articulate their members' interests, they will share power with workers' councils in the workplace and with organs of community power at the local and national levels.

In "Radical Democracy" Mihailo Marković echoes Resnick's concerns, but on a broader and more philosophical scale. He agrees that radical versions of democracy—those that "abolish all existing relationships of political, economic, and cultural domination and bring about conditions for full individual and group self-determination in all areas of social life"—are likely to be realized only in materially and culturally developed societies. But, unlike Resnick, his point of departure is more informed by the lessons of the failures of the new social formations that grew up in, or were imposed upon, the East European countries. Drawing in particular upon the successes and shortcomings of the Yugoslav experience, Marković formulates a model of federated democracy: direct democracy at the lower levels (the workplace, cultural associations, local government), and representative democracy at the higher levels, thus combining liberal values (tolerance, separation of powers, civil liberties) with egalitarian ones (equality, equal participation in affecting decisions, egalitarian distribution of the bases of self respect). Given the East European experience, Marković is less sanguine than Resnick about the capabilities of political parties to achieve democratic aims.

The chapters by Marković and Resnick were written before the onset of the most recent developments in Eastern Europe. With their permission, we have slightly altered their essays, without affecting their substantive content. That substance stands independently of the continuing and unpredictable flux in the former "actually existing socialisms." The editors believe these remain important contributions to our topic.

The final essay in the collection is concerned with a particular justification of democracy. Democracy is standardly justified on the grounds that it efficiently translates citizens' preferences into public policy. But what happens if their preferences fail to dovetail with their objective interests? In "Objective Interests" D. Goldstick, writing from the standpoint of Marxist theory and sensitive to charges that Marxist and Leninist theories legitimate paternalism and even minority dictatorship, distinguishes between desires and interests. On the basis of scrupulous conceptual analysis involving counterfactuals, he defends democratic practice (at least in societies that are economically and culturally advanced) because, in a way that is consistent with the values of individual autonomy and freedom, it performs admirably in getting people to desire what is in their objective interests. He states,"Something [is] in a person's objective interests just in case that person would on balance desire it if sufficiently informed about its potential effects." Goldstick argues that people's concrete desires, so informed, as well as their unspecified or "abstract" desires, motivate people in the direction of socialism.

Whether democracy and socialism go together in the way Goldstick contends may not fetch the universal assent of our contributors. The intellectual commitments and priorities of the authors are fairly diverse, but they are united in their concern for rational, critical discourse and in their belief that democracy must be understood normatively, as a set of principles rather than as a rhetorical flourish. In line with the theme of this volume, they collectively enjoin the perspective that democratic theorists need to inform their empirical enterprise with elaborations of the normative bases—equal concern and respect for persons, the values of community and citizenship, the satisfaction of human interests—of democratic politics.

Chapter 1

Rehabilitating Democratic Theory: The Prospects and the Need

Ron Perrin

The turn to normative democratic theory entails two related but distinct judgments of value. The first is explicit, if not tautological, and involves the claim that such public "goods" as equality, liberty, and popular sovereignty serve to ground and distinguish the politics of democratic societies. The second, however, is more subtle and more controversial. It reflects the presumption that democratic theory entails more than study of the formal and institutional arrangements that encompass the determination of public policy, the resolution of political conflict, and the orderly succession of governments. Although these matters are legitimate and necessary concerns for any systematic knowledge of democratic systems, the case for a normative theory rests on the capacity to also maintain a rational and public dialogue about the meaning and significance of "democracy" itself. Those who continue to be engaged by the problems and possibilities inherent in establishing a case for why democracy is or ought to be the preferred form of human governance are bound, by that commitment, to provide some rational court of reference within which that claim might be heard and assessed. Normative democratic theory, in other words, must be grounded in a communicable understanding of the meaning and source of democratic values.

Currently both of these claims need a mutual redemption. The plausibility of a deliberately and acknowledged value-oriented politics rests on the capacity to establish a credible cognitive foundation for the study of democratic values. If we are to understand why this is so and why the recognition that it is so is itself problematic, we must first understand something of the intellectual climate in which political theory finds itself.

The New Realism

A preoccupation with the formal and procedural properties of democratic states has been dominant within Anglo-American political theory throughout the twentieth century. Its expressions have been varied, with the functionalist, behavioralist, and structuralist schools alternately capturing center stage in the journals and departments of political science. But the common spirit throughout has been an insistent realism that takes the system as it finds it, thereby precluding before the fact any critical role for theory by limiting the study of democracy to the observable and describable phenomenon of the extant state. Typically the adherents to this "new realism" have been careful to avoid any discussion of the meaning or source of democratic values, even when avowing some personal commitment to them.[1]

> Our own values are those of the citizen of a society that aspires toward freedom. Hence we have given special attention to the formulations of conditions favorable to the establishment and continuance of a free society. . . . But we are not concerned with the justification of democratic values, their derivation from some metaphysical or moral base. This is the province of political doctrine, not political science.[2]

Here the discussion of values assumes an incidental relationship to the analysis of the institutions and processes of the democratic state. As such, freedom becomes a by-product of the constitutional system of checks and balances, open and competing parties, and the like. The problem with this strategy is very much like the problem of its close cousin, the economic theory of laissez-faire. There, having once declared that the general interest emerges from the unhampered competition of individual interests, the theory is obliged to accept whatever emerges from this competition as a legitimate expression of the common weal. But how are we to *know* that we have found freedom or the general interest without some prior sense of what we are looking for?

The Twofold Challenge

This, of course, is the real issue. Critics of normative democratic theory deny the possibility of such prior understanding on the grounds that it necessarily commits us to judgments that cannot be verified in experience. Faced with the alternative of validating the system as they find it (often with an acknowledgment of its shortcomings) or committing themselves to the metaphysical assertions of transcendental ethics or natural law doctrine, they choose the safer course of realism.[3]

Let me acknowledge, as clearly as possible, that I have no quarrel against the realist's desire to bring the study of democratic values down to earth. Nor do I mean to invite closure on the public debate about what these values entail and signify. Rather, my objection is with the trivialization of this study and debate that inevitably occurs when the critical role of theory is disbarred before the mute facticity of practice and with the implications of exempting the nature and source of democratic values from serious study. As Sheldon Wolin has reminded us, "when beliefs are simultaneously relegated to the status of unexamined preferences and declared undemonstrable according to the most respected method of validation, their tendency is to become ritualistic dogmas."[4]

It is worth noting that as an attempt to escape the pitfalls that democratic theory presumably encountered when it sought to establish its foundations in the unverifiable assumptions of transcendental philosophy or natural law doctrine, the new realists naively drew upon a model of theoretical inquiry that was equally suspect. As John G. Gunnell has noted, Harold D. Lasswell and Abraham Kaplan were enamored of developments in the philosophy of science—which Gunnell alternately describes as "scientism" or "empiricism"—that unwittingly endorsed "the authority of the 'facts' as the objects and benchmark of science." "Like the logical empiricists from whom they drew support for their position, political scientists believed that, no matter how useful theories might be in thinking about facts, these facts at least presented themselves in some unproblematical manner."[5] From this perspective, the problem for political theory is not so much a matter of its acquiescence before the given institutions and processes of politics; rather, as the new realists opted for a model of political theory that represented an amalgam of logical positivism, operationalism, and instrumentalism they became, as the subtitle of Gunnell's book suggests, "alienated" from the practice of democratic politics.

These preliminary observations and disclaimers suggest that the rehabilitation of normative democratic theory must begin by confronting the realist's reduction of intelligible experience to those features of experience that can meet the test of empirical validation. Only when our understanding of what rational experience entails has been released from the thrall of the narrowly construed social sciences can we proceed with any confidence to inquire about the values of democracy and, most fundamentally, raise the question of what is of value in democracy itself.

Moreover, the study of democracy will never be adequate to its subject matter if it insists on reducing the reality of our political experience to those processes, institutions, and public policies that are subject to empirical description. For, as it is with the organization of all societies, democracy, or more precisely, the democracies, are nothing without their histories.

We can, in principle, conceive of two identical parliamentary democracies. And yet we readily understand that the "nature" of these two systems will differ dramatically in accordance with the diverse circumstances of their origin (e.g., restoration England and absolutist France), the intentions of their founders, the shifting interpretations of those intentions by subsequent generations, and the relative priorities assigned to conservative versus liberal conceptions of social justice over the decades and centuries of their development.

Thus, the meaning of "democracy" is available to us only in the lives of the democracies. All of these factors, along with the multiplicity of religious, ethnic, and ideological elements that feed into and shape the political culture, are permeated by presumptions and expressions of value. To be sure, the manner and meaning of the way they converge to establish the character of any given democracy are subjects of enormous complexity and can never be finally resolved. This, in part, explains why the new realists wish to relegate normative theory to the ranks of the inscrutable. But, as I hope to show, there are good reasons to question the realists' claim that the pursuit of normative and historical questions inevitably consigns us to the realm of the doctrinal and the unverifiable.

However, our task of rehabilitation cannot be limited to the question of whether one can provide a cognitive foundation for the study of democratic values. Normative democratic theory is equally preoccupied with the relationship of its content to practice, with the possibility of establishing the political community within which freedom, equality, and social justice might flourish. It is here that the theory encounters its second challenge. For within the setting of democracy in America, the realists' constraining of democratic theory to the formal properties and institutional processes of the nominal democratic state has been accompanied by an eclipse of communal and public interests that threatens to make the democratic project suspect.

In the United States a growing body of literature continues to document and sound the breakup of the American political community and the erosion of its moral and cultural foundations.[6] This literature describes a social world in which the domination of its politics by a host of interest groups mocks any pretense that ours is a healthy environment of social and cultural pluralism. It describes how the continued erosion of the socio-cultural infrastructure of extended families, ethnic neighborhoods, and moral communities—religious and secular alike—has exposed and released that unbridled self-interest that de Tocqueville fearfully observed on the nether side of the virtues of independence and egalitarianism. Within this body of scholarship and commentary the recent work of Robert Bellah and his associates strikes me as particularly compelling. In their *Habits of the Heart,* Bellah and his colleagues ground their theoretical observations and conclusions in a series of selected case studies.[7] Not the least of *Habits'* many strengths, then, is its authors' ability to enlist the personal accounts and histories of their fellow citizens in the service of reflecting upon the damaged ethos of American democracy. What emerges is a striking depiction of how thoroughly the consequences of what Bellah et al. choose to describe as "ontological individualism" have undermined the civic foundations of the democratic community.

With the adjective "ontological," the authors seek to convey the extent to which the attitudes and assumptions of their subjects express the conviction that "the individual has a primary reality whereas society is a second-order, derived or artificial construct."[8] But the real force of their study is its ability to trace the practical implications of that conviction as it manifests itself either, and often alternately, in the utilitarian pursuit of economic self-interest or in the commitment to an expressive standard of individualism that measures personal development in the ability of each to develop his or her own "unique core of feeling and intuition."[9] Given the wholesale displacement of the public by the private and of the social by the selfish, which is chronicled in *Habits* and its allied studies in sociology, social history, and philosophy, we cannot avoid the question of whether there is any longer a community of shared values and interests that might sustain a democratic polity.

The coincidence of the new realism with the breakdown of social cohesion is not entirely accidental. We have already seen that in the former instance the matter of general interests is denied any cognitive status, a circumstance that fits quite well with the case studies depicted in *Habits of the Heart*. In effect, Bellah's subjects are living out the rationality of the new realism.

Thus, the rehabilitation of normative democratic theory cannot meet the challenge posed to its cognitive claims without simultaneously demonstrating that its commitment to become a practical voice in a revitalized public dialogue has not been preempted by the ethos and practice of individualism.

In the remainder of this essay I hope at least to indicate the direction the rehabilitation of normative democratic theory might take in response to the twofold challenge outlined above. In the first instance I suggest that the test of its cognitive claims may be met by drawing upon the resources available in the dialogue between Hans-Georg Gadamer and Jürgen Habermas.[10] Then, building upon that discussion, I briefly draw upon some central themes in Jeffersonian democracy and indicate their significance in light of the issues raised by Bellah and his associates.

Tradition and Knowledge

I have argued above that the meaning of any given political order is encased within the unique and value-laden history of that order, a circumstance that contributed to the rejection of normative theory by the new realists. However, the complex specificity of differing political cultures poses an insurmountable obstacle to understanding only to the extent that social scientific inquiry insists on emulating the inductive methods of the natural sciences. For reasons extending beyond the confines of this essay, Gadamer and Habermas reject as implausible the effort to model the social sciences after the natural sciences, and both insist that a normatively oriented theory need not yield before the inherent complexity of its subject matter. On the latter point I find Gadamer's analysis the more accessible and telling.

Gadamer reminds us that there is a more fitting cognitive milieu for those who wish to study the "moral and historical experience of man," namely the human sciences (*Geisteswissenshaften*), or the "humanities." These, he insists, provide the proper cognitive milieu for those who would understand the "moral and historical experience of man."[11] Although the bulk of his work is devoted to explicating this theme with illustrations drawn from the classics and literary studies, its implications for democratic theory are obvious. For, no less than the enduring works of art and literature, the various attempts to redeem the principle of popular sovereignty, to fulfill the aspiration to social justice, and to realize the ideals of freedom and equality in human affairs must be read as expressions of our moral and historical experience.

Two themes in Gadamer's reconstruction of the humanities have particular relevance for our attempt to rehabilitate normative democratic theory. The first is his recognition of the irreducible role that our culturally bound expectations and presumptions (our "prejudices") play in our understanding of all historical phenomena. Gadamer is quick to point out that prejudice does not necessarily entail false judgment. His intention is simply, or (for those still committed to the goal of objective knowledge in social science) not so simply, to highlight the selective function our biases and memories bring to our efforts to comprehend and describe our past.[12] For this reason, as he repeatedly insists, within the purview of the humanities "all understanding is interpretation."[13]

Gadamer's second theme, which serves to check the impulses of a blind prejudice, is the role of tradition in historical understanding. He observes that to affirm the historical character of our biases and expectations need not consign us to a hopeless relativism. On the contrary, because our tradition is the source of our values, the task of normative evaluation requires that those who undertake it are continually validating the claims of their past.[14]

Within the context of our concern here, this suggests that the study of democracy is foreshadowed by our preoccupation with freedom, equality, and justice. But these are, of course, given to us within the same tradition we seek to understand. Viewed through the prism of the humanities, normative democratic theory is not a process of speculating upon transcendent values; rather it is a discussion that democracy is having with itself. Commenting on Hegel's observation that the classical "is that which signals itself and hence also interprets itself," Gadamer notes "that means ultimately that the classical is what is preserved precisely because it signifies and interprets itself. . . ."[15]

In the same vein, then, when we engage the classics of democracy (e.g., Locke's *Second Treatise of Government*, Rousseau's *The Social Contract*, *The Federalist*, or Jefferson's *Declaration of Independence*), we are not obliged to limit their significance to the circumstances of their origination, for example, their connection with eighteenth-century doctrines of natural law. Rather, if we acknowledge their status as the founding texts of the modern democratic tradition, we must interpret their reflections on natural and civil rights, the meaning of popular sovereignty, and the common good from the perspective of our own place within that tradition. This is why there can never be closure of the debate over what democratic rights, political self-determination, and the general interest entail. Only in that debate does the tradition live. "The truth is that there is always contained in historical understanding the idea that the tradition reaching us speaks into the present and must be understood in this mediation—indeed, as this mediation."[16]

Thus, Gadamer's highlighting of the central place of the traditional interpretation nexus in our understanding of those activities (e.g., literature, history, and philosophy) that alternately express and engage our humanity enables us to transcend the terms and conditions of the new realism. Indeed, he helps us to see that there is little of the "realistic" in the attempt to limit political theory to the present organization of society. Because that organization is itself the product of all those prior interpretations through which the tradition lives, any science of politics that limits itself to the here and now can only be sustained by an act of abstraction from the very reality it seeks to understand. In that guise theorists are asked to stand outside the historical continuum that frames and constitutes their subject matter. Not only is such an act impossible, its presumption in the new realism exposes operationalism, behavioralism, and structuralism as modern varieties of the doctrinal metaphysics against which their adherents continually rail.

However, before the insights available in Gadamer's hermeneutics can become foundational for a value-oriented democratic praxis, the activity of interpretation he counsels must be guided by some selective principle. Strictly speaking, a normative theory cannot affirm every moment of the past without sacrificing the critical role that is an elemental feature of any evaluation. The history of democracy, for example, records the domination of one or more social groups by political and economic elites just as it describes the affirmation of human rights. Not incidentally, every such realignment of power and authority is accompanied by the attempt to legitimize itself through the sanction of tradition. Within the tradition of American democracy, the defense of slavery, no less than the movement for abolition, was couched in the language of human rights and freedoms. What is more, the preoccupation with tradition can easily translate into a mindless nostalgia that effectively preempts any reflective or critical engagement with the past.[17]

With these last considerations in mind, any attempt to appropriate Gadamer's hermeneutics for the rehabilitation of normative democratic theory must establish some cognitive standard by means of which the theorist can distinguish between those expressions of the democratic tradition that are valid and those that are not. This, as I understand it, is the significance of Jürgen Habermas's critical response to Gadamer. Habermas insists that when we move to the level of social–political theory our engagement with tradition must be mediated by our practical interest in emancipation as well as by the circumstances of our location within the tradition.

The Critique of Tradition

This essay is not the place to evaluate the more ambitious features of Habermas's development of the relationship between knowledge and human interests. I am not yet prepared to accept, for example, Habermas's claim that the interest in emancipation constitutes the transcendental, universal, and a priori condition for a critical social theory.[18] But, fortunately, within the context of a normative democratic theory we are spared the effort required to confirm or refute that assertion. This is because the history and tradition of modern democracies give us the interest in emancipation; we do not have to discover it through some logical or phenomenological exercise. Without this interest we lose sight of what makes democracy distinctive; the cynics among us who make of democracy simply another form of power politics would rule the day. But if all political theory is ultimately the study of power then political theory becomes a theory without categories. Power is power and that is that. The role of theory as a guide for the organization of power or the medium whereby we might gain some insight into the uses and abuses of political power requires the ability to discriminate between the respective goals or "interests" of various political systems. And, again, within the tradition of democracy we are given the interest in emancipation.

To be sure, that interest assumes different expressions as the sources and terms of political domination change. For example, the earliest expressions of modern democratic theory took shape against the backdrop of the Reformation and Enlightenment and were thereby marked by the struggle against the absolutist union of Christianity and monarchy. This circumstance lent a note of urgency to the claim that the origins of civil society in a social contract could be established by the appeal to natural laws that were transparent to any rational individual. What is more, the mark of individual autonomy was understood to reside in the capacity to comprehend the dictates of the natural law together with the ability to establish a civil order that would endow those dictates with a force at once moral and political.

In this regard the significance of "liberty" as a primary value in democratic theory is less a feature of the philosophical merits or demerits of natural law doctrine than it is of the historical and emancipatory interest in supplanting the rule of dogma and arbitrary force by reflective standards of reason and the principles of constitutional law.

To further trace the developing theory and practice of democracy, and not incidentally provide further illustration of what is implied in Habermas's thesis (his work is notorious for its lack of concrete illustrations), let me note that subsequent to its early concern to establish the legitimacy and limits of the modern state in appeals to natural law the theory came to incorporate the insistence that a democratic society must provide for the opportunity of all to develop their uniquely human capacities to the fullest. As with its original formulations, this modification cannot be comprehended as an intellectual development alone; it must, as C. B. Macpherson has shown, be seen in light of the practical limitations in the exclusively libertarian construction of democracy. Within the nineteenth-century context of an industrial–capitalist order, the free pursuit of individual interests produced a social order in which the interests and personal development of one class of individuals came to prevail at the expense of those who constituted the class of laborers. In this setting it became increasingly difficult to maintain the claim that the common good was secured solely through the achievements of liberty.[19] At that time, the implicit egalitarian assumptions within democratic theory became highlighted with the claim "that each individual was equally entitled to the opportunity to realize his human essence . . . that men's capacities were substantially equal, and that they were entitled to equal opportunity in this world."[20]

Following the lead of Gadamer and Habermas I think it is helpful to view this development as an instance wherein the interest in emancipation directed a new interpretation of the democratic tradition.

In sum, although the interest in emancipation emanates from within the democratic tradition, it can provide what Paul Ricoeur terms an "ethical distance," which allows theory to "transvalue what has already been evaluated."[21] This is what occurred with the transvaluation of natural law theory by the utilitarianism of Jeremy Bentham and John Stuart Mill. And this is what must occur now if we are to rescue the possibility of a democratic community from the corrosive forces of the unchecked utilitarianism that is documented by Robert Bellah and his associates.

Democracy, Community, and Human Nature

In the concluding chapter of *Habits of the Heart*, Bellah and his colleagues call for a "transformation of American culture" from the disconnectedness of the consumption and self-centered utilitarian ethos of modernity to an ethos that privileges the setting and values of community, or (more accurately) a matrix of interdependent communities in which the mores of mutual commitment and civic responsibility might be renewed. The authors rightly observe that the latter dispositions were present in the early decades of our national experience, first in the biblical tradition expressed through the protestant communities of New

England and second in the tradition of civic republicanism. The latter, with its presupposition that the identification and mutual achievement of common purposes can acknowledge the freedom and equality of all only when all citizens are committed to ensuring the vitality of the res publica, or public things, is central to the rehabilitation of normative democratic theory.

Any recollection of the republican tradition in American life must be qualified by an awareness of its precarious cultural and social status, even in the period of its origination. As Bellah notes, the claims of utilitarian individualism (personified, for example, in the character of Benjamin Franklin) have as lengthy a pedigree. And any suggestion that the great majority of the inhabitants of early America enjoyed the graciousness of circumstance required to live the republican life of civic virtue is an affront to the women and men whose indentured, wage, slave, and domestic labors created the time and space for such a life. Nonetheless, because citizenship is currently and, at least nominally, a universal status, it seems fair and urgent to wonder, once again, whether a republican praxis is beyond the capacities and interests of anything approaching a social majority. Are there any reasonable grounds to assume that the fashioning of a communitarian politics engaged in clarifying and expressing the meaning of democracy is congenial to the American temperament?

Within the context of the American political tradition (or better, traditions), the most considered, affirmative response to this question is found in Thomas Jefferson's observations on human nature, morality, and society; their significance and selection here reflects their place within that tradition. The following commentary is pursuant to the course anticipated in my discussion of Gadamer and Habermas. But I also find Jefferson's thought particularly relevant to the problems and the prospects for a further transvaluation of democratic theory, or (as Bellah might put it) the transformation of American culture, for two reasons. First, key presuppositions and claims in Jeffersonian democracy are remarkably devoid of the social contractarian and utilitarian assumptions that characterized the earlier and now suspect expressions of normative democratic theory. Second, despite the twists and turns they have undergone, the variations of interpretation offered by historians of all persuasions, and the uses and abuses to which they have been subjected for ideological and partisan ends, central elements of Jeffersonian democracy persist amid the fractured dialogue of contemporary American society. As such they remain part of a collective memory to be expressed, for example, in the nostalgia Bellah's subjects often express for the virtues of neighborhood and community; or in the almost ritualistic homage educators and politicians pay to the premise that only a broadly educated public is capable of meaningful self-government; or in the abiding suspicion of government—large and federal—that so many Americans continue to display and which Ronald Reagan so skillfully exploited throughout his presidency; and in the special place the family farm and farmer occupy in the iconography of the American culture.

However, lest the following observations be woefully misunderstood, I offer an important caveat. Although I find in Jefferson significant and telling precepts for a normative democratic theory—one that highlights the value of communal goods and the virtue of service to those goods—I do not claim that Jeffersonian democracy is the product of a deliberate and systematic political philosophy. As was the case with his contemporaries (John Adams, James Madison, and Alexander Hamilton), for Thomas Jefferson politics was forever the midwife of theory, experience the trigger of reflection, and history a resource to be selectively mined for whatever instruction it might bring to the tasks of independence and nation-building.

If we must assign Jefferson to any particular school of thought, we would do best to see him as a precursor of American pragmatism. We should observe how much his thought displays those features of pragmatism George Santayana would later characterize as "naive naturalism."

> Now the philosophy by which Americans live, in contrast to the philosophies which they profess, is naturalistic. In profession they may be Fundamentalists, Catholics, or idealists, because American opinion is largely pre-American; but in their hearts and lives they are all pragmatists, and they prove it even by the spirit in which they maintain those other traditional allegiances, not out of rapt speculative sympathy, but because such allegiance seems an insurance against moral dissolution, guaranteeing social cohesion and practical success. Their real philosophy is the philosophy of enterprise.[22]

Jefferson's disposition to tailor thought to the perceived imperatives of the moment, to enlist reason in the service of practice, was unbounded. It expressed itself in matters great and small, as the following excerpt from a letter to his son-in-law indicates.

> In political economy I think Smith's wealth of nations the best book extant. In the science of government Montesquieu's spirit of laws is generally recommended. It contains indeed a great number of political truths; but almost an equal number of political heresies; so that the reader must be constantly on his guard. . . . Locke's little book on government is perfect as far as it goes. Descending from theory to practice there is no better book than the Federalist. Burgh's political disquisitions are good also, especially after reading De Lorne. Several of Hume's political essays are good also. There are some excellent theories written by Turgot and the economists of France. For parliamentary knowledge the Lex parliamentaria is the best book. [23]

Here Jefferson's thought is engaged by the enterprise of reading for the law. To that end the political literature of the eighteenth century is a great unclassified library, a legacy of information to be pruned and appropriated at will. Typically, no pause is given to the questions that would occupy a modern theorist–scholar. How, for example, is one to reconcile the embryonic capitalism of Adam Smith with the claims of the physiocrats, here represented by Turgot? By what principle is the student to discriminate between the true and the heretical in Montesquieu? However, as the Santayana citation indicates, neither logical consistency nor the cognitive status of first principles is of consequence. Rather the project itself, in this case the choice and successful pursuit of a vocation, is left to discriminate between the true and the false.

Thus we search in vain if we expect to find in Jefferson an altogether distinctive and internally coherent theory of democracy or an American application of classical democratic theory. Despite the repeated efforts of Jefferson scholars to confine his thought to one camp or another, he was neither a Lockean liberal democrat nor a Rousseauean republican.[24]

Once the consideration of Jefferson's thought is freed from the need to either make of him America's first political philosopher or an American exemplar of one of the contending eighteenth-century political doctrines, it is possible to identify in his various works principles for a normative democratic theory that fit remarkably well into the context of the Gadamer–Habermas dialogue. Jefferson's selective reading of the Scottish moralists and of the political economies and philosophies from France and England, as well as his studies of the classical works of Greece and Rome, provide a splendid illustration of historical understanding as Gadamer has described it. What from a more conservative point of view would seem to be a willful disrespect for the integrity of those works is, in effect, a lively reworking of the problematic relationship between human nature, morality, and society. We are to understand Jefferson as humanist, not as theorist or philosopher, and as humanist he gives us a clear example of the humanistic tradition interpreting itself.

If we inquire further into the motivating and discriminating principle of Jefferson's thought, the answer proves to be a passion akin to Habermas's interest in emancipation. The pervasive force of this interest in Jefferson's life is reflected in his desire to have his epitaph cite, from among his many public accomplishments, only his authorship of the *Virginia Statute for Religious Freedom* and the *Declaration of Independence* together with his founding of the University of Virginia. For Thomas Jefferson, the significance of each deed lay with its potential to address the three great tyrannies of mankind: religion, government, and ignorance.

More telling, however, is the fact that when we read Jefferson's letters and public papers through our own interest in emancipation, and thereby strive to reconstruct his understanding of human nature and society, we discover the intimations of a democratic theory that departs significantly from the basic tenets of liberal democracy.

At the very heart of Jeffersonian thought is his insistence upon the innate and fundamental morality of human beings. Impatient with the attempts of philosophers and theologians to derive morality from reason or faith—such efforts are a reversal of the natural state of affairs, "as if a tree taken up by its roots, had its stem reversed in the air, and one of its branches planted in the ground"[25]—Jefferson proclaimed morality "the brightest gem with which the human character is studded, and the want of it as more degrading than the most hideous of the bodily deformities."[26] Anticipating the rejoinder that one cannot ascribe to human nature a characteristic obviously lacking in so many, he went on to observe that "some men are born without the organs of sight, or of hearing, or without hands. Yet it would be wrong to say that man is born without these faculties, and sight, hearing and hands may with truth enter into the general definition of man."[27]

Gary Wills has correctly identified the spirit of the Scottish Enlightenment and its conception of the "moral sense" in passages such as the one above.[28] But of greater importance for our concerns is the extent to which the Jeffersonian insistence upon our innate morality, reflects a decidedly antiutilitarian bias. For, among those "rational" attempts to explain morality, which he reviewed and finally rejected, is the appeal to self-interest.

> Self-interest, or rather self-love, or *egoism*, has more plausibly substituted as the basis of morality. But I consider our relations with others as constituting the boundaries of morality. With ourselves we stand on the ground of identity, not of relation, which last, requiring two subjects, excludes self-love confined to a single one. To ourselves, in strict language, we can owe no duties, obligation requiring also two parties. Self-love, therefore, is no part of morality. Indeed it is exactly its counterpart. It is the sole antagonist of virtue, leading us constantly by our propensity to self-gratification in violation of our duties to others.[29]

This pragmatic or "naturalist" appropriation of the Scottish moralists' concept of the moral instinct, the logic of common sense, and the concern to establish legitimacy for public works and public obligations stands, as I have already suggested, in stark contrast to either the classical Hobbesian version of utilitarianism or the nineteenth-century variations of Jeremy Bentham and John Stuart Mill.

Furthermore, Jefferson's depiction of human nature is equally removed from the "state of nature" premises of liberal democracy. Rather than posit a hypothetical (or spurious historical) asocial moment that only the Social Contract can alleviate and, conversely, which the legitimacy of the Contractual State requires, this Jeffersonian notion entails the assumption of a naturally social and communitarian nature. Twenty-seven years before he wrote the above reflections on morality, Jefferson had written that ". . . man was destined for society. His morality, therefore, was to be formed to this object. He was endowed with a sense of right and wrong, *merely relative to this*" (my emphasis).[30] With this claim Jefferson was drawing upon his immediate experience with the communities of the Native Americans. These, he felt, displayed a natural human capacity for self-government in the absence of institutionalized political authority. "They demonstrated the compatibility of sociability and independence, of liberty and social cooperation: their self-sacrificing love for the natural community developed without coercion and rested solely on the identity of the personal and the communal interest."[31]

Thus, in this view of the matter, the right of self-government is neither a matter of individual utility nor philosophical speculation. On the contrary it is grounded in the recognition of what human beings are, or would be, if their moral and communal capacities were allowed to express themselves.

One of the few recent political theorists to trace the practical implications of Jefferson's concept of human morality and sociability is Hannah Arendt. In *On Revolution,* Arendt documents the way this concept found its working corollary in Jefferson's proposal for a system of elemental democracies.[32]

To forestall the rise of an "artificial aristocracy of wealth and birth," Jefferson repeatedly proposed the establishment of a system of "ward-republics," which would serve the educational and political needs of a free society. These wards would be the school districts of his time, offering free education and serving to identify the best students, who would then attend district schools where a "natural aristocracy" would then be selected to attend the university. Of equal importance is Jefferson's proposal to make these wards the foundation of national and state politics.[33]

At a first reading, these educational and political proposals, which Jefferson argued would have "laid the axe to the root of pseudo-Aristocracy," seem antiquated and quixotic. Maybe so, but as one revisionist study of Jefferson's thought observes, "the ward-republic is the logical outgrowth of Jefferson's concept of man."[34]

If morality is understood as the most elemental feature of our nature, and further represented as an aptitude and disposition for society, then any organization of society that does not invite our engagement and reflect our determinations is at best an abridgment and at worst a denial of our humanity. The little republics of Jefferson's theoretical design would have been, then, the necessary enabling instruments of his democracy.

Here we encounter what many read as the fatal flaw in Jeffersonian democracy. Any communitarian politics presumes locale, the relatively confined space within which individuals can meaningfully interact and within which the fact of their daily transactions gives silent testimony to the reality of their common fate.[35] But Americans are, as de Tocqueville observed, a "restless" lot, not given to the settled ways and habits such a vision of community seems to imply.[36] What is more, the cultural and economic autonomy that contributes to the identity and security of a communal politics seems to be at variance with the complex interdependencies of modern life.

Anything approaching a full exploration of this phenomenon would require another study. However, Michael Walzer has recently intimated the direction such a study might take, a direction that I find congenial with the thrust of my concerns in this essay. Walzer notes that republicanism "is a doctrine adapted (in both its classical and neoclassical forms) to the needs of small, homogenous communities, where civil society is radically undifferentiated."[37] The current forms that voluntary association take—churches, unions, neighborhood organizations, and so on—do not display that overt political character the republican tradition prized. "[T]here are virtually no examples of republican association and no movement or party aimed at promoting such association."[38]

However, no less than Robert Bellah and his colleagues, Walzer understands that the vitality of democracy is drawn from strong local identities and associations. Might we not, he suggests, envision a "republic of republics," wherein the policies of the liberal state contribute toward the "strengthening of local governments . . . in the hope of encouraging the development and display of civic virtue in a pluralist variety of social settings?"[39]

Here the choice is not between two traditions, the narrative of civic republicanism versus that of liberal utilitarianism. Rather it would involve the commitment to embrace and live within a tension between them, a tension that promises to mitigate the collectivist tendencies that characterize the unqualified exercise of communitarianism as well as the socially destructive tendencies of an unbridled utilitarianism.

One way to recognize the importance of such a tension is to reinstate the "civic Jefferson" alongside the "liberal Jefferson" in the tradition of Jeffersonian democracy.

It is time to take stock of what might be learned from these reflections and observations. First, it is possible and plausible to establish a cognitive foundation for normative democratic theory without appealing to the unverifiable and transcendental principles of metaphysics. Second, one can locate within the mainstream of the American political tradition an alternative to the utilitarian conceptions of human nature and society whose practical consequences are becoming destructive of our moral, political, and natural environment.

But what, one can legitimately ask, entitles me to assume that I have made any contribution to the rehabilitation of normative democratic theory, much less its practice? To that some response, however brief, is still warranted.

With regard to the cognitive foundation I have tried to sketch, I am convinced that some such direction may well emerge from the search for a new paradigm in the social sciences.[40] To date that effort has primarily taken shape (as my references to Gadamer and Habermas illustrate) in some arresting, but largely speculative, studies and critiques in the theory of knowledge. What is required, I suggest, of the myriad contemporary efforts to chart a new course for political theory, is the kind of concrete models and examples whose use I have tried to illustrate with the discussion of Jeffersonian democracy. In effect, the now discrete activities and disciplines of history and political theory need to be unified through the interest in emancipation. The fact that progress is being made toward that end is, I believe, demonstrated in works such as the essay by Michael Walzer.

The climate for a renascent normative democratic theory is further enhanced today by the extent to which many who have long kept faith with the new realism are taking a more critical look at both their earlier positions and the political "reality" they presumed to describe. This development can be charted in the work of a representative theorist such as Robert A. Dahl. Whereas Dahl was once prepared to dissolve the normative problems of democratic theory within the structure of polyarchy, more recently he has seemed willing to respond to the substantive and practical difficulties in his own model.[41]

What then, finally, of the conditions that might bring the issues and themes of Jeffersonian democracy to the practical agenda of American politics where they might then serve as an active voice within a rehabilitated theory and practice of democracy? For one, there are clear signs that a politics at variance with either those of liberal democracy or neoconservatism may at last be opportune. As Walter Dean Burnham argues, to my mind persuasively, the political parties (Democratic and Republican) that presently embody those two theoretical persuasions are constrained by that very fact from initiating policies that would resolve the growing crisis of "economy, empire and culture" in the United States.[42] Furthermore, little in the historical experience of American political movements suggests that a majority of citizens would respond favorably to either the social–democratic or Marxist vision of community and self-government. Although one of the various socialist alternatives might, and no doubt will, continue to be invoked as a theoretical alternative to the bankrupt politics of the welfare and the neoconservative state, these alternatives are likely to remain alien options in the minds of most Americans.

Granted this, and I realize that many are not prepared to do so, the resolution of our current crisis must draw upon indigenous resources. To recognize in Jeffersonian democracy elements of a native alternative to the prevailing ideologies has, of course, been a major concern of this essay. But if my choice and reading of Jefferson have been selective, they have not been cavalier. To cite just two developments, the public's reception of works such as *Habits of the Heart* and the fact that, for better or worse, a large measure of political responsibility is shifting from the federal to state and local governments suggest that, for reasons both moral and political, a reengagement with the full spectrum of Jeffersonian democracy might serve to clarify and instruct the next future of democracy in America.

Notes

1. With the term "new realism" I have in mind that body of thought and persuasions Richard Bernstein characterizes as "empirical theory" in his outstanding study, *The Restructuring of Social and Political Theory* (Philadelphia: University of Pennsylvania Press, 1978). I favor the former construction here because it conveys the practical and spiritual kinship between the empiricists of the twentieth century and the realist turn in political theory inaugurated by Machiavelli.

2. Harold D. Lasswell and Abraham Kaplan, *Power and Society: A Framework for Political Inquiry* (New Haven, Conn.: Yale University Press, 1950), pp. xiii–xiv.

3. One of the clearest expressions of this concern and its implications for political theory is Robert A. Dahl's *A Preface to Democratic Theory* (Chicago: University of Chicago Press, 1956). See especially pp. 44–51.

4. Sheldon S. Wolin, *Politics and Vision* (Boston: Little, Brown and Co., 1960), p. 206.

5. John G. Gunnell, *Between Philosophy and Politics: The Alienation of Political Theory* (Amherst: University of Massachusetts Press, 1986), p. 70.

6. See, for example, Christopher Lasch, *The Culture of Narcissism* (New York: Norton, 1978); also Daniel A. Bell, *The Cultural Contradictions of Capitalism* (New York: Basic Books, 1976). For a more recent study that frames the process of socio-cultural dislocation within the context of developments in philosophy and ethics, see Alasdair MacIntyre, *After Virtue* (South Bend, Ind.: University of Notre Dame Press, 1981; 2nd edition, 1984).

7. Robert N. Bellah, Richard Madsen, William M. Sullivan, Ann Swidler, and Stephen M. Tipton, *Habits of the Heart* (Berkeley: University of California Press, 1985).

8. Bellah et al., *Habits of the Heart*, p. 334.

9. Bellah et al., *Habits of the Heart*, p. 334.

10. For summary and critique of the issues involved and positions taken, see Dieter Misgeld, "Critical Theory and Hermeneutics: The Debate between Habermas and Gadamer," in J. O'Neill, ed., *On Critical Theory* (New York: Seabury Press, 1976); Thomas McCarthy, *The Critical Theory of Jürgen Habermas* (Cambridge, Mass.: The MIT Press, 1978); Jack Mendelson, "The Habermas–Gadamer Debate," *New German Critique*, 18, (1979). In my discussion here I am following the lead of Paul Ricoeur, who proposes a mediation between the two positions in "Ethics and Culture: Gadamer and Habermas in Dialogue," *Philosophy Today* (Summer 1973).

11. Hans-Georg Gadamer, *Truth and Method* (New York: Crossroad, tr. by Sheed and Ward Ltd., 1974), p. 22.

12. Gadamer, *Truth and Method*, pp. 235ff.

13. Gadamer, *Truth and Method*, p. 350.

14. Gadamer, *Truth and Method*, pp. 324–25.

15. Gadamer, *Truth and Method*, p. 257.

16. Gadamer, *Truth and Method*, p. 293.

17. ". . . a hermeneutic which would cut itself off from the regulative idea of emancipation would be no more than a hermeneutic of traditions and in these terms a form of philosophical restoration. Nostalgia for the past would drive it unpityingly toward the positions of Romanticism which it had started out to surpass." Ricoeur, "Ethics and Culture," p. 165.

18. See Jürgen Habermas, *Knowledge and Human Interests* (Boston: Beacon Press, 1979), "The Appendix," especially pp. 310–12.

19. See C. B. Macpherson, *Democratic Theory: Essays in Retrieval* (Oxford: Oxford University Press, 1973), pp. 198–201.

20. Macpherson, *Democratic Theory*, p. 10.

21. Ricoeur, "Ethics and Culture," p. 165.

22. George Santayana, *Obiter Scripta*, cited in William Barrett and Henry D. Aiken, *Philosophy in the Twentieth Century* (New York: Random House, 1962), vol. 1, pp. 369-71.

23. Thomas Jefferson, "Letter to Thomas Mann Randolph, Jr." May 30, 1790, *The Papers of Thomas Jefferson* (Princeton, N.J.: Princeton University Press, 1961), vol. 16, p. 449.

24. Merrill D. Peterson carefully chronicles "what history made of Thomas Jefferson" in *The Jefferson Image in the American Mind* (New York: Oxford University Press, 1960). For more recent and representative portrayals of the relationship between Jefferson's thought and the principles of classical republicanism, see Gary Wills, *Inventing America: Jefferson's Declaration of Independence* (New York: Random House, 1978), and Gordon S. Wood, *The Creation of the American Republic, 1776–1787* (New York: Norton, 1969), chapters 2 and 3. Both Wills and Wood argue that Jefferson was more committed to the republican values of civic virtue and the innate sociability of human nature than to the Lockean principles of individualism and self-interest, a view that is challenged in John P. Diggins, *The Lost Soul of American Politics: Virtue, Self-Interest and the Foundations of Liberalism* (Chicago: The University of Chicago Press, 1984). Diggins's study illustrates the difficulty of any attempt to reduce Jefferson's political thought to a unitary standard. To make the case that Jefferson was not a classical republican, Diggins must establish the highly questionable assumption that "classical political thought aspired to make man dependent upon the state, to whose civic ideals private interests would be subordinate." Having done so Diggins can then and quite rightly note that "Jeffersonian liberalism aspired to free man from the state to pursue his own interests." (Ibid., 40-41). However, this spurious contrast between republicanism and liberalism breaks down as soon as we recognize that Jefferson did not confine the notion of interests within their private and Lockean context. See pp. 13–14 above. Implicit throughout my discussion of Jefferson is my conviction that he was as committed to the republican virtue of public service and the republican ideal of community as he was to the liberal virtue of self-sufficiency and the ideal of personal liberty. Currently, for reasons I make clear in my narrative, the reinstatement of the former has become an imperative for the rehabilitation of democratic theory.

25. Thomas Jefferson, "Letter to Thomas Law, June 13, 1814," *Jefferson Writings*, by

Merrill D. Peterson, ed. (New York: Literary Classics of the United States, 1984), p. 1336.25. Peterson, *Jefferson Writings*, pp. 1337–38.

26. Peterson, *Jefferson Writings*, p. 1338.

27. Peterson, *Jefferson Writings*, p. 1337.

28. Wills, *Inventing America*, part 3.

29. Peterson, *Jefferson Writings*, pp. 1336–37.

30. Thomas Jefferson, "Letter to Peter Carr, August 10, 1787," Peterson, *Jefferson Writings*, p. 901.

31. See Yehoushua Arieli, *Individualism and Nationalism in American Ideology* (Cambridge, Mass.: Harvard University Press, 1964), p. 135.

32. See Hannah Arendt, *On Revolution* (New York: Viking Press, 1962), pp. 234–44. My attention was drawn to Arendt's study by Richard K. Matthews's more recent work, *The Radical Politics of Thomas Jefferson* (Lawrence: University of Kansas Press, 1984). Matthews's is a more extended treatment of the themes developed in this essay and is particularly valuable for its discussion of Jefferson's troubling and troubled relationship to slavery.

33. The details of Jefferson's proposed system are contained in "The Letter to John Adams, October 28, 1813," Peterson, *Jefferson Writings*, p. 1308.

Impart to these wards those portions of self-government for which they are best qualified, by confiding to them the care of their poor, their road, police, elections, the nomination of jurors, administration of justice in small cases, elementary exercises of militia, in short, to have made them little republics, with a Warden at the head of each for all those concerns which, being under their eye, they would better manage than the larger republics of the county or state. A general call of ward-meetings by their Wardens on the same day thoughout the state would at any time produce the genuine sense of the people on any required point.

34. Matthews, p. 87.

35. See Daniel Kemmis, *Community and the Politics of Place* (Norman: University of Oklahoma Press, 1990).

36. Alexis de Tocqueville, *Democracy in America* (New York: Vintage Books, 1945), vol. 2, chapter 13.

37. Michael Walzer, "The Communitarian Critique of Liberalism," *Political Theory* 18, no. 1 (February 1990): 20.

38. Walzer, "The Communitarian Critique of Liberalism," p. 19.

39. Walzer, "The Communitarian Critique of Liberalism," p. 20.

40. In addition to his analysis in *The Restructuring of Social and Political Theory*, Richard Bernstein has provided a sensitive and informed depiction of the search for new cognitive foundations in *Beyond Objectivism and Relativism* (Philadelphia: University of Pennsylvania Press, 1983).

41. See Robert A. Dahl, *Dilemmas of Pluralist Democracy* (New Haven, Conn.: Yale University Press, 1983) and *Democracy and Its Critics* (New Haven, Conn: Yale

University Press, 1989). Dahl now feels that it is important for democratic theory to articulate a conception of substantive values and the common good. However, as he develops these themes, he remains within the context of what I have termed "the new realism." For example, the common good is described in the language of operationalism: "the common good among the members of a group is what each person would choose if they possessed the fullest attainable understanding of the experience that would result from their choice and its most relevant alternatives." (*Democracy and Its Critics*, p. 308).

42. Walter Dean Burnham, *The Current Crisis in American Politics* (Oxford: Oxford University Press, 1982), p. 310.

Chapter 2

The Politics of the Enlightenment:
A Pragmatist Reconstruction

Timothy V. Kaufman-Osborn

It is no longer easy to embrace the Enlightenment's happy assurance that the advance of reason heralds the achievement of universal emancipation. Today, more often than not, Condorcet's hymn to scientific rationality is interpreted as an insidious prophecy of technocratic domination, while Kant's celebration of humanity's escape from heteronomy is represented as a tragedy whose call to autonomy merely reinforces agencies of normalization.[1] In such fashion does the frustrated promise of modernity spawn a flurry of dystopian caricatures mocking the myth of inevitable progress toward the consummation of human destiny.

Behind this backlash rests the often tacit but widely shared conviction that the significance of modern science for contemporary culture is best articulated through Max Weber's rationalization thesis. According to that thesis, the difference between the ancient and modern worlds consists in the latter's discovery that forms of practice once considered impervious to theoretical guidance are in fact susceptible to technical control in accordance with the objectifications of scientific discourse. As scientific rationality completes its conquest of the metaphysical rivals that once limited its pretensions to universality, the traditional understanding of culture as a fragile complex of works produced through reference to models furnished by an independent nature is displaced by the idea of civilization as a construct whose wholesale fabrication renders irrelevant the distinction between artifice and its pregiven material. As the dualism of theory and practice collapses within the realized ideal of a totalistically ordered system, the disillusioned intellect is confounded by the obdurate embodiments of its own achievement. Denied the reconstructive opportunities preserved in a less mindful era, reason finds itself with nothing to do other than descriptive social science. Weber's metaphor of the iron cage is an apt symbol for an age whose infatuation with science's fruits cannot quite dispel its gnawing fear that modernity's will to know, shaping every domain of practice to its own imperatives, has now produced forms of organizational and technological power that can be neither mastered nor dismissed.

I am not unsympathetic toward this fashionable account of the political import of modern science. However, I am also persuaded that the Enlightenment's promise was thwarted at least in part because its more illustrious champions read science as a surrogate for premodern doctrines whose theological and cosmological foundations were then proving suspect. As I show in this essay, men as disparate as Descartes, Locke, and Kant failed to see how thoroughly their interpretation of the human meaning of modern science was informed by inherited presuppositions regarding the relationship between knowledge and experience.

Were we to rethink that relationship, might it prove possible to advance a chastened defense of the Enlightenment's emancipatory aspirations? In answering that question, I draw on a suspect source: American pragmatism and, more particularly, the work of John Dewey. Thinking as pragmatists, we can challenge Enlightenment epistemology's insistence on the subordination of ordinary noncognitive experience to the imperatives of cognition; and, in doing that, we can question our inveterate conviction that practice has value only when subjected to rationalistic reconstruction. Pragmatism, in sum, furnishes the conceptual tools necessary to criticize what Weber calls the dynamic of rationalization. What this signifies for democracy's prospects I explore, first, by sketching in broad strokes a pragmatist reading of the contemporary bureaucratic state; and, second, by noting how that reading might inform the struggle to refashion the provision of reproductive health services.

Science and Emancipation

Anticipating by half a decade the argument advanced by Max Horkheimer and Theodor Adorno in their *Dialectic of Enlightenment*, John Dewey acknowledged in 1939 that it was "no longer possible to hold the simple faith of the Enlightenment that assured advance of science will produce free institutions by dispelling ignorance and superstition: the sources of human servitude and pillars of oppressive government."[2] Yet unlike Horkheimer and Adorno, Dewey never abandoned his conviction that the cause of emancipation is bound up with our understanding of modern science and its conduct. Why?

Dewey situates the origins of modern science against the backdrop of late medieval culture. Within this context, Aristotle's qualified naturalism, which located the embodied at the lowest point in the hierarchical order of Being and the disembodied at its apex, was transmuted into the supernaturalism of Roman Catholic dogma. The transformation of this theoretical monopoly into concrete hegemony was effected by a Church that "never forgot to remind its adherents of their lost condition due to their fallen estate," and hence their "need for the work of redemption supernaturally entrusted to it."[3] To its inhabitants, the essential outlines of this order appeared unquestionably given because its class divisions mirrored those of a divinely created and hierarchically ordered nature in which each discrete species held an inviolable position entailing specified duties toward its superiors as well as privileges over its inferiors. What distinguished medieval culture from its ancient counterpart, consequently, was not its reading of the structure of social relationships into nature, but rather its invention of more potent institutional means to assure the indisputability of that homology.

The rigidity of this order was reinforced by a Thomistic ontology that placed severe constraints on the role of sensory experience in the elaboration of knowledge; for, even at its most exacting, observation could do no more than intimate the existence of a superior realm whose teleological objects escaped the deficiencies of all that is tainted by matter. Because that ontology also held that all existents are naturally disposed to realize the good of the species to which they belong, it necessarily read the deliberate introduction of change within specific spatiotemporal contexts as a source of deviation from immutable form. The institutional and the ontological thus conspired to prevent the novel from disconcerting received categories of sense-making.

Although many other causes contributed, the crumbling of this order was hastened when the initiators of early modern science began to use purposive experimentation in generating knowledge. Such practice, whose deliberate invention of hypothetical conceptions raised it above the trial-and-error empiricism of ancient *technai*, effectively subverted the distinction between theory and practice that premodern philosophy had derived from that between reality and appearance:

> The division of the world into two kinds of Being, one superior, accessible only to reason and ideal in nature, the other inferior, material, changeable, empirical, accessible to sense-observation, turns inevitably into the idea that knowledge is contemplative in nature. It assumes a contrast between theory and practice which was all to the disadvantage of the latter. But in the actual course of the development of science, a tremendous change has come about. When the practice of knowledge ceased to be dialectical and became experimental, knowing became preoccupied with changes and the test of knowledge became the ability to bring about certain changes. Knowing, for the experimental sciences, means a certain kind of intelligently conducted doing; it ceases to be contemplative and becomes in a true sense practical.[4]

When combined with the use of instrumentalities abstracted from various humble crafts, the conduct of experimentation suggested that Western philosophy's scorn for concrete particulars was no longer assured of cosmological authorization; intimating that "every existence deserving the name of existence has something unique and irreplaceable about it," it hinted that no individual being exists merely "to illustrate a principle, to realize a universal or to embody a kind or class."[5] No longer could nature be uncritically invoked to justify class divisions whose intelligibility presupposes a categorical distinction between the sublimity of the heavens and the grossness of the earth, and therefore a strict disjunction between those who work with their hands and those who work with their intellects. In short, the practice of modern science substituted "individual facts equal in rank for the feudal system of an ordered gradation of general classes of unequal rank."[6]

Correlatively, Galileo's representation of nature as a mathematically apprehensible scene of mechanical interactions between homogeneous objects undermined antiquity's identification of knowledge with unmediated apprehension of transcendental substances. Supplanting theories whose aim was to replicate the structure of Being with intellectual constructs whose purpose was to account for correlations of change, early modern science intimated that self-evidence could no longer be taken as the defining trait of noetic objects; things in their immediacy were now to be read as signs of what is to come. In sum, if the critical force of science's epistemic revolution consisted in its demystification of indefensible legitimations of socioeconomic privilege and political domination, its constructive meaning consisted in its indifference to ancient teleology and, by extension, its liberation of distinctively human powers: "It was not till ends were banished from nature that purposes became important as factors in human minds capable of reshaping existence."[7] As "an organ of inspiring imagination, through introducing ideas of boundless possibility, indefinite progress, free movement, and equal opportunity irrespective of fixed limits," the conduct of modern science projected the reality of "a world which is not all in, and never will be, which in some respects is incomplete and in the making, and which in these respects may be made this way or that according as men judge, prize, love and labor."[8]

Epistemology and Emancipation

Why is it that the promise of modern science now appears so hollow? Why is it that "science lies today like an incubus upon such a wide area of aspirations?"[9] These questions are perhaps best answered by pointing to the institutionalized relationships of power definitive of a capitalist political economy. That, however, is not the concern of this essay. My aim, instead, is to show how the capacity of these relationships to skew enjoyment of the fruits of modernity is strengthened by readings of modern science that deny the critical thrust implicit in its conduct.

On a pragmatist reading, post-Cartesian philosophical debate about the possibility of knowledge, i.e., epistemology, is best understood as an effort to render intelligible the notions of knowledge and nature intimated by modern scientific inquiry without abandoning either the presuppositional core of classical metaphysics or the theological baggage assimilated to it by medieval Catholicism. If this reading is adopted, it then becomes clear that the dispute between rationalist and empiricist interpretations of modern science is merely a smokescreen. To take professional philosophical partisans at their word is to fail to see that their conflict takes place on territory they occupy in common.

To defend this claim, it is necessary to isolate three interlocking premises of the epistemological problematic, each of which has its ultimate roots in classical philosophy. The first consists of the conviction that "inferred or discursive conclusions depend for their status as knowledge on being derived by inherently necessary procedures from premises that are immediately and self-evidently known to be true."[10] Whether identified as Cartesian universal truths achieved through a priori intuition or as Lockean sense data apprehended through simple ideas, epistemology is defined by its search for a privileged starting point from which to deduce all subordinate claims:

> How largely indeed has historic philosophy been a search for an indefeasible seat of authority. Greek philosophy began when men doubted the authority of custom as a regulator of life; it sought in universal reason or in the immediate particular, in being or in flux, a rival source of authority, but one which as a rival was to be as certain and definite as custom had been. Medieval philosophy was frankly an attempt to reconcile authority with reason, and modern philosophy began when man, doubting the authority of revelation, began a search for some authority which should have all the weight, certainty and inerrancy previously ascribed to the will of God embodied in the divinely instituted church.[11]

Epistemology's endless squabbles about the reality of innate ideas, the indubitability of raw sense percepts, the truth of reason's regulative principles, and so forth, all testify to Europe's unwillingness to let God go, that is, to abandon the hope that we may someday discover a self-certifying world whose secure foundations irrevocably exclude the possibility of doubt, revision, and rejection.

The second constitutive premise of epistemological debate consists of "belief in the inherent correspondence of knowledge with Being or Reality at large."[12] When early students of epistemology, following Galileo, elected to conceptualize all existents as so much dumb homogeneous matter moving through uniform space and time, it proved necessary to repudiate the classical understanding of *physis* as that which determines the growth of seed to mature form; the physical, in other words, was recast as the material. But this rejection of the Aristotelian claim that every being is what it is in virtue of the intelligent form that defines its end entails the withdrawal of reason from the cosmos. Consequently, captains of epistemology had to relocate the reality of mind.

Descartes' response to this dilemma asserts that all being is either incorporeal substance whose essence is thought or corporeal substance whose essence is extension. Although he thereby cuts the ground out from under classical ontology, he is not prepared to jettison belief in the privileged capacity of knowing to reveal the truth of being. How, then, will he explain the capacity of mind, understood as one kind of substance, to know the truth about the radically distinct kind of existence that is matter? To answer this question, Descartes shed the classical conviction that knowledge consists of participation in, or achievement of identity with, the form that defines the essence of what is known. But he retained the ocular metaphors that account for the traditional representation of knowledge as unmediated vision. The upshot, implicit in Descartes' description of knowing as "looking with the eyes of the mind,"[13] is apparent in his characterization of mind as "consciousness," that is, as a form of self-revealing activity whose site is the individual soul. Defining ideas as "intuitions," Descartes transformed reason from a medium through which the cosmos' structure is revealed into a private inner stage on which consciousness discloses its immaterial apprehensions. Knowledge, on this account, is the inherent transparency of ideas given without mediation to the mind.

Although locating the stuff of knowledge in sense perception rather than innate ideas, John Locke's empiricist reformulation of this second element of the epistemological problematic differs only in form from its rationalist foil. He perpetuated the fundamental implication of the Cartesian *cogito ergo sum* by identifying the mind with the self. He defined knowledge as a sort of perceptual consciousness—specifically, "perception of the connexion and agreement, or disagreement and repugnancy of any of our Ideas."[14] And, finally, he insisted on the need to confirm the truth of all beliefs by reducing them to certain "simple ideas" that, from a pragmatist perspective, are best understood as epistemological equivalents of Newton's irreducible "physical corpuscles." In sum, like his Continental counterpart, Locke was an epistemological conformist who, persuaded that "reality" is antecedently given, conceptualized knowledge as the mind's submission to its fixed structure. Considered together, their work suggests not a radical break with the past but rather an interiorization of its most cherished assumptions. For just as "Descartes' thought is the *nous* of classic tradition forced inwards because physical science had extruded it from its object," so too "Locke's simple idea is the classic Idea, Form or Species dislodged from nature and compelled to take refuge in mind."[15]

The final shared premise underlying epistemological debate consists of "belief in a knowing self, ego, or subject, the seat and organ of knowledge, equipped with a variety of powers (later attenuated to states and processes), to whose structural constitution the conclusions of specific inquiries had to conform if they were to be entitled to rank as knowledge."[16] At first glance, Dewey is referring here to Kant's quest to isolate the universal conditions of all cognitive endeavor.

(That enterprise is best read as a forlorn attempt to compensate for the elimination of "ideal forms and rational ends from Nature" by reinstating "the intrinsic rationality of the universe via the route of examination of the conditions under which knowledge is possible."[17]) However, Dewey's more fundamental concern was the subjectivism latent in all epistemological constructions of knowing. When ontologically reified, the mechanistic presuppositions of modern science suggested the unreality of the qualitative (as opposed to the quantitative) traits of human experience. Consequently, these dimensions came to be represented not as real attributes of the activities and objects they qualify, but rather as mere mental projections. Although this transformation of nature into a neutered aggregation of mechanical actions and reactions did much to puncture the illusion that the world is a soulful medium designed to furnish metaphysical comfort, it did not eliminate the philosophical puzzle posed by the contextually qualified character of everyday experience.

To account for the tenacity of such experience in a disenchanted universe was the service performed by the Enlightenment's most original invention: the idea of human nature. The "search for a sure and inexpungable abode for the qualities which provided life with meaning and value led to the creation of an ego-centric" ontology that postulated the discrete individual as autonomous author and exclusive host of "all objects and all subject matter having any connection, direct or indirect, with qualities, ends, goods and evils, prudential or moral."[18] Paradoxically, however, this being was invested with the essentialist status ascribed by classical cosmology to the very qualities (qua metaphysical forms) that modern science could no longer ascribe to nature itself:

> The power and capacities which belong to human nature in its differentiation from cosmic nature were not just referred to "individuals" in the sense in which *private* may be properly distinguished from public, and the socially singular from the socially incorporated; that which was called "individual," and thereby in effect the human generally, was interpreted and described in terms borrowed from the ancient theories of mind, which had been taken up into Christian theology and which through the Church had found their way into the popular culture of the western world. Because of this latter influence, the practical, the essentially moral and social, operation of this and that daring pioneer in breaking away from old customs and from accepted tradition, which was the legitimate heart of modern individualism as a *social* manifestation, was transformed into a metaphysical doctrine of the inherent constitution of human beings.[19]

However, because this doctrine could no longer draw sustenance from the cosmo-theological narratives that once wrapped humanity within a qualitatively rational structure of Being, the modern self took shape as form without determinate content. As a value-positing seat of rationality radically set apart from an inherently end-less nature, this peculiarly Protestant soul could not help but assume an instrumentalist posture toward everything other than itself.

Identifying its autonomy with its capacity for consciousness, that soul jealously guarded its independence from every other sovereign ego, becoming "not merely a pilgrim but an unnaturalized and unnaturalizable alien in the world."[20] To see what is at stake in the fabrication of this creature, consider its implication for our understanding of epistemic error. Classical philosophy, especially of an Aristotelian stripe, contended that there

> were higher and lower forms of knowledge; but all stages of knowledge were alike realizations of some level of Being, so that appearance in contrast with reality meant only a lower degree of Being, being imperfectly or not fully actualized. With the beginnings of modern thought, the region of the "unreal," the source of opinion and error, was located exclusively in the individual. The object was *all* real and *all* satisfactory, but the "subject" could approach the object only through his own subjective states, his "sensations" and "ideas." The Greek conception of two orders of existence was retained, but instead of the two orders characterizing the "universe" itself, one *was* the universe, the other was the individual mind trying to know the universe.[21]

Descartes and Locke alike, agreeing that epistemic failure expresses a defect in the knower rather than in the known, replaced the ancient hierarchy of cognitional forms with a unidimensional doctrine affirming that instances of knowing either fully grasp their object or grasp it not at all. Equally persuaded that misapprehension is to be understood as reality "mimeographed at many removes upon a badly constructed mental carbon paper which yields at best only fragmentary, blurred, and erroneous copies,"[22] they set in motion the distinctively modern quest for a monologic method that, by securing the intellectual self-purification of an inconstant subject, will guarantee its accurate perception of disqualified matter. Only the subject's willingness to submit to the discipline of a systematically interrelated code of abstract rules can ensure its ability to master, both epistemically and technically, whatever remains outside the confines of self-consciousness.

The Domination of Science

Exposure of epistemology's reliance on presuppositions surreptitiously imported from the past is not an end in itself. The peculiar form of "consciousness" represented by this school of philosophic endeavor is "but a symbol, an anatomy whose life is in natural and social operations. To know the symbol, the psychical letter, is important; but its necessity lies not within itself, but in the need for a language for reading the things signified."[23] Accordingly, a pragmatist reading of the epistemological project aims to show that its allegedly "absolute and fixed distinctions of existence and meaning" are optional affairs "which are historic and temporal in their origin and their significance"; for that project's fundamental dualisms—sensation and thought, subject and object, mind and matter—"are not invented *ad hoc*, but are simply the concise reports and condensed formulae of points of view and practical conflicts having their source in the very nature of modern life."[24] In the last analysis, the transcendence of epistemology is a political affair.

Epistemological debate is best read as a rarefied transcript of the inarticulate categories of self-interpretation presently used by men and women who, ensnared within dualistic institutionalized confines, find unavailable the forms of experience that might otherwise temper the alienation of contemporary life. Sensing that traditional moral and religious doctrines have been decisively sapped by the encroachments of a rationalizing science, the prototypically modern self either retreats within an "inner life" in search of protection against the fragmentation of cultural life or, alternatively, exhausts its energies in a frenzied pursuit of material gain. Seeking an object of assurance to moderate its oscillation between rigid dogmatism and radical skepticism, that ego all too often presses on scientific rationality the hopes and fears it once projected on another world. Credited with the certainty characteristic of unreflective faith, granted access to a more profound plane of reality than that grasped by ordinary experience, and ascribed an omnipotence that reaffirms the insignificance of the privatized self, science becomes the commanding deity of a cult whose spread hastens the decay of pre-Enlightenment authorities but cannot satisfy the foundationalist urges that called them into being.

The growing irrelevance of the modern self in the face of this reified agency is intimately bound up with the notion of reason that defines the Western philosophical tradition and hence with that tradition's reformulation as epistemology. To see this, consider the political dynamic set in motion by modern science when, epistemologically construed, its rationality is credited with privileged access to the real:

> Philosophy, like all forms of reflective analysis, takes us away, for the time being, from the things had in primary experience, as they directly act and are acted upon, used and enjoyed. Now the standing temptation of philosophy, as its course abundantly demonstrates, is to regard the results of reflection as having, in and of themselves, a reality superior to that of the material of any other mode of experience. The commonest assumption of philosophies, common even to philosophies very different from one another, is the assumption of the identity of objects of knowledge and ultimately real objects. The assumption is so deep that it is usually not expressed; it is taken for granted as something so fundamental it does not need to be stated.[25]

The "intellectualist fallacy," expressing our obsessive preoccupation with the distinctive form of experience that is cognition, has "systematically hypnotized European philosophy since the time of Socrates into thinking that all experiencing is a mode of knowing, if not good knowledge, then a lowgrade or confused or implicit knowledge."[26]

The epistemological version of this fallacy has introduced new and insidious dimensions into this "turning of presence-in-experience over into presence-in-a-knowledge experience."[27] Characteristically, ancient philosophy distinguished its theoretical wisdom from what Plato called "right opinion" by grounding the latter in experience acquired through the everyday conduct of a skilled craft; the body's intelligent habits, although deemed epistemically inferior to philosophical insight, were nonetheless acknowledged as a genuine form of knowing. By way of contrast, modern epistemology holds that bare presentation to individual consciousness, whether of idea or sense datum, constitutes the exclusive source of cognition. When joined to its representation of consciousness as the privileged site of rationality in a universe of neutered matter, epistemology finds itself committed to the unqualified universality of the knowing experience: "If the notion of perception as a case of adequate knowledge of its own object-matter be accepted, the knowledge relation is absolutely ubiquitous; it is an all-inclusive net."[28]

The political import of this conclusion becomes apparent when it is wedded to the traditional conviction that the definitive traits of known objects are supremely valuable because they are the sole ultimate realities. It then follows that "all subject-matter, all nature, is, in principle, to be reduced and transformed till it is defined in terms identical with the characteristics presented by refined objects as such."[29] What this means in practice is best disclosed by the use to which Locke's empiricism is put by his Enlightenment successors. Although Locke insisted in his *Essay Concerning Human Understanding* that the "relations" established between simple ideas are the "workmanship of the understanding," this qualification was more or less forgotten by his French followers, who reduced these indispensable elements of scientific knowledge, like the epistemic atoms they link, to sensational form via a doctrine of extreme associationalism. When merged with the representation of consciousness as a blank tablet whose accuracy is guaranteed by its passivity, figures like Condorcet and Helvetius readily concluded that the mind could be moulded into any shape by merely regulating its impressions, sensations, and observations.

The French Enlightenment's celebration of infinite perfectibility was predicated on epistemological presuppositions that stripped noncognitive experience of its authority to either constrain or criticize the tyrannical pretensions of scientific knowledge. Persuaded that experience's value turns on its assumption of the formal features that define knowledge whose indubitability is apparent to all, the Enlightenment's champions too often succumbed to the temptation to equate realization of transparent, simple, and systematic order with the fulfillment of reason's promise. Or, to put this more bluntly, the terror of the French Revolution and Bentham's Panopticon are the unsurprising fruits of modern scientific rationality when, epistemologically construed, it mandates the colonization of all unrationalized experience.

Herein lies the explanation for modernity's peculiar "combination of thorough distrust of passion and faith with complete faith in reason and all-absorbing passion for knowledge."[30] Scientism (i.e., the idolatrous conviction that method-based knowledge furnishes the ontological ground as well as the exclusive organizing principle for all practice) is deeply implicated in a culture whose desperate desire to dispel doubt invites exploitation by those who know how to profit from the search for lost orientations:

> Like everything precious and scarce, it [modern science] has been artificially protected, and through this very protection it has been determined and appropriated by a class. The philosophic theories which have set science on an altar in a temple remote from the arts of life, to be approached only with peculiar rites, are a part of the technique of retaining a secluded monopoly of belief and intellectual authority.[31]

Ironically, it is this same worship of science that, when defiled by recalcitrant practice, explains the present revolt against reason. Such disillusionment, which Dewey finds most disturbingly articulated in Max Weber's "extreme hypostatization of the elements in human action that may be labelled irrational,"[32] is an expression of the frustration we feel when modern science proves unable to satisfy the cosmo-theological cravings now wedded to its cause. Our sense that the future's promise of unqualified progress remains unredeemed hints that modern science has been made to "reoccupy a position"[33] first staked out by medieval Catholicism through its eschatological account of the meaningfulness of human history considered as a whole. Accordingly, demystification of the superstitious cult of science represents a first step toward realizing a form of intelligence whose exercise will challenge rather than facilitate the conduct of domination.

Demystifying Science

A pragmatist critique of the epistemological interpretation of modern science, as well as the political dynamic it spawns, turns on the contention that experience does not comprise the discrete sensations or ideas of a self-contained psyche sustaining only external relations to a grid of independent objects. Correlatively, the pragmatist denies that immediate presentation of reality to consciousness is the defining mark of knowledge and, correlatively, that the content of everyday experience is itself an object of cognition. Rather, experience in its primary form is an affair of noncognitive doings and undergoings sustained by embodied agents located within concrete situational contexts; and thinking is a distinctive kind of conduct that transforms what is *had* in immediate experience into what is known. To explicate this position, John Dewey points to the difference between quenching one's thirst and inquiring into the chemical composition of water; between enjoying a conversation and researching the psychological make-up of its participants; between enjoying a painting and determining the compositional elements that account for its aesthetic form.[34] Each of these examples suggests a rejection of epistemology's peculiar version of the Western philosophical tradition's chronic contention that *to be* and *to be known* are one and the same thing. If we distinguish between what is given in the immediacy of primary experience and the form of experience that follows its refashioning by thinking, it becomes apparent that the character of the former cannot be gotten at directly but rather must be inferred. For as soon as we analytically remove some thing from the complex web of relationships of which it is a part to render it a discursive object, we have suspended its defining characteristic, (i.e., its qualitative status as what is experientially *had*): "Things in their immediacy are unknown and unknowable, not because they are remote or behind some impenetrable veil of sensation of ideas, but because knowledge has no concern with them. Immediate things may be *pointed to* by words, but not described or defined."[35] The more experience is had unreflectively, the more it is absorbed within the ongoing practices of human beings and hence absent from the deliberate attention that thinking entails: "Existences *are* immediately given in experience; that is what experience primarily *is*. They are not given *to* experience but their givenness *is* experience. But such immediate qualitative experience is not itself cognitive; it fulfills none of the logical conditions of knowledge and of objects *qua* known."[36]

When epistemology fails to acknowledge the distinction between the presence-in-experience of noncognitive things and their reflective constitution as epistemic objects, it cannot help but affirm the antecedent reality of a discrete knower standing in a relationship of subjective perception to its externalized objects of cognition. It cannot help but deny the reality of experience, which, because "innocent of the discrimination of the *what* experienced and the *how*, or mode of experiencing," admits of "no division between act and material, subject and object, but contains them both in an unanalyzed totality."[37] Our primary encounter with the world, in other words, is grounded in our dealings with it rather than in our reception of representations of it; we are experientially implicated within that world before we become subjects capable of conceptualizing a realm of independent objects to be mastered either intellectually or practically.

To hold otherwise is to think of reality (i.e., "what is there") as an entity whose truth can be known apart from our experience of it. As such, the epistemologist concludes, it can be used as a criterion against which to check the validity of competing accounts of its character. That belief in turn simply adds fuel to the fire that is the philosophical tradition's familiar denigration of conventional belief. For if opinion is "the state to which knowledge is condemned in a merely finite and phenomenal world," then philosophy is defined by its "invidiously superior attitude towards the convictions of the common man."[38]

To think of experience as does the pragmatist is to see that "reality" *is* that which is disclosed in prereflective experience. As Dewey's "postulate of immediate empiricism" states,

> ...things—anything, everything, in the ordinary or nontechnical use of the term "thing"—are what they are experienced as....If it is a horse that is to be described, or the *equus* that is to be defined, then must the horse-trader, or the jockey, or the timid family man who wants a "safe driver," or the zoologist, or the paleontologist tell us what the horse is which is experienced. If these accounts turn out different in some respects, as well as congruous in others, there is no reason for assuming the content of one to be exclusively "real," and that of the others to be "phenomenal"; for each account of what is experienced will manifest that it is the account *of* the horse-dealer, or *of* the zoologist, and hence will give the conditions requisite for understanding the differences as well as the agreements of the various accounts.[39]

The qualitative dimensions that make each of these experiences what it distinctively is belong neither to the experiencing self nor to the object experienced but rather come into being as a result of the transaction sustained between them. Over time, as Dewey's examples suggest, such qualities sort themselves into kinds such that we can intelligibly speak of what it means, for example, to be a jockey. But the fact that ordinary experience comes to be segregated into types (e.g., the productive, the political, the religious, the scientific) poses no specifically epistemological dilemma for pragmatism. As a doctrine of what William James called "radical empiricism," pragmatism recognizes the claims of all modes of experience rather than according any one privileged access to the real.

Consequently, there is no good reason to hold that science, as opposed to (say) art, is peculiarly entitled to disclose or express the truth of things: "We do not have to go to knowledge to obtain an exclusive hold on reality. Esthetic and moral experience reveals the traits of real things as truly as does intellectual experience."[40] Science is not a self-justifying and self-sufficient agency whose unconditional stranglehold on truth places its practice beyond either criticism or regulation. As one among many ways of gaining entry into experience, it merely explains the world so far as it can be rendered intelligible through its distinctive way of abridging the immediacy of prereflective experience. Its abrogation of the qualitative dimensions of existence, as when the physicist insists that the law of gravitation refers not to the behavior of common sense objects but rather to the movement of homogeneous masses, is a temporary expedient that states the conditions under which things present themselves but does not reveal their essences. To insist that the vocabulary of the physicist comprises the language to be used in determining the adequacy of claims formulated in any other language is to permit the hegemonic pretensions of the Western philosophical tradition to universalize the otherwise unobjectionable contention that the world can be grasped mathematically for the purpose of facilitating control. That in turn must provoke the equally universalistic rejoinder of metaphysical idealism, which, like its materialist counterpart, signifies nothing more than the nagging persistence of questions that no longer need answering.

The pragmatist account of the relationship between knowing and experience situates the forms of analysis peculiar to modern science within the context furnished by the qualitative and noncognitive. If that ground is neglected or denied, the conduct of science becomes abstract; it becomes deficient in that it requires reference to a more encompassing context to bring its project to completion. "Knowledge that is ubiquitous, all-inclusive and all-monopolizing, ceases to have meaning in losing all context."[41] Specification of that context's character is the purpose of Dewey's concept of the situation. All thinking, no matter how sophisticated, emerges out of and draws its initial material from a specific spatially and temporally qualified experiential context. Contrary to empiricist epistemology, what is given within such a situation is not a confrontation between uninterpreted sense data and a self who, to the extent that its contact with the world is defined by its reception of such unrelated data, must be as fragmented and discontinuous as the discrete objects it knows. Were that in fact an adequate account of experience, there could be no backdrop against which to articulate the meanings that define any particular encounter. Instead, what is given in experience is always a situation whose parts are more or less bound together by the presence of a pervasive quality, or qualities, that, depending on the fund of habitual meanings previously woven into the world through the dynamics of collective practice, renders it either recognized and understood or unfamiliar and puzzling.

The insufficiency of this fund accounts for the capacity of an unanticipated happening to disrupt the smoothness of everyday conduct and so render an individualized situation problematic. Better, it is this rupture of established expectations that makes the world conspicuous *as* a world, that is, as a complex of discriminable objects. Accordingly, the task of thinking is to reweave the world by fashioning new meanings that can show their full worth only by achieving expression in embodied conduct. By enduring the consequences and so learning of the import of its hypothetical meanings, the agent opens up the possibility of fulfilling thinking's telos in a reinstatement of the world's significance:

> Just what role do the objects attained in reflection play? Where do they come in? They *explain* the primary objects, they enable us to grasp them with *understanding*, instead of just having sense contact with them. But how? Well, they define or lay out a path by which return to experienced things is of such a sort that the meaning, the significant content, of what is experienced gains an enriched and expanded force because of the path or method by which it was reached.[42]

Intellectual instrumentalities of even the most refined forms of thought are therefore derivative. Although inquiry may entail "a long course of reasoning, many portions of which are remote from what is directly experienced, the vine of pendant theory is attached at both ends to the pillars"[43] of prereflective experience. Just as the meaning of the words used in any specific situation is comprehensible only through reference to the larger context of ongoing practices within which it is embedded, so too each instance of knowing secures its initial (although not necessarily its final) meaning through reference to the delimited situation out of which it first emerged. The fruits of thinking are not self-sufficient; they remain unripe until they become part of a new situation in which their import, as an integral element of this reconstituted whole, is had immediately as sensed significance. Because "meaning is wider in scope as well as more precious in value than is truth, the world which is lived, suffered and enjoyed, as well as logically thought of, has the last word in all human inquiries and surmises."[44]

Pragmatism, Modernity, and Democracy

A pragmatist construction of the relationship between knowledge and experience furnishes the conceptual leverage necessary to think critically about the dynamic of rationalization. That dynamic, which presupposes the transformation of science into scientism, is predicated on the hegemonic universalization of what Weber calls *Zweckrationalität*, that is, means–ends rationality, aimed at the achievement of technical control. This form of reason, Weber argues, dissolves traditional structures of meaning through its disenchantment of the world, yet fails to replace that which it destroys with anything that can give either meaning or unity to human experience. Consequently, the natural and social worlds are conceived exclusively as matter to be manipulated while, at the same time, the sphere of judgment, reduced to a potentially limitless number of nonrational preferences, is denied the ability to ground the power acquired through such objectification. Although incapable of justification by the canons of scientific reason, the Baconian vision of the totalistically administered society secures its fulfillment within the bureaucratized nihilism of Weber's "iron cage."

A pragmatist will not contest the descriptive adequacy of this reading of modernity; nor will a pragmatist deny the existence of powerful configurations of interest that benefit from acceleration of the dynamic of rationalization. However, by questioning the conviction that science constitutes the exclusive vehicle through which human existence can achieve value, the student of pragmatism does hope to counter the tyrannical pretensions of a reason that insists on remaking all conventional experience in the image of its artificial simplifications: "It is important for a theory of experience to know that under certain circumstances men prize the distinct and clearly evident. But it is no more important than it is to know that under other circumstances twilight, the vague, dark and mysterious flourish."[45] Encouraging us to inquire into the sense-making or sense-denying qualities engendered via incorporation of instrumental rationality into the noncognitive experience of everyday life, the pragmatist reminds us that "standardizations, formulae, generalizations, principles, universals, have their place, but the place is that of being instrumental to better approximation to what is unique and unrepeatable."[46] In sum, if insinuation of the modes of analysis and instrumentalities of science eviscerates the vitality of primary experience, that experience is thereby deprived of its ground as well as its authority.

The more explicitly political bearing of this argument can be suggested by offering a bare-bones indication of the character of a pragmatist critique of Weber's nemesis—the bureaucratized state of late modernity. Dewey defines "mind" as the cumulative fund or resource built up through abstraction and arrangement of the meanings intimated by concrete instances of intelligent conduct. "Intelligence," defined as "all the ways in which we deal consciously and expressly with the situations in which we find ourselves,"[47] thus gets its bearings from mind; for mind comprises the contextual background, which—in addition to accounting for the intelligibility of objects of focal aware-ness—furnishes preliminary guidance to conduct in its reworking of problematic situations. It is, as such, the handmaiden of intelligence's doings.

Yet mind "has not remained a passive spectator of the universe, but has produced and is producing certain results. Ideas that descend from the prescientific era are still with us and are crystallized in institutions."[48] For example, the mind of modern science, epistemologically construed, has achieved its most powerful articulation in the bureaucratic institutions of the modern state. It is there that we locate an objectified expression of epistemology's commitment to an inverted reading of the relationship between mind and intelligence. Within such institutions, mind sheds its derivative status and assumes the form of a hypostatized reality detached from its ground in primary experience.

One posture assumed by the state's agencies of bureaucratic administration toward the society they manage presupposes the epistemological distinctions between reality and appearance, reason and opinion. Because it hypostatizes the subject–object dualism generated by its own reflection, epistemology can have no sense for the interwoven textures of prereflective experience and so cannot escape a manipulative conception of action. So too, as a superimposed structure of ossified reason, the bureaucratic state can neither create nor sustain an integral link between itself and its charges. Presupposing the antecedent reality of the disjunction between its power and the ground from which that power was first extracted, the officers of that state cannot help but confront society as an externalized object to be mastered instrumentally through reference to the statistical uniformities its own rule produces. Tacitly holding that their subjects are incapable of sufficient self-organization because of their status as recalcitrant bits of matter not yet shaped to form, the officers must conclude that only progressive penetration of means–ends rationality into every sphere of collective action can thwart society's decomposition into phenomenal disarray.

Correlatively, realization of the state's autonomy—secured through expropriation of whatever means of collective action might otherwise be deployed to counter the purity of its abstraction from the sphere of unreason—progressively vitiates society's ability to unlearn its need for constant supervision and discipline. Recapitulating in secular form the theological conviction that God is mind perfected, the bureaucratic state equates the fulfillment of national purpose with its accumulation of the power that ensures its exclusive right to represent the real.

Ruling via efficient application of administrative directives, the bureaucratic state gives practical expression to the Western philosophical tradition's defining fallacy:

> Since it is the express and proper business of the philosopher to subject things to reflection with a view to knowledge, he is prone to take the outcome of reflection for something antecedent. That is to say, instead of seeing that the product of knowing is *statement* of things, he is given to taking it as an *existential equivalent* of what things really are "in themselves," so that the subject-matter of other modes of experience are deviations, shortcomings, or trespasses.[49]

Distinguished from the variability and heterogeneity of ordinary qualitative experience, knowledge's most refined objects effect abstract substitutions by formulating mathematical equations, the purpose of which is to fashion the matter of experience in a way that highlights its susceptibility to calculation and control. When an epistemological bureaucrat converts the formalized statements of administrative science into the desiderata to which social relationships must conform to ensure their self-constitution as clear and distinct objects presented to the state's centralized organ of sight, knowledge's subordination to the cause of richer primary experience is once again forgotten. Over time, re-formed by the institutionalized mind that administers it, society comes to accede to its own organization as a systematic totality comprising specialized functional units hierarchically arranged in accordance with a comprehensive plan. Those specific social practices that submit without complaint to the imperatives of bureaucratic reason are construed as formally equivalent exemplifications of some general rule, whereas those that resist are either disciplined or dismissed as "anomalous."

Albeit unwittingly, ruler and ruled conspire to eliminate whatever impedes reason's consummation. The solitary self, recognizing that the qualitative dimensions of ordinary existence must now be confined to the shadows of the private sphere, acknowledges that its participation in public truth can be assured only by agreeing to define democracy as the levelling of difference. The bureaucratic state, equating reason with universal submission to its codified rules, defines the goal of politics as the avoidance of disorder through monopolistic marshalling of the physical and psychical energies necessary to its efficient hegemony. As what was once means becomes an end to which all owe their being, the state perfects its supremacy over those whose collective conduct grounds its power but who no longer share the forms of experience that might enable them to recall that this is so.

The irrationality Weber locates at the heart of rationalization is a contingent matter whose persistence turns, at least in part, on our collective conviction that experience's achievement of complete reality entails its wholesale reconstruction in accordance with the form and content of instrumental knowledge. Pragmatism's rival account of the relationship between intelligent conduct and experience exposes the totalistic thrust implicit in the epistemological ego's desire for unrestricted objectification of the world's contents. Affirming the ontological subordination of the abstract to the concrete, the relational to the immediate, that account validates the truth-making capabilities of embodied selves whose partial comprehensions remain incomplete until reabsorbed within the attentive habits of noncognitive experience.

Epistemology's dualisms serve chiefly to safeguard us from the intensity, ambiguity, and depths of experience that is lived rather than observed. What, therefore, might it mean to embrace the pragmatist invitation to sculpt epistemic and institutional structures that enhance rather than detract from the capacity of experience to achieve the vital state of informed engrossment that Dewey calls "cultivated naiveté?"[50] This is not the place to offer an exhaustive account of pragmatism's specifically political import.[51] I do, however, wish to make clear that if the modern bureaucratic state is in fact well understood as a complex of institutions that identify reason with the consummation of monocratic control, then any serious commitment to realize the promise of democratic politics must take as its initial premise a repudiation of that complex. This is not to call for a revolution in the sense of a violent overthrow of the state; that is a fantasy we can no longer afford. Rather, it is to call for a revitalized sense of everyday life's political character as well as a critical celebration of the capacity of ordinary citizens to assume responsibility for articulating their own organs of joint action.

Movements animated by a collective desire to go beyond state-centric politics, to recover the powers of action systematically expropriated by inegalitarian and rigid bureaucratic institutions, need not be created ex nihilo. The reality of that aspiration is evident in a wide range of associations that, whether using the language of contemporary feminism, humanistic Marxism, environmentalism, etc., question the anthropocentric notion that transformation of all nature into culture in accordance with the strictures of means–ends rationality is a condition of human freedom.

Pragmatism does not set itself up as a rival to such movements. Instead it offers a way to interrogate the state's objectivism without slipping into its alter ego, that is, the sort of subjectivism that spawns privatistic withdrawal from the public world. As we have seen, pragmatism holds that the capacity of ordinary actors to craft rich qualitative sense from the everyday situations in which they find themselves is the ultimate test of knowledge's value. It therefore suggests that when the insinuation of "knowledge" within the world of primary experience confuses and immobilizes, it is cognitively disqualified; in a strict sense, it can make no claim to truth.

How might this recognition inform a specific movement aimed at challenging the institutional vehicles through which the epistemological construction of reason is given objectified form? The medicalization of pregnancy and childbirth in the United States is a familiar story that need not be retold here. Suffice it to say that throughout the twentieth century, this domain of experience has been thoroughly colonized by the claims of expertise seeking maximal instrumental control. At the same time, the secularizing thrust of rationalization has relativized and hence vitiated the forms of ethical discourse (e.g., Christian fundamentalism) that might have furnished women with the resources of meaning necessary to question professionalized medicine's systematic appropriation of this domain. The transformation of reproduction through the introduction of new technologies continues apace, as infertile women are given the opportunity to have fertilized ova implanted in their wombs; as amniocentesis makes it possible to "know" a fetus before delivery; as extensive surveillance of women throughout pregnancy, from prenatal genetic screening to ultrasound imagery to fetal monitoring during labor, becomes the order of the day.

The cumulative effect of these interventions is readily interpreted in the terms of this essay. The Western philosophical tradition is distinguished by its conviction that the legitimacy of noncognitive experience turns on its assumption of the form and content definitive of knowledge's reified objects. Because this tradition has generally regarded women as embodied expressions of unrefined nature, their experience has proven especially vulnerable to rationalistic invasion. Thus, as the inexpert skills once deemed adequate to reproduction are progressively discredited, as midwives are replaced by obstetricians and gynecologists, the shared intelligence of women gives way to the bureaucratically structured centers of social control that are modern hospitals. Confronted by these obdurate expressions of mind, women become epistemological subjects whose experience assumes the form of subordination to unknown objects within self-enclosed institutional complexes whose paradigmatic values are predictability, control, and security.

It may appear irrational to question the benefits made possible by such technological and institutional innovation. It is especially difficult to do so given that such "progress" is intensely ambiguous in import. To a couple who has suffered years of infertility, in vitro fertilization cannot help but appear a blessing. Acknowledging that, a pragmatist's perspective cannot pretend to generate simple or definitive answers to the contextualized dilemmas of everyday practice. What it can do is to call attention to the costs of such blessings; for more often than not their adoption, especially within the confines of medicine as currently institutionalized, will undermine the capacity of experience to affirm and enrich the qualitiative sense of its own integrity.

The authority of modern medicine, based in the representation of its practice as a self-legitimating domain of expertise, is at least partly contingent on its refusal to acknowledge the ontological priority of the noncognitive doings and undergoings of embodied agents situated within qualitatively idiosyncratic contexts. To recall the distinction between the presence-in-experience of noncognitive things and their reflective constitution as objects of knowledge is to open up the possibility of asking how the incorporation of knowledge's fruits within reproductive technologies is concretely *had*. It is to contend that the legitimacy of medical practice turns on its capacity to supplement, refine, and expand (as opposed to replace, dominate, and impoverish) the fund of habitual meanings already woven into the world of the patient. It is to question the medical profession's negation of conventional opinion by affirming the "reality" of what is disclosed in the body's prereflective experience. It is, finally, to suggest that the practice of medicine is abstract and hence deficient so long as the patient's experience fails to take shape as genuine suffering (i.e., as an undergoing that enhances the significant sense of the world rather than reducing it to senselessness).

To become alert to the many ways in which contemporary institutions express an epistemological construction of the relationship between knowledge and experience is to grasp one of the fundamental mainstays of our inegalitarian and antidemocratic polity. It is to appreciate the need to recreate the constitutional foundations of that polity by fashioning new institutions that respect the claims of ordinary experience and its struggle to sustain some sense of itself. To stay with the example suggested here, to participate in the establishment of a women's health clinic is to bring into being a medium of practice wherein professional medicine's objects may begin to reaffirm their status as embodied agents. And to reappropriate expropriated powers in this domain is perhaps to initiate a critical dynamic that may in time animate comparable conduct in others. It is therefore to take a small but not insignificant step toward recovering the integrity of a civil society whose knowledge, expressed in the common sense of its members, remains embedded in the ground that nurtures it. Pragmatism can give no detailed instruction in the tactics and strategies appropriate to this more encompassing end. However, by recovering the prephilosophical distinction between knowing and the modes of noncognitive experience it can either enrich or subvert, it renders a bit less stubborn the bars of Weber's iron cage.

Abbreviations

In the following notes, numerical citations (e.g., 61/12) refer to the cataloging system used by the Morris Library at the University of Southern Illinois to organize Dewey's unpublished manuscripts. Except where otherwise specified, all other citations use the following abbreviations:

AE   *Art as Experience* (New York: Paragon Books, 1979).

CE2   *Characters and Events*, vol. II (New York: Octagon Books, 1970).

EEL   *Essays in Experimental Logic* (Chicago: University of Chicago Press, 1916).

EN   *Experience and Nature* (New York: Dover, 1958).

ENF   *On Experience, Nature, and Freedom*, Richard Bernstein,editor (Indianapolis: Bobbs-Merrill Co., 1960).

EW2   *John Dewey: The Early Works*, vol. II (Carbondale: Southern Illinois University Press, 1967).

FC   *Freedom and Culture* (New York: Capricorn Books, 1963).

IDP   *The Influence of Darwin on Philosophy* (New York: Peter Smith, 1951).

LTI   *Logic: The Theory of Inquiry* (New York: Henry Holt & Co., 1938).

LW1   *John Dewey: The Later Works*, vol. I (Carbondale: Southern Illinois University Press, 1981).

PC   *Philosophy and Civilization* (New York: Minton, Balch & Co., 1931).

QC   *The Quest for Certainty* (New York: Paragon Books, 1979).

RP   *Reconstruction in Philosophy* (Boston: Beacon Press, 1957).

Notes

1. For a helpful review of this anti-Enlightenment literature, see Richard Bernstein, "The Rage Against Reason," *Philosophy and Literature* 10, no. 2 (October 1986): 186–210.

2. Dewey, *FC*, p. 131. For Dewey's explicit comparison of American pragmatism with "the French philosophy of the enlightenment," see "The Development of American Pragmatism," in *PC*, p. 34. For his claim that the "faith" of the Enlightenment "may have been pathetic but it had its own nobility," see "Time and Individuality," in *ENF*, p. 227.

3. Dewey, "Antinaturalism in Extremis," in *Naturalism and the Human Spirit*, Y. H. Krikorian, ed. (New York: Columbia University Press, 1944), pp. 1–2.

4. Dewey, *RP*, p. 121.

5. Dewey, "Philosophy and Democracy," in *CE2*, p. 854.

6. Dewey, *RP*, p. 66.

7. Dewey, *RP*, p. 70.

8. Dewey, *RP*, p. 74; "Philosophy and Democracy," in *CE2*, p. 851.

9. Dewey, *EN*, p. 382.

10. John Dewey, "How is Mind to be Known?" *Journal of Philosophy* 39 (1942): 3.

11. Dewey, "Philosophy and Democracy," in *CE2*, p. 853.

12. Dewey, 54/6, p. 12.

13. Descartes, quoted in Anthony Kenny, *Descartes* (New York: Random House, 1968), p. 125.

14. John Locke, *An Essay Concerning Human Understanding*, Peter Nidditch, ed. (Oxford: Clarendon, 1975), p. 525.

15. Dewey, *EN*, p. 229.

16. Dewey, "The Experimental Theory of Knowledge," in *IDP*, p. 80.

17. Dewey, *LTI*, p. 529.

18. Dewey, 61/21, pp. 12-13.

19. Dewey, 59/9, p. 31.

20. Dewey, *EN*, p. 24.

21. Dewey, *EN*, pp. 136–37; "The Experimental Theory of Knowledge," in *IDP*, p. 101.

22. Dewey, "The Development of American Pragmatism," in *PC*, p. 18.

23. Dewey, "Consciousness and Experience," in *IDP*, p. 244.

24. Dewey, "The Antecedents and Stimuli of Thinking," in *EEL*, p. 134; "The Significance of the Problem of Knowledge," in *IDP*, pp. 273–74.

25. Dewey, *EN*, p. 19.

26. Dewey, "The Need for a Recovery of Philosophy," in *ENF*, p. 54.

27. Dewey, *ENF*, p. 54.

28. Dewey, "Naive Realism vs. Presentative Realism," in *EEL*, p. 263.

29. Dewey, *EN*, p. 21.

30. Dewey, "Beliefs and Existences," in *IDP*, p. 181.

31. Dewey, *EN*, p. 382.

32. Dewey, 55/11, pp. 13–14.

33. I draw this phrase from Hans Blumenberg, whose *The Legitimacy of the Modern Age*, Robert Wallace, tr. (Cambridge, Mass.: MIT University Press, 1983), is strikingly Deweyan in important respects.

34. These examples are to be found in Dewey's "Introduction" to *EEL*, p. 2.

35. Dewey, *EN*, p. 86.

36. Dewey, *LTI*, p. 522.

37. Dewey, "Data and Meanings," in *EEL*, pp. 136–37; *EN*, p. 8.

38. Dewey, "Beliefs and Existences," in *IDP*, pp. 189, 192.

39. Dewey, "The Postulate of Immediate Empiricism," in *IDP*, p. 227.

40. Dewey, *OC*, p. 295; *EN*, p. 19.

41. Dewey, *EN*, p. 23.

42. Dewey, *EN*, pp. 4–5.

43. Dewey, *EN*, p. 2a.

44. Dewey, "Philosophy and Civilization," in *PC*, p. 4.

45. Dewey, "Experience and Philosophic Method," in *LW1*, p. 369.

46. Dewey, *EN*, p. 117.

47. Dewey, *AE*, p. 263.

48. Dewey, "Psychology," in *EW2*, p. 15; "Unity of Science as a Social Problem," in *International Encyclopedia of Unified Science*, Otto Neurath, ed. (Chicago: University of Chicago Press, 1938), p. 35.

49. Dewey, "Experience and Philosophic Method," in *LW1*, p. 375.

50. Dewey, *EN*, p. 37. For Dewey's best indication of the character of such experience, see his "Interpretation of the Savage Mind," in *PC*, pp. 173–87.

51. For an attempt to outline a pragmatic account of politics, see my *Politics/ Sense/Experience: A Pragmatic Inquiry into the Promise of Democracy* (Ithaca, N.Y.: Cornell University Press, 1991).

Chapter 3

Democracy and Citizenship

John P. Burke

Must a good society be a democracy? It is not difficult to imagine a society that is a good society in many important ways but in which democracy is not one of the characteristic "goods." One cannot, after all, simply assume that democracy is a defining feature of a tolerably good society. And many "goods" may be selected as enjoying priority over democracy even on the assumption that democracy deserves some status as a good. The history of Western political philosophy from Plato onward contains examples of ideal societies, constructed at the level of theory, that are not of a democratic form. Indeed, with Plato democracy is neither neglected nor absent but deliberately expunged from the Republic to be presided over by philosopher kings. Far from an ideal, democracy is pathological, a malady. Others, while indulging in idealistic and utopian thought, have not found it necessary to include democracy on their list of political and social goods. Many thinkers have joined Plato unabashedly in deeming democracy a malady.

Descending from thought to existing practice, as Platonic philosophical prejudice might express it, there are indisputably many societies whose members, supporters, and rulers have been regarded (by others) correctly as nondemocratic and (by them) preferably so. One cannot automatically impute cynicism about democracy to their views. Whatever the attractions democratic theory and democratic forms may hold for some of the members of twentieth-century liberal societies, the historical fact is that numerous people in Western (and not only Western) societies have chosen not to indulge in either democratic theory or democratic social forms.[1] In many of these societies democratic thought and activity are not normative ideals and some neither encourage nor sanction democracy. This is so as a matter of historical and contemporary fact.

Thus political imagination need not be particularly vigorous in conceiving a good but nondemocratic society. Existing and past societies need only be observed and invested, abstractly and hypothetically, with appropriate properties.

What would such a society look like? We may at the outset stipulate that the society values freedom, equality, and justice, and that it has institutions to give effective force to those values. The society may be free of disease to a very large extent, may have reduced poverty and human misery considerably, and may have achieved a rather high standard of living for all or most of its members. "We might argue that any good society cannot contain overwhelming misery, poverty, disease, repression, exploitation; that its members must have some rather high level of comfort, culture, freedom, security, and peace."[2] The society may be highly productive economically, scientifically, technologically, and artistically. It does not exploit or war upon neighboring societies. It simply has no democracy.

This may seem a fantastic assemblage of parts—a good society minus democracy—a monster. To be more precise, at least three objections may be here entertained even to this limited beginning. First, it may be said that disagreement about what would constitute a good society would be so deep and so extensive as to rule out even taking this imaginary first step. Barrington Moore, Jr., formulates this objection and disposes of it in a manner adequate for present purposes.

> Human beings have rather more difficulty in agreeing upon what they do want than what they do not want. The good society connotes one that has a variety of positive virtues, from satisfying the lower to the higher appetites. Over such questions there can be legitimate and endless differences of opinion. On the other hand, people are much more ready to agree that they would like to escape from pain and suffering, especially from useless and avoidable suffering. As used here, the conception of a decent society has an even more restricted and negative aim than the elimination of useless suffering. It means no more than the elimination of that portion of human misery caused by the working of social institutions. The historically recurring forms of suffering due to such causes can be grouped very roughly under the headings of war, poverty, injustice, and persecution for the holding of unorthodox opinions.[3]

Disagreement about a good society does not rule out agreement on a decent society. Put in Moore's terms, my question becomes: "Can a decent society be nondemocratic?" This leads to two further objections.

It may be said that it is conceptually impermissible to imagine a good, or decent, society in the ways mentioned above if there is no democracy. That is, it may be argued that such concepts as freedom, equality, and justice entail the concept of democracy. This seems to me to be possibly true, but I am not certain of it. All that may be true (or need be true) is that a nondemocratic but "decent" or "good" society understands and institutionalizes freedom, equality, and justice in ways different from the manner in which those values are realized and understood in a democratic society. In other words, the democratic understanding of freedom, equality, and justice may be different, a variant of these, but not the definitive and defining expression of them. This does not entirely, if at all, dispose of this possible objection, but I do not propose to do more at this point than acknowledge this objection.

Finally, it may be objected that there is no conceptual impossibility involved in the postulation of a decent nondemocratic society but that, more seriously, there is a real incompatibility. Democracy, it might be argued, is necessary to the existence of such goods as mark the good or decent society. It either enables these to exist or flourish or it is a necessary concomitant of them, or some other supposed complementary. This objection may insist on pointing out that democracy is an historical achievement alongside the growth of freedom, equality, and justice and that it is simply ahistorical to imagine a nondemocratic decent society. Or the objection could take a "functionalist" or systemic form: democratic practices, values, and institutions are necessary for the functioning of a society in which such goods as freedom, equality, and justice are parts of a system.

To dispose of this objection would be difficult. If it has merit, presumably that would be because of some historical truth about democratic societies, an historical truth that in no way seems entirely obvious. This much seems to be correct—that if democracy has been achieved or is yet to be achieved, then that is an historical achievement and there is something ahistorical about proposing to imagine a decent nondemocratic society. But even if the charge of being ahistorical is well-founded, this need not be fatal to a conceptual exercise in political philosophy.

What objection or criticism is it reasonable to direct to a nondemocratic but, in other respects, decent or tolerably good society? Is it that such a society would be a "better" society if only it were democratic? Better in what sense? Would it be "better off" in some economic or technological sense? Would it be politically superior to a society that was exactly like it but not a democracy? To raise such questions is to invite exploration into the value of democracy. It is the value of democracy I now propose to consider.

Certain features of the social and political thought of John Stuart Mill and Jean-Jacques Rousseau are first examined as they bear on democracy, the individual and the public, and on citizenship. I then examine a contemporary exercise of democracy and citizen participation, analyzing the public discourse on education and its reform.

John Stuart Mill

Some, although presumably not all, democrats believe democracy has moral justification. For them the value of democracy consists in its moral aptness for human beings and human affairs. For them, however efficient or inefficient democratic practices and institutions may be, the true value of democracy rests on moral grounds. Democracy alone, or more so than its rivals, is in accord with other fundamental values such as freedom, equality, and the autonomy of the human individual. A major moral objection to a nondemocratic society is thus that it is paternalistic, and the classic objection to paternalism is found in Mill's *On Liberty*.

John Stuart Mill is not consistently viewed as a democrat. Maurice Cranston has said flatly "Mill was a liberal, but not a democrat."[4]   But Mill favored weighted voting, with more influence being registered by the more educated. He was an advocate of women's liberty; he anticipated that universal suffrage would become a reality and hoped that education would prepare for such a development. These features of his thought do not necessarily negate credentials as a democrat. What is true is that Mill's central concern is not democracy but rather liberty. He argued for liberty, he said, not on grounds of abstract right but on grounds of utility. The greatest good of the greater number of people could best be assured by individual liberty of thought, expression, and manner of life. Foregoing a claim for liberty based on "abstract right" meant that Mill thought that what justified individual liberty was an improvement of the individual and, thereby, the rest of society. What concerned Mill was the dominance of the majority of people in society, the stifling hold of the customary and the conventional, over the minority.

Mill's espousal of liberty is thus not absolute but qualified. Liberty is justified because of social utility, of which the flourishing of individual development is an assumed element. But if individuals are to flourish in an environment of liberty, they must be "capable of being improved by free and equal discussion." Thus liberty is for those "in the maturity of their faculties." Mill explicitly excludes from the proper domain of liberty "children and barbarians." For the latter, paternalism and benevolent despotism, respectively, are in order.

On the whole, however, Mill objects to paternalism as an unwarranted intrusion into the competence of mature, educated individuals to develop their capacities and in turn to enrich the society's well-being. In discussions of Mill it is often questioned which commitment of Mill's runs deeper—liberty or utility. He maintained that he deemed individual liberty to be justified against the despotic inroads of convention, custom, and majoritarian intolerance because not only did individual liberty enhance (and enable in the first place) individual development and flourishing (a self-realizationist ideal), but it contributed to social utility. He asserted that he regarded utility—the greatest good of the greater number of people—to be the ultimate appeal on ethical matters. In foregoing a rights-based libertarian defense ("abstract right"), he shows his awareness of its availability and implies its ethical inferiority to a utilitarian defense. And yet the enthusiasm with which he defends the libertarian position, the passion with which he argues for a privileged sphere of the individual which society may not invade, have suggested to some, not unreasonably, that in this work, at least, Mill's libertarianism may overshadow his utilitarianism. But if

Mill meant what he asserted, that utility justified liberty in that allowing individual liberty to have scope in a society would in fact enrich that society and make that society better off than it would otherwise be, and utility was the ultimate appeal in ethical matters, where must Mill stand on democracy?

It seems clear that Mill as democrat must cite the principle of utility. If, hypothetically, Mill could have become persuaded, perhaps through the influential offices of Harriet Taylor,[5] that a democratic form of society and democratic activities not only allowed for the flourishing of individuality and individual well-being of all sorts, but that democracy really was in the utilitarian interests of the whole or the larger part of society, consistency would force Mill to embrace democracy with a utilitarian justification for it. Mill could have endorsed democracy as a normative ideal because of its perceived or anticipated improved social consequences over its nondemocratic rivals. That Mill did not, unambiguously, endorse democracy may suggest only his overriding concerns about majoritarian tendencies in his own society, his observations about the efficacy of existing democratic forms and processes in his own day, and a conception of human nature in which individual excellences, talents, and gifts are not distributed, either actually or potentially, as the egalitarian might suppose. To this we must add, of course, that Mill's utilitarianism, if it is the ultimate justifying philosophy for him, also supports paternalism where the circumstances warrant caring for (children) and administering for and ruling over (barbarians and "backward states of society"). As Mill himself recognized elsewhere in *On Liberty*, "the spirit of improvement is not always the spirit of liberty." It is tempting to conclude that even on this qualified representation of Mill as democrat his championship of individuality and his antipathy to the majority does not permit him to recognize and articulate a "mediating" conception between two such extremes. Such a bridging notion may be that of citizenship.

Jean-Jacques Rousseau

We have physicists, geometricians, chemists, astronomers, poets, musicians, and painters in plenty; but we have no longer a citizen among us; or if there be found a few scattered over our abandoned countryside, they are left to perish there unnoticed and neglected.[6]

Of what does Rousseau complain in this excerpt from his *First Discourse*? Rousseau's complaint gives expression to a distinction that is old in Western civilization, that between citizen and noncitizen. Aristotle drew the distinction between citizens and those who are laborers and artisans (not slaves, but those nonetheless involved in productive work activities). For Aristotle, the class of laborers, mechanics, and artisans is necessary for the existence of the polis, but it would be mistaken to classify them among the body of citizens for the reason that the productive worker "lives the life" characteristic of such product- and service-providers and has neither the time nor the capacity (presumably, for Aristotle "by nature") to engage in what is distinctive of the life of the citizen. What is distinctive of the life of the citizen? Aristotle defines the citizen as the one who is able to achieve a distinctive excellence by (whose virtue is) being free to share in the deliberative and judicial offices of the polis. Slaves, artisans, women, children, and foreigners are excluded from citizenship because they all, although for different reasons, are unable to participate in the realm of political action—deliberation, judgment, and decision-making about matters that affect not the individual or the household, but the community as a whole.[7]

Rousseau's fondness and admiration for (what he took to be) ancient Greek ideals and community are too well known to require comment. Rousseau's categories of noncitizens are instructive—we would today call them specialists, experts, professionals, technicians, managers, artists. Rousseau, then, deplored a wealth of professional practitioners of the arts and sciences and a dearth of citizens. Admittedly, it was his object in the *First Discourse*, if not to win the essay prize proposed by the Dijon Academy (which he did), then to defend an eccentric or at least unorthodox, anti-Enlightenment view on the role of the arts and sciences in the improvement or debasement of the human condition.

But Rousseau continued to uphold the value of citizenship not only above the value of the arts and sciences but even above the value of democracy. Although Rousseau is widely regarded as belonging more deservedly to the mainstream of democratic theory than does Mill, Rousseau too is a democrat in a very qualified sense. In the *Social Contract* he maintains that no true democracy ever existed or ever will because democracy is against the natural order of things. If there were a nation of gods, democracy would be suited to them, but such a perfect government is not suited to humans.[8] But Rousseau is consistent here. Like the Hobbes of the *Leviathan,* Rousseau defends the doctrine of absolute sovereignty, but Rousseau, unlike Hobbes, places the sovereignty in the people. The government, for Rousseau, is an administrative agency, and popular sovereignty and governmental administration can coincide only in the small-scale republic. Democracy, as a form of government, then, is suitable only for a small state. Rousseau's favored form of government is elective aristocracy by which he means an arrangement whereby the wisest govern the multitude, an arrangement he regards as the best and most natural. Governance by the wise is a thesis that Rousseau and Mill share, however much the latter may have thought Rousseau's confidence in the absolutism of popular sovereignty was misplaced.

Rousseau was a democrat not in the sense that he identified it as the best form of government. It was not, or if it was, it was also unattainable by human beings. He was instead a democrat in the sense that the people as a body, sans factions and special-interest groups, were to conduct the public business, the work of Aristotle's polis, of deliberation and decision-making concerning issues that affected them as a community, not as private persons or special-interest groups. The sovereignty of the people was by right absolute, indivisible, inalienable. In such consisted their citizenship; falling short of the absoluteness of popular sovereignty, the people would be subjects but not citizens.

Democracy cannot be described as having absolute value for Rousseau, but a case can be made for citizenship as having that place in his social thought, if anything deserves such a place. The First and Second *Discourses* and the *Social Contract* all subscribe to the natural freedom and equality of the individual. If we indulge Rousseau in his fiction of the state of nature and concede that the social contract is not some historical pact or convention, all he needs to maintain is that the supposed original natural liberty and equality of individuals are transcended and transformed in organized civil societies. Rousseau's answer to the modern problem of political philosophy—the legitimacy of the state—is given in terms, the only terms that can retrieve or restore natural liberty and equality, of absolute popular sovereignty. In the exercise of this sovereignty, in the certifying of an issue in accordance with the general will, the people give expression to the only liberty and equality that are salvageable given that we have to contend with government, whether that is democracy or elective aristocracy. In the exercise of this sovereignty, the people constitute themselves a citizenry.

> When our work is over we are in a position to enjoy all kinds of recreation for our spirits. There are various kinds of contests and celebrations regularly throughout the year. In our homes we find a beauty and good place which delights us every day and which drives away our cares. Our love of what is beautiful does not make us soft. We regard wealth as something to be properly used rather than something to boast about. And here each individual is interested not only in his own affairs, but in the affairs of the city as well. This is a peculiarity of ours. We do not say that a man who takes no interest in politics is a man who minds his own business. We say that he has no business here at all. We in our own persons take our decisions on policy or submit them to proper discussions. For we do not think that there is an incompatibility between words and deeds. The worst thing is to rush into action before the consequences have been properly debated.[9]

Readers of Rousseau's *Discourses* and *Social Contract* will recognize the theme of the integration of the citizen with the community that operates as a normative ideal in much of his work, but may wonder precisely where in the corpus of the "citizen of Geneva" such a passage is to be found. The passage is not Rousseau's but is attributed to Pericles, speaking of Athens, as recorded by Thucydides. This Periclean homage to a civic community, an idealization to be sure, is fully in the spirit of Rousseau. For Rousseau represents the communitarian "pole" (in contrast to Mill's individualism) in modern liberal democratic theory.

This is an image of a civic community far removed from American society today.[10] To confirm this one need look no further than the state of public discourse on contemporary education and its reform.

Excursus: Citizen Discourse on Public Education

It is difficult to think of a public issue with which Americans feel more comfortable and more entitled to debate, because the United States is accepted by them as a liberal democracy, than public education. On numerous other public policy issues, even those with no obvious need for specialists or expertise, Americans seem prepared, even willing and eager, to defer to authorities whose credentials may derive from their academic or professional discipline or from political office and leadership. But when it comes to public education and its possible need for reform, everyone feels that he or she is something of an expert in making the diagnosis and writing the prescription for reform.

This confidence is misplaced, as the following analysis of public discourse shows. It is not that there are education experts whose expertise is blithely ignored. Indeed, "education experts" is dissonant in a way not unlike that of "wisdom experts" in Socratic dialogues critical of the Sophists of Plato's time. Rather it appears that citizenship is questionable or is in a sorry state.

In 1984 the people of Washington State were invited to offer their observations of what was wrong and right with the public schools in their area, their beliefs about what and how to change, and their imaginary ideals of the public schools ten years hence. These forums were held all across the state and certain scholars from academic disciplines were asked to reflect on the meaning of this exercise in democracy, this citizen debate about reforming public education.[11]

Followers of democratic practices, especially critics of democracy, will not fail to recognize this description of an all too familiar exercise in democracy. I do not propose, of course, to generalize from this one issue in Washington State to the fortunes of democracy and citizenship in American society as a whole. But neither should any suitable inferences be blocked in advance.

It is legitimate to examine the citizen discourse on public education because people believe education (especially public education) is essential to a functioning democracy. They believe that citizens of a democracy have a right and a civic responsibility to contribute to the financial support and the reform of education for the sake of democracy. People believe they are competent to contribute to decision-making about public education. Finally, there is a kind of competence regarding education that, prima facie, it is proper to assume citizens possess.[12]

An analysis of the citizen discourse on the status and the future of public education in the state of Washington recalls two haunting images drawn from the works of philosophers separated by nearly 2500 years. In his 1981 book, *After Virtue*, the contemporary philosopher Alasdair MacIntyre offered the following scenario, entitled "A Disquieting Suggestion."

Imagine that the natural sciences were to suffer the effects of a catastrophe. A series of environmental disasters are blamed by the general public on the scientists. Widespread riots occur, laboratories are burnt down, physicists are lynched, books and instruments are destroyed. Finally a Know-Nothing political movement takes power and successfully abolishes science teaching in schools and universities, imprisoning and executing the remaining scientists.[13]

A later attempt to revive science finds only fragments—pieces of knowledge, experiments, and theories in a state of severe disorder. What would pass for scientific practices would be in disarray and public discourse about scientific terms and expressions would show disagreement and confusions about meanings. According to MacIntyre this imaginary world may be described as a "world in which the language of natural science ... continues to be used but is in a grave state of disorder."[14]

This provocative and disturbing scenario of the possible destruction and the clumsy revival of science was used by MacIntyre to introduce the hypothesis that moral philosophers should find "disquieting," namely, that the language of morality in our actual world "is in the same state of grave disorder as the language of natural science in the imaginary world." He then argued that we have lost our theoretical and practical comprehension of morality although we continue to use many of the traditional terms and expressions of morality.

MacIntyre's imaginary scenario stipulated that an antecedent state of healthy, ordered, coherent science suffers catastrophe. He hypothesized that a similar catastrophe has befallen moral theory, implying that moral theory and practice once enjoyed an antecedent state of healthy, ordered, coherent existence. By invoking the provocative imagery of MacIntyre, I do not suggest that public education has suffered a catastrophe that has gone unrecognized, although that may be true. I do *not* imply there has ever been an antecedent civic community in America in which public discourse on education was coherent and orderly, a state that has somehow undergone catastrophe or a state from which we may have imperceptibly lapsed. But I do maintain that public thought and discussion of public education are in a state of disorder. Community responses to questions about public education appear as fragments of conceptual schemes; some fragments are uprooted from their natural contexts; and some conceptual schemes do not harmonize.

Let me illustrate.

Participants imagined the 1994 classroom environment was challenging, with exciting learning and enthusiastic students. But a majority wanted stronger basic skills training and more testing of students, testing for both promotion and graduation. It is difficult to visualize basic skills training enkindling enthusiasm, and although tests do produce excitement, nervousness is the form it normally assumes. A majority of people questioned favored a curriculum with more emphasis on academics, more emphasis on vocational programs, and stronger graduation requirements. But they rejected a longer school day or year. But if school day and year are not extended, educational activity would have to be intensified. The question unaddressed is how.

Washington residents reported that teachers should be awarded more recognition for outstanding teaching performance and that more incentives should exist to encourage and to reward educational achievements. A sizable majority favored increased pay to reflect the "professional" status of educators and to attract highly qualified and motivated people to teaching. What teacher would not be gladdened at such news? But many people also wanted a longer work year for teachers, more emphasis on teacher evaluation, a longer probationary period for beginning teachers, stricter certification requirements, and more years of teacher training.

These are not necessarily contradictory values and goals, although it is difficult to visualize a public school whole in which these are coherent parts. Even with the prospect (or only the promise?) of increased pay and recognition, what intelligent person would rationally select the field of public education if it also involved more years of training, longer probation, stricter certification, a longer work year, and more evaluative scrutiny of teacher performance?

People favoring more testing and stricter standards for students also professed to favor individualized instruction, attention to individual learning needs, and sensitivity to individual student pacing. Some realized smaller class size may be a necessary condition for individualized attention. But the uniformity that seems requisite for meaningful testing and the imposition of standards they did not see as difficult to accommodate alongside individualized learning. Moreover, few were concerned that the emphasis on test scores would prompt teachers to "teach to the test," aiming to produce able test-takers, in part to receive favorable teaching evaluations in turn.

Washington residents reported they wanted to see more extensive and more substantive, meaningful community participation in the public education process. At the same time, a majority regarded the public school programs as disappointing in the provision of assistance to students needing remedial work, special education, gifted education, and bilingual programs. The latter would seem to require more "specialists," not just greater attention or "extra help" on the part of those from the community wanting to participate. Community participation may be a source of "satisfaction"; the question is whether it can be effective in accomplishing some of the claimed objectives.

To a participating scholar–observer in the citizen discussions and debates about public education in Washington, two things were quite clear. People in the various communities expected much from public education, and there was a strong desire for reform. They may have been expecting more from public education than what has been its most obvious historic mission: ensuring a certain level of literacy for the general public. For what they demanded was no less than improved basics, solid academics, individualized and special education, technological and global education.

The launch of a Soviet satellite in 1957 provoked calls in the United States for excellence in education, especially for improved mathematics and science instruction, and yet the business world and the academic world continue to be the recipients of graduates of the public school system: poorly trained and poorly prepared in critical thinking, and analytical and communication skills. In *A Nation at Risk*, David Gardner concluded that the schools were a major factor in the decline of American power in comparison to other world industrial powers.[15] But current calls for educational reform reflect nationalism (which is not the same as citizenship!) and concerns for declining U.S. economic productivity in the face of the perceived economic growth and health of Japan and Europe. Admittedly, into the discourse on public education there creep mentions of the need for an informed citizenry to participate in democratic processes, and of an ideal for individuals to be so educated as to maximize their potentials. Neither the theoretical need of a democracy for an informed citizenry nor the sorry state of citizenship would appear to harbor the galvanic force of the Sputnik of the 1950s.

American society is often characterized as pluralist. Some mean by this that it is a society with a plurality of special-interest groups, but it can also signify a commitment to a plurality of values, a pluralism reflected in the citizen discussion about public education in Washington State. Thus, one might interpret the public responses as reflecting commitments to values such as equality, individualism, freedom, or democracy.[16] Do those who sought improved basic skills training reflect the ideal of equality in education and equality of opportunity for a post-schooling life? Might the frequently expressed desire for "excellence" in education reveal a commitment to the ideal of individualism? If so, does the demand for better, and better-qualified, teachers similarly give voice to a recognition of individualism or to a dimly sensed recognition of teachers as an elite corps, a priesthood poised to impart and transmit a gnostic learning to enable the public school student to "succeed" and live the good life? Finally, does the call for greater community participation in the schools and educational decision-making deserve to be viewed as an ideal of democracy—participatory and planning democracy? Even if the demands and desires reflect and embody a pluralism of social values and ideals, and this appears uncertain, the effective fulfillment of such demands, and their reconciliation where they conflict with one another, would force one to confront the uneasy coexistence of the social ideals that constitute American pluralism.

This is not the place to probe the pluralistic value commitments of American society or to seek consistency among them. The point for present purposes is to reflect on a public education debate as an exercise in citizenship, in democratic participation. What was particularly striking to a scholar observing and participating in that process was the extent to which the people's demands upon and expectations of public education were like no demands or expectations applied to other public agencies or services. In the same vein, people tended to detach the schools from their real-world contexts, isolating them from the surrounding society. It is, of course, plain upon reflection that the public schools are microcosms of that society outside the classroom, the school grounds, and the campus. The ideal public school the citizens were asked to imagine in the 1990s cannot harbor peacefully, in isolation, in its classes, halls, and lunchrooms a set of conflicting pluralistic ideals.[17] Nor can a society contrive to sustain the image of public education desired by those participating in the education debate, if that substance is riddled with conflicting value commitments, themselves unresolved outside the schools.

The second haunting philosopher's image, called to mind by the public education debate, and with which I frame this excursus, is drawn from Plato's allegory of the cave in his *Republic*. The allegory is a powerful image of a society's education and a severe (Platonic) criticism of education. Plato has Socrates describe conventional education in terms of prisoners in a cave dwelling. There is an exit from the cave, toward the light, but the way out of the cave is very long. The cave dwellers have been so since childhood, their necks and legs in fetters, so they remain in the same place and can see only ahead of them, unable to move heads or legs. Light in the cave is provided by a fire that burns behind and above them. Between the fire and the prisoners is a path across the cave together with a low wall, "like the screen at a puppet show in front of the performers who show their puppets above it." On the path and along the wall are people carrying all kinds of artifacts, statues of people and animals. Some of the carriers are talking and others are quiet. The carried objects cast shadows on the wall the prisoners face, and the occasional talk of the carriers bounces echoes off the wall. The prisoners take the shadows and the echoes to be reality and they praise and honor those prisoners who could see most clearly the passing shadows and could best remember the order in which the shadows appeared regularly. Unless one of the prisoners were to be liberated from the chains and forced up to the light at the entrance, the prisoners would continue to assume the shadows and echoes were reality. Glaucon remarks to Socrates that this is a strange picture and strange prisoners. "They are like us," Socrates replies.[18]

Although the allegory has historically supported many interpretations, a savage indictment of conventional education is among them, and no one can seriously restrict the allegorical meaning to Plato's metaphysics of appearance and reality. The familiarity of the allegory does nothing to diminish its forceful criticism. Plato's allegory retains a capacity to provoke and disturb us about contemporary education. One may hope that public education does not resemble that to which the cave dwellers were subjected. "They are like us," Socrates had admonished Glaucon. One might wish that current debate by citizens about the point and purpose of public schooling did not resemble so closely MacIntyre's hypothetical scenario. My object is not to deflate public enthusiasm for democratic participation in the schooling process and schooling reform. Those who are serious about educational reform must reflect critically upon such public discourse to attempt to discern what these "revealed preferences" really mean and what they might involve for educational reform itself. Those who are serious about democracy must concede that the state of contemporary public discourse about education sounds a tocsin about the quality of citizenship in a nominally democratic society.

Citizenship

Why discuss public education or, more accurately, the public discourse about education, an apparent digression in an examination of democracy and citizenship? What is the place of Mill and Rousseau in this discussion?

Although Mill and Rousseau stand in the mainstream of the history of Western political thought about democracy, neither can or should be regarded unambiguously as democrats; they contribute to the understanding of democracy, particularly the value of democracy and citizenship. Rousseau's insistence on the absoluteness of the sovereignty of the people reinstates citizenship as a central category in political thought. Citizenship, the concern of the people (in a democracy, at least) for the public business, takes precedence over democracy in Rousseau's political conception. Mill too presents a persuasive case for the instrumental and qualified rather than the absolute value of democracy. He also articulates a moral critique of paternalism without rejecting wholly its necessity under some conditions. To appreciate Mill's utilitarianism and individualism is to see him as giving citizenship priority over democracy.

> Mill's attitude towards democracy is thus deeply ambivalent. On the one hand he, like Tocqueville, is a firm believer in participatory citizenship, and wishes to see as much popular involvement in decision-taking as possible. In one very important respect he was a more consistent and thorough democrat than many who claimed that title: he made no distinction between men and women. By universal suffrage he meant universal suffrage, and not male suffrage....On the other hand he shared middle-class fears of the working class and the "mass of brutish ignorance" which it supposedly embodied.[19]

As interpreted here, Mill represents an individualist pole in democratic theory, whereas Rousseau represents a communitarian pole. Democratic theory oscillates between these two "opposite" poles. Some notion of citizenship may be fruitful in mediating between these two poles. Interpretations of Mill and Rousseau aside, what is clear is that democratic theory is riven by the individualist and communitarian debate. To explore this rift here would take us too far afield.[20]

Concern for education is perennial for democratic thought. Democrats, nondemocrats, and antidemocrats have agreed that governing requires some sort of fitness. Whatever may be the fitness(es) for governing, democrats must seek fitness for self-governing in the education of the populace. Governing may not require public education, but self-governing of a *large* state almost certainly requires public education. Democrats must look to education as the chief means by which people become citizens, members of a functioning democracy. Thus, most attention to education within democratic theory is focused on civic education, even moral education, because of the role of education in sustaining a democracy.

The object of my excursus has been different. I have looked at public education neither in its own right nor because of its capacity to furnish requisite civic or moral education to a nominally democratic society. Rather I have examined public education indirectly (and thus democracy indirectly) by exploring the public discourse on education, because such discourse comes closest to citizen debate in this society at present. This is the voice of the putative sovereign in a democracy. Public education discussions are worth heeding not so much to discover a breakdown of civic education (as communitarian democrats may urge), but because of what is revealed about citizenship.

The existence of a widespread public discourse on public education indicates the presence of a democracy. The quality of the public discourse about education is a barometer of the quality of citizenship in that democracy. People assume they are members of a democracy and that it is incumbent upon them as members to contribute to the support and (sometimes) reform of education. As putative citizens of a democracy their active role in education is both their right and their responsibility. Because people believe they are competent to participate in decision-making about public education and educational reform, their deliberations in public forums provide some measure of the quality of citizenship in that society. Without imputing to them a theory of democracy or citizenship (or not much of a theory), it is thus appropriate to explore citizen discourse on public education in an effort to gauge citizenship in a professedly democratic society. The public debate about the present and future public schooling in Washington State cannot be pressed unduly to yield generalizations about liberal democratic American society or about democracy in general. But all communities in the state were involved, and this public exercise in deliberation and hypothetical decision-making about a public issue—education—comes closest to an ideal of citizen participation.

The thesis to which this discussion points is that the value of democracy lies in the conditions it affords for citizenship. Citizenship concerns questions of what must be shared and endured together in the public realm, what sorts of accountability we all hold each other to on matters of public concern. What level of shared participant activity do we regard as essential for constituting ourselves an effective society in addressing the public agenda? Elaine Spitz has articulated some essential properties of the "full-fledged citizen in a democracy."

> Three characteristics distinguish him from others: (1) The capacity to share in a specified community's life; (2) a stake in that community; (3) a willingness to share with the community the common experiences, both the duties and the rewards of group life. The citizen stands able, involved, and committed.[21]

I must add, however, that the citizen is one whose observations and participant activity are directed to issues that affect the public weal. Not all special interests and not all issues that might associate people in a community are issues to which the "general will" ought to be directed—only those that concern the common good. The belief that there are identifiable public matters that transcend individual and special interest without enveloping and engulfing all individuals in a vast assimilative community is central to democratic political theory.

Although citizenship need not entail democracy, democracy does entail citizenship; to assert this is to claim that the value of democracy is grounded in citizenship. This means more than that citizenship is complementary to democracy—something without which democracy is unfruitful. At the level of democratic theory, citizenship mediates between the individual and the community. At the level of practice, citizenship in a democracy provides the individual with a form of community that does not compromise the autonomy of the individual.

Democracy, Rousseau, and Mill converge in citizenship. Citizenship provides a kind of community that appears otherwise unavailable within the large nation state and that has led many theorists, notably Rousseau, to deny that democracy can have a place outside a small setting. If the theorists of planning democracy and participatory democracy are correct about the value of involvement, and if citizenship embraces such involvement and a recognition of its value, then citizenship has its own value independent of the value community is supposed to have and distinct from the value of citizenship as a surrogate for community.

None of the foregoing discussion constitutes an argument for or against democracy even if it is true that democracy entails citizenship. Even if the latter thesis is only suggested rather than supported by the present line of thought, one may venture the (weaker) hypothesis that a shift of attention from democracy to citizenship as a way of evaluating a society may be illuminating and fruitful. Normative political thought should perhaps examine a society for the quality of citizenship it affords rather than ask how desirable is democracy or ask whether a society is or is not a democracy. Or course, if the stronger thesis is correct (that democracy entails citizenship), then the weak hypothesis recommending assessment of a society in terms of its citizenship will have implications as well for democrats and for democratic theory.

Must a decent society be a democracy? Democracy may not be "the society nobody wants," in Barrington Moore's phrasing. But democracy need not be a utopia either.[22] It may be sufficient that democracy can afford the conditions for effective citizenship in matters of public life. "Feasts to which many contribute may excel those provided at one man's expense."[23] Thus the decent society does not entail democracy. There can be a decent society without democracy but no decent society without citizenship.

Notes

1. For the sake of simplicity in the present discussion, I ignore any problems that arise from considering the relationship of liberalism to democracy and thus refer to "liberal democratic theory" and "liberal democratic society." Sheldon Wolin, however, is a good example of a political thinker who has consistently appreciated that liberal values and democratic values are frequently in conflict with each other. See *Politics and Vision: Continuity and Innovation in Western Political Thought* (Boston: Little, Brown, 1960) and his more recent *The Presence of the Past: Essays on the State and the Constitution* (Baltimore: Johns Hopkins University Press, 1989).

2. Richard T. DeGeorge, "Marxism and the Good Society," in *Marxism and the Good Society*, John P. Burke, Lawrence Crocker, and Lyman H. Legters, eds. (New York: Cambridge University Press, 1981), p. 9.

3. Barrington Moore, Jr., "The Society Nobody Wants: A Look Beyond Marxism and Liberalism," in *The Critical Spirit: Essays in Honor of Herbert Marcuse*, Kurt H. Wolff and Barrington Moore, Jr., eds. (Boston: Beacon Press, 1967), pp. 401–2.

4. Maurice Cranston, "John Stuart Mill and Liberty," *The Wilson Quarterly* 11, no. 5 (Winter 1987): 88.

5. Cranston, p. 85.

6. Jean-Jacques Rousseau, *A Discourse on the Arts and Sciences* in *The Social Contract and Discourses*, G. D. H. Cole, tr. (New York: E. P. Dutton, 1950), p. 169.

7. Aristotle, *Politics*, Book III.

8. Rousseau, *Social Contract*, Book III, chapter 4.

9. Thucydides, *The Pelopennesian War*, tr. Rex Warner (Baltimore: Penguin, 1954), pp. 118–19.

10. A communitarian such as Robert Bellah may deplore the absence of such community, but it is not unreasonable for a democrat to wish not to be governed by someone's (or even a great many) "heart habits." See Robert N. Bellah, Richard Madsen, William Sullivan, Ann Swidler, and Steven Tipton, *Habits of the Heart: Individualism and Commitment in American Life* (New York: Harper & Row, 1986).

11. Citizens Education Center Northwest (Seattle, Wash.) played the major role in organizing the community forums and a summer seminar (sponsored by the Washington Commission for the Humanities), and in distributing discussion papers.

12. In support of this last claim, see Amy Gutmann, *Democratic Education* (Princeton, N.J.: Princeton University Press, 1988). This incisive, persuasive, and comprehensive discussion of why education in a democracy must itself be democratic is both intellectually provocative and philosophically responsible. See also her "Undemocratic Education" in Nancy L. Rosenblum, ed., *Liberalism and the Moral Life* (Cambridge, Mass.: Harvard University Press, 1989), pp. 71–88.

13. Alasdair MacIntyre, *After Virtue* (South Bend, Ind.: University of Notre Dame Press, 1981), p. 1.

14. MacIntyre, p. 2.

15. David Gardner, *A Nation at Risk* (Washington, D.C.: National Commission on Excellence in Education, 1983).

16. For an insightful discussion on how liberal values are already "situated" in the policies and practices of the public schools, see David C. Paris, "Moral Education and the 'Tie That Binds' in Liberal Political Theory," *American Political Science Review* 85, no.

3 (September 1991): 875–901.

17. Elsewhere I have argued that discussion of workplace democracy cannot isolate the workplace from its undemocratic surroundings. *Research in Philosophy and Technology*, Paul R. Durbin, ed. (Greenwich, Conn.: JAI Press, 1982), vol. V, pp. 37-41.

18. Plato, *Republic*, Book VII (514).

19. Anthony Arblaster, *The Rise and Decline of Western Liberalism* (Oxford: Basil Blackwell, 1984), p. 280.

20. See the fine collection of essays on the controversy in Nancy Rosenblum, ed., *Liberalism and the Moral Life* (Cambridge, Mass.: Harvard University Press, 1989).

21. Elaine Spitz, *Majority Rule* (Chatham, N.J.: Chatham House, 1984), p. 4.

22. Paul E. Corcoran has observed that utopian thought has seldom been expressed in the form of political democracy. If this is so, then whatever the value of democracy, it is not that it is a utopia. "The Limits of Democratic Theory," in *Democratic Theory and Practice*, Graeme Duncan, ed. (New York: Cambridge University Press, 1983), pp. 20-21.

23. Aristotle, *Politics*, Book III (1281 b).

Chapter 4

Democracy, Equality, and Racism

Lyman H. Legters

When Gunnar Myrdal placed his monumental and path-breaking *An American Dilemma* on the doorstep of American society nearly a half-century ago, the work bore the subtitle, "The Negro Problem and Modern Democracy."[1] The conspicuous implication for any reader, even before he or she had advanced beyond the lengthy acknowledgments, was that the problem existed, was necessarily there on the agenda of a modern democratic society, awaiting and indeed crying out for solution. It would be possible to argue about the relative importance to be assigned to Myrdal's book (and other less weighty contributions of similar sort) on the one hand, and to activist strivings of diverse sorts undertaken by the victimized African-American population on the other hand, in accounting for the persistent presence of "the Negro problem" in the intervening lifespan of this particular "modern democracy." From any perspective, it would be difficult, however, to deny the combination of prescience and forcefulness with which *An American Dilemma* forecast the agenda of American political and social life for the ensuing four-and-a-half decades that we can now scrutinize with the considerable advantage of hindsight.

What we see from this perspective is, first of all, that the problem is nowhere near solution but that, secondly, the problem is universally acknowledged (however diverse may be the terms in which the problem is addressed). To the degree that Myrdal's book contributed both a warning signal to, and a prescription for improving the health of, the particular "modern democracy" that was his subject, one can hardly ask more of a mere book. But what is left to contemplate, in a slightly less obvious implication of Myrdal's subtitle, is the notion that there is some particular injunction resting on a modern democracy to solve the problem of racism, precisely because it is a democracy. One has to go to Myrdal's text for a fuller exploration of the notion that American society, not alone because it bears a historical responsibility but especially because of its claim to democratic status, must feel a special urgency about the problem of race and racism. As I have suggested, this is a weaker implication of the subtitle, but it does raise several of the most interesting intellectual and theoretical problems adumbrated in *An American Dilemma*.

When Myrdal comes, as he does fairly infrequently, to deal with democracy as a concept, it is clear at least that he regards racism and democracy as incompatible. It is not equally clear why he thinks so. In one place,[2] referring as he often does to the American Creed (always in upper case!), Myrdal convincingly argues that attitudes that pass through institutionalized arrangements—school, church, state—formally committed to such values as racial equality will come out on the high rather than the low side of a society's median style of response to a problem such as racial prejudice. Contrary to what might be expected from a poll of prevailing attitudes, the power of certain ideals, institutionally transmitted into the arena of public policy, will, according to Myrdal, have some efficacy in counteracting the contagion of prejudicial attitudes left alone, as it were, to infect and stain a democratic polity. The ideals—Myrdal enumerates progress, liberty, equality, and humanitarianism as elements of the American Creed—operate in the institutional sector and "gain fortification of power and influence in society. This is a theory of social self-healing that applies to the type of society we call democracy."[3] Thus far, however plausible the notion of self-healing may be, we have no indication of what democracy amounts to other than its identity with the American Creed and the norms attributed to it.

At another point,[4] as part of his argument for the pivotal importance of suffrage for African-Americans, Myrdal calls attention to a historical peculiarity of the American polity, namely that the civil service, which in several European countries had predated the emergence of democratic forms and had therefore to be encroached upon by popular sovereignty, was in America a creature of democratic impulses and unable, given this reversal of temporal sequence, to fall back on a professional tradition of independence and impartiality. Accordingly, American habit placed exceptional emphasis upon the value of votes, as distinct from an independent rule of law (*Rechtsstaat*), as the means of holding bureaucracies accountable. Thus, democracy, which had impaired the functioning of an impartial and independent civil service, also provided the available remedy for those disadvantaged by a less than evenhanded administration of the law. Hence the centrality given by Myrdal to the acquisition and exercise of suffrage by African-Americans, the classic means of access to the system, and the mechanism of leverage still (at the time of his writing) largely closed to them.

An extension of the same point applies especially to the exercise of the judicial function by judges and juries closely tied to local pressures and the direct impact of popular (democratic?) influence. While maintaining as an aspect of the Creed "that Negroes are entitled to justice equally with all other people," Myrdal observes that democracy can cut both ways. "The extreme democracy in the American system of justice turns out, thus, to be the greatest menace to legal democracy when it is based on restricted political participation and an ingrained tradition of caste suppression."[5] It is therefore, at least in part, a charge against democracy (though not necessarily against the American Creed) that—and here Myrdal quoted W.E.B. DuBois—"The Negro is coming more and more to look upon law and justice, not as protecting safeguards, but as sources of humiliation and oppression."[6]

In the concluding portion of the book we encounter Myrdal's notion of the promise held out by democracy and (indistinguishably) the American Creed. "What America is constantly reaching for is democracy at home and abroad.... In this sense the Negro problem is not only America's greatest failure but also America's incomparably great opportunity for the future.... If America in actual practice could show the world a progressive trend by which the Negro became finally integrated into modern democracy, all mankind would be given faith again."[7]

As a last prelude to a closer examination of the relationship between democracy and racism, I want to insist upon two observations with particular reference to Myrdal. The first is that his methodological sophistication forbids us to take these statements as mere exhortation. It would of course bring no discredit to him if we were to say simply that his moral passion for racial equality provoked these phrases as a species of sermon that should not be scrutinized too closely. But it must be acknowledged that his scientific commitment, already several notches beyond the arid empiricism of conventional social science, commands us to take his statements seriously in their own terms.[8]

The second is that, however inadequate Myrdal's conceptualization of democracy may turn out to be, his book was not designed as an exercise in democratic theory. Although it is important to examine and perhaps also criticize his notion of democracy, it would be churlish to intimate that any such shortcoming impairs the magnificence of his accomplishment. Rather, it is precisely because of his work's permanent importance, and because American performance has fallen so far short of Myrdal's hopes, that it is worthwhile to inquire more deeply into his conception of democracy and its relationship to the racism he so unsparingly deplored.[9]

Democracy as Description and as Norm

A fascinating peculiarity is associated with the concept of democracy within the stream of the history of political thought. Although we use the term all the time, usually taking it for granted that it is securely rooted in Enlightenment and post-Enlightenment political philosophy, it turns out that the so-called classical model of democracy does not exist. Symptomatically, in his *History of Political Thought,* George Sabine cites in his index only the eighteenth-century Jean-Jacques Rousseau between his references to ancient (mainly Greek) democracy and his several references to democracy and communism.[10]   On a more systematic footing, both C. B. Macpherson and Carole Pateman, looking for the traditional (or classical) model of democracy that is frequently invoked, conclude that the classical model is a fiction and one that raises serious questions about the theorists who confidently cite it, describe its inadequacies, and then set about to improve upon it.[11]   Even John Stuart Mill, who on most accounts could be counted on to fill the void, turns out in Graeme Duncan's words to be a less than adequate stopgap. "Mill did more than put a democratic facade over capitalistic inequality, but he cannot be characterized as unequivocally democratic even according to his own lights. He was not a democrat of whom it could be said that he genuinely wanted democracy but failed to see the large social changes which should be needed if it was to become a reality."[12]

That leaves us with Rousseau and perhaps James Madison and Thomas Jefferson. The latter two, on Robert Dahl's showing,[13] can best be viewed as theorists of republicanism, in their different ways of course, and not of democracy. Rousseau's vision of a democratic polity, while embodying normative standards, could only be envisaged, by Rousseau himself, as a workable scheme for a city–state or a close community and is therefore substantially ruled out as a model for large and complex modern societies. Incidentally, some recent critical interpretations cast Rousseau as the inspiration for something called "totalitarian democracy";[14] although this is less than germane to the present theme, it invites mention because it expresses the riskiness often perceived in a normative theory of democracy. The anxiety manifest in the very expression "totalitarian democracy" is certainly well-founded in light of more recent social excrescences that owed something to populist impulse, but that anxiety may simply tell us less about Rousseau and his democratic model than it does about those fears that have so often attenuated and restricted the applications of democratic norms.   I agree that normative democracy, Rousseau's or any other, is risky as are all other ambitious social visions. But I shall suggest further on that the most serious risks lie elsewhere, namely in emptying the concept of democracy of its normative thrust in favor of built-in safeguards, which spring from a negative notion of liberty,[15] that limit full-scale democracy and in fact turn it into something else. It may turn out that because of the riskiness or for the sake of realizing positive social goals (e.g., racial equality) people may wish to forsake democracy as both norm and goal. But it is best, in that case, to be clear about what is afoot and not simply resort to artificial preservation of the ideal by redefinition.

With respect to the search for a classical, normative theory of democracy, I have sometimes urged greater attention to Karl Marx as author of a coherent and radically normative theory of democracy.[16]   This suggestion is most often greeted, and frequently by Marx's firmest supporters, with criticism of the shortcomings of Marx's democratic theory. Even as I agree with such critics, I must ask who offers a more coherent and at the same time pertinent democratic model to the contemporary world. The only sensible answer seems to come from those who, however wrong they may be in positing a classical body of democratic thought that must be rethought in empirical terms, want to substitute an entirely empirical account for risky and discomfiting normative elements of democratic theory.

The empirical accounts,[17] sensible though they may be in their own terms, proceed from the common assumption that we may know what democracy is by examining those systems that we are wont to call democracies. Instead of asking whether or not the traditionally labeled democracies of Western Europe and North America live up to a normative conception of democracy, they take the conceptual measure for granted and seek the general attributes of democracy within the systems that popular usage has admitted into that category. By this procedure, the norms are set not by any conceptual prescription, according to which existing political orders could be measured as to their adherence to the concept, but by a process of empirical generalization from the practices we have already agreed to call democratic. In this manner, the progress of democracy in the world is charted by the degree to which societies or polities of questionable acceptability move toward the model, namely us, that we already accept as defining. Accordingly, other systems also claiming democratic status can, by this technique, be dismissed out of hand as ideological pretenders. The criticism of our model that is apt to undergird their claim can likewise be disregarded on grounds of hostility, wrong-headedness, propaganda, or all of these.

We are reminded, in this connection, of the absence in contemporary socialist societies of Soviet type of any convincing theory of socialism. When reading purportedly theoretical reflections on socialist societies, from native but obviously not from dissenting viewpoints, we find instead an account of the development of that particular socialism, fortified of course by the necessary citations from classical socialist thinkers. Instead of telling us what socialism ought to look like and then measuring reality against that norm, we are given straight description based on the unstated premise that socialism is whatever the so-called socialist societies became as they developed. It is, then, not much different when Americans and Western Europeans describe their societies, analyzing their workings however meticulously, and profess to have told us what democracy is.

In fairness, it must be conceded that some of the empirical accounts of both democracy and socialism are more sophisticated than I have implied. Moreover, small doses of the normative do creep into many accounts, at least in the form of suggestions for improvement in the practices and institutions that seek to effectuate a democratic social and political order.[18] Such proposed improvements must come from somewhere, and if they are not fulfilled in current practice, there must be some discoverable source whereby deficiencies can be noticed and somehow measured: thus, the vast literature of political science on electoral schemes for a more faithful reflection of citizen preferences. Yet, no matter how sophisticated the empirical inquiry, that method or approach offers no route from the merely descriptive to the judgment as to whether or not a particular polity deserves at all to be classified as a democracy.

If we are thus driven to the conclusions that descriptive techniques are wanting and that no inherited theory is fully adequate to the modern world, what procedure can we adopt? What approach will provide a sufficiently firm notion of democracy that we can then proceed to examine the sense (if there is one) in which democracy forbids racism?

Clusters of Values

It would be difficult, and possibly also perverse, to begin with anything but the proper meaning of the term: Democracy means, and has meant historically, popular rule. The first consideration that follows is that some means must be used to ascertain what decisions or choices the citizenry may wish to make concerning those matters that arise if the community is to be governed. (Although societies differ as to the dividing line between public and private affairs, governance implies all those things that fall within the public arena as understood in any given society.) Whatever means are adopted for registering preferences, when the hypothetical unanimity of the citizenry is breached a rule is required to determine how differences are to be resolved. The majority principle, while not in itself any more appealing than some other numerical formula, has the singular merit of allowing each citizen equal weight in reaching decisions for the whole community. (Any cutoff point other than 50 percent would unbalance the weights of affirmative and negative preferences.) We thus arrive at a principle—majoritarianism—that is essentially banal and is yet the essential ingredient in any process aimed at effectuating the rule of the people.[19]

Thus far we have spoken of the citizenry as the body of people whose preferences count in the public realm. That way of defining "the people" avoids certain problematical features of majoritarianism—such as the position of children or those whose handicaps prevent the exercise of citizenship, not to mention the exclusion of slaves or aliens from the performance of citizen roles. It might be argued in defense of this sense of "the people" that it is necessary to classify Athens, the primary classical example of democratic rule, within the meaning of majoritarian, hence democratic, governance; also that it is appropriate for each polity to establish a category, citizenship, that is to some degree exclusive. But that also introduces another set of problems, especially if one imagines a body politic so exclusionary as to enthrone a narrow or numerically small segment of the population as an effective oligarchy ruling under the cloak of democracy. Such a circumscribed understanding of citizenship obviously allows for a restricted model of democracy that would be entirely compatible with slaveholding, gender-based inequality, and assorted discriminations based on race, religion, property-holding, and the like, provided only that it is the definition of citizenship itself, and not distinctions within the class of citizens, that provides the restrictions.

If outcomes of that sort are not formally incompatible with a citizen-based majoritarianism, we would still not want to acknowledge it as democratic just because the formalities are covered. It can hardly qualify as "the rule of the people" when most, or any significant fraction, of the population is excluded by denial of citizenship. To the majoritarian principle we thus need to add the widest possible definition of citizenship as a guide to the identification of a democratic order. Even then it may remain ambiguous on certain counts: a class of slaves might still be admitted, on much the same grounds that serve to place children outside the class of active citizens, without fatally damaging a democratic claim. It must at any rate be clear that the thrust of admittance to citizenhip be inclusive rather than exclusive in tendency.

If majoritarianism must count as a defining feature of the democratic model, the notion of maximal extension of citizenship in constituting the body politic is more of a recommendation[20] growing out of reflection on what would enhance and what would impair the central democratic imperative. Of similar nature is the injunction that participation is an essential feature of a democratic procedure. The notion of participation carries with it no prescription as to forms or types, no endorsement of particular participatory schemes, except perhaps the recognition that representation and its attendant need for voting, necessary though these may be in complex and widely extended societies, are ipso facto attenuations of the democratic principle of self-rule by citizens. When the achievement of equal and universal suffrage is still at issue, as it was for minorities when Myrdal was writing, the struggle for access to that basic lever of democratic politics and representative government remains crucial and is deserving of the attention paid it by the disenfranchised and their allies. Only when it is achieved is the shallowness, the inadequacy, of voting rights as guarantors of democratic decision-making fully revealed. That revelation must in turn lead, at least for those committed to authentic democracy, to a quest for additional modes of political action that will enable citizens to actuate their self-rule in a multitude of ways and on a daily basis. What these modes should be is, as noted above, not prescribed. But effective rule of the people or the citizenry clearly depends on a greater intensity and, as it were, density of participatory activity (absent of course any coercive devices for securing such participation by citizens) than is or can be present in an electoral system serving, with or without the manipulative features endemic to such systems, the principle of representative government. Participatory mechanisms and habits are, then, another recommendation, growing out of political thought, for the authentication of democracy.

It will not have escaped attention that the democratic requirements mentioned so far are procedural in character, that although normative in their thrust they say nothing about the substance of public life in a democracy—whether it will be more or less just, more or less honest, more or less decent and humane.

Myrdal's usage makes it evident that he expected democratic norms and procedures to operate favorably in behalf of the eradication of racism in a putatively democratic social order. It is not equally evident that he wanted to rest his expectations on some article of faith involving innate human decency as a quality to be liberated and maximized by democratic procedures. Rather, it seems to me, the grounding of his hopes for the eradication of racism through democracy is to be sought in his all but interchangeable use of the terms democracy and the American Creed.

It is difficult to imagine neither a hypothetical situation nor actual historical instances in which a reasonably scrupulous observance of the procedural rules of democracy, even the fairly ambitious ones enumerated here, has failed to obviate racist policies and practices. This is of course no riddle but just the obvious recognition that a set of procedural rules designed to assure social decisions that are in accord with the preferences of the citizenry offers no security against reprehensible choices if those are the prevailing sentiments of the majority. Apartheid, residential and school segregation, and employment discrimination are all conceivable choices of conceivable majorities, thus also possible outcomes of democratic procedures—much as Myrdal and we might wish otherwise.

Myrdal's way out of the dilemma was to invoke a set of related values, compatible with but not entailed by democracy, that he lumped together as the American Creed. He was guilty no doubt of sowing some confusion in his near identification of it with democracy; but if we separate out his notion of a Creed and focus on its connection with democracy, it may prove that his solution, unclear though it was, is not the worst one available.

The underlying notion involved a cluster of values, all compatible with democracy but none of them peculiar to it or impossible of realization in other political systems. Myrdal's expectations of improvement in race relations and in the status of African-Americans were built, apparently, on the belief that this cluster of values—including justice, fairness, and equality, at a minimum—would provide the substance of democratic procedure in action (though, again, he was not plain about democracy as procedure) to be realized over time as a fulfillment of those creedal commitments. Overly optimistic as he may have been about the overall impact of equal voting rights and about the purely political struggle in general, this is not a bad way of associating democracy with social goals that have validity independent of narrowly conceived democratic norms.

The fact is that political philosophers endorsing democracy have usually associated particular substantive values with their images of a democratic practice, thereby achieving a much more fully rounded picture of a good society than could be derived from democratic principles alone. What is crucial, however, is the choice of associated values from a historical experience and a constitutional commitment that Myrdal thought he had discerned in American society. Whether he was right or wrong is not our concern. But he did, in this manner, endorse a particular cluster or set of associated values he deemed favorable to the eradication of racism. I want to suggest other bases for choosing the associated values, such as justice and equality, that do indeed seem most pertinent to the eradication of racism in a putative democracy.

One of the reasons for the confusion in American political thought between democracy and liberalism is that a common choice of a primary associated value among political theorists has been the set of rights connected with property holding. Historically, that value is central to liberalism and, to the extent that liberals have led the thrust toward democracy in the advanced societies of the triumphant bourgeoisie, it is doubtless understandable that the claims of democratic principle have been honored only to the degree that they do not call property rights into question. Hence, the evolution of those political entities that we are accustomed (speaking in a nonnormative way) to call democracies has been bound up with the retention, irrespective of the cost to genuine democracy, of property rights as part of the inventory of inviolable individual liberties.[21] Democratic thinking has thus in effect been blinded to the nonessential character of property rights from a rigorously democratic standpoint and, still more importantly, to the sense in which property rights as understood in advanced capitalism do violence to democratic presuppositions about the equal weighting of citizens' preferences in the making of public decisions.

Another example of inappropriate association of values, one of slightly different nature, inheres in the widespread presumption that order or stability is a *conditio sine qua non* of a democratic system. There is of course a sense in which any political and social order can function only under conditions of orderly procedure, predictability about the acceptance of decisions properly arrived at, and avoidance of violence as a means of settling public disputes. It is thus true on grounds of common sense that democracy depends for its proper functioning on a measure of order in public affairs. This emphasis on order tends, on the other hand, to ignore the fundamental social fact that orderliness, stability, and predictability are partly functions of differential perception among social groups and classes. What looks like order to one social group may look terribly disorderly to another; one person's stability may be another's instability; predictability for one may be purchased at the price of unpredictability for someone else. There is no doubt that, according to strict democratic principle, the majority's notion of order is entitled to prevail, even if it entails disorder for some minority. But there is also something wrong with claiming general validity for a rule about order, as distinct from a particular majoritarian decision for a particular version of order, that applies unevenly to citizens and classes of citizens. Thus, although it would be difficult to argue that stability, like property rights, may even be inimical to democracy, it is possible to maintain that it is, in social context, too weak as an associated value to merit a central place in the cluster around democratic principle.

What then of the values Myrdal endorses, translating his historical reading of an American Creed into the present terms of discourse, as central and even essential to democratic practice? Both equality and justice would seem to deserve such placement, not so much because of the questionable rank accorded those values in American historical experience but rather because they are necessary to the realization of democratic principle. Both help to assure that the preferences of citizens will be recorded with equal weighting in the public arena and, cutting the other way at the same time, that adherence to democratic procedure will have worthy social purpose beyond mere observance of accepted rules of the game. A radical or strict democratic commitment would thus entail the adoption of those associated values without which democracy will fail to realize itself and to serve substantively valuable social purposes. That Myrdal got to this particular cluster by a different route seems less important than the fact that he got there.

Democracy and Racism

It must be clear that a bare majoritarian understanding of democratic procedure would afford little protection for minorities, and that even the addition of the other procedural principles—the widest extension of citizenship and provision for participation—would not safeguard democracy against racism. As we all know, majorities can be racist, both in attitude and in policy preference, and even if, in the name of democratic rules, they restrain themselves from manipulating the boundaries of citizenship and act to assure citizen participation in governance, a great deal of room is left for overbearing majority decisions adversely affecting ethnic minorities.[22] So much has this been the case historically, though admittedly under conditions of highly imperfect democratic performance, that it is understandable that ethnic minorities have sometimes grown dubious about democracy itself. Where then are we to seek the remedies to racism?

The theoretical plane is of course not the place to look for remedies to actual evils. But it is not irrelevant, given the possibility of persuasive appeal to the principles of a community, that theoretical ammunition against racism appears unambiguously in the egalitarian injunction that is, of all the values belonging to the democratic cluster, most central to the realization of democracy. To say this is not to claim that suasion is unfailingly or even occasionally efficacious, but a radical commitment to democracy does provide a powerful argument insofar as it can invoke or require careful attention to the problematics of equality among citizens.[23]

More to the point perhaps is the notion of participatory democracy, which provides the theoretical warrant for active engagement by minorities and their allies in the actualities of popular governance. To the degree that the participatory accent is missing from the practices of a self-styled democratic social order, the commitment to it is little more than a license to struggle—both for the principle itself and for the minority gains that can emerge from the struggle. This, I suggest, is one way of characterizing what has actually happened, most dramatically in the civil rights campaigns of the recent past. Far from being just another one among the many claims to specific individual rights, that struggle was a fight for egalitarian participation, that is, self-determination, by citizens in their own governance. To the degree that the civil rights effort was a proximate success, it registered gains for minority status and for the principles that are most central to the adequate functioning of a democratic order; to the degree that it failed, it at least called attention to the deviation of American practice from its professed values.[24]

The final point that needs to be made here requires the introduction of a new consideration. Analysis may pretend for its own purposes that its object is standing still. But we know that actuality is in perpetual flux. One of the names for this state of affairs in a professedly democratic polity is majority building. The participatory injunction is perhaps the most relevant one here: As citizens find or demand ways to participate in their own governance and gain the skills and values of civic activism in the process of practicing these modes of action, they are engaged in the task of forging majorities for particular positive goals and for the implementation of the professed values of the community.[25] It may seem all but irrelevant to enjoy suffrage or even to command access to means of communication necessary to the circulation of the arguments in question. It may, in short, require a species of civil disobedience, and has of course done so many times, to gain attention and to discomfit the opposing majority.[26] So long as this process remains within the rules of the game (i.e., eschews violence and outright revolutionary effort), it is no doubt a counsel of gradualism with all its attendant frustration. Nevertheless, it is an essentially democratic process. It is not inconceivable that a revolution might indeed have to be made in the name of an authentic and encompassing conception of democracy, especially in places that reveal weak commitments to even the formalities of democracy. Meanwhile, in any event, democratic principle and the goal of racial equality meet in mutually reinforcing ways precisely in this struggle.

Notes

1. (New York: Harper, 1944). This is the edition used throughout.
2. Myrdal, p. 80. The notion of institutional racism, a post-Myrdal formulation, is in effect the obverse of his anticipation and casts social institutions in a much less hopeful role, though it could certainly be argued that institutional racism comes into its own, in a manner of speaking, only after the correctives to the situation Myrdal observed have taken some effect. For examples, see *Social Development Issues* 4, no. 1 (Winter 1980), special issue on "Institutional Racism and American Policing"; for a different view, see Nathan Glazer, *Affirmative Discrimination* (New York: Basic Books, 1975), especially pp. 68–69.
3. Myrdal, p. 80.

4. Myrdal, pp. 432 ff.

5. Myrdal, p. 524. Italicized in original.

6. Myrdal, p. 525, quoting from W. E. B. DuBois, *The Souls of Black Folk* (Chicago: A.C. McClurg, 1903), p. 176.

7. Myrdal, p. 1021.

8. Methodological matters are quite fully elaborated in *An American Dilemma*, introduction. But see also Gunnar Myrdal, *Objectivity in Social Research* (New York: Pantheon, 1969).

9. I should add that this does not purport to be a close reading of Myrdal. Rather I am using his notions, all marginal to formal political theory, for their suggestive value. For extended treatments of Myrdal, see David W. Southern, *Gunnar Myrdal and Black–White Relations* (Baton Rouge: Louisiana State University Press, 1987), and Walter A. Jackson, *Gunnar Myrdal and America's Conscience* (Chapel Hill: University of North Carolina Press, 1990).

10. *A History of Political Theory* (New York: Holt, Rinehart and Winston, 1960), p. 918; the point is of course only symptomatic but nevertheless striking.

11. C. B. Macpherson, *The Life and Times of Liberal Democracy* (Oxford: Oxford University Press, 1977); Carole Pateman, *Participation and Democratic Theory* (New York: Cambridge University Press, 1970), especially p. 17.

12. Graeme Duncan, *Marx and Mill* (Cambridge: Cambridge University Press, 1973), p. 259.

13. Robert A. Dahl, *A Preface to Democratic Theory* (Chicago: University of Chicago Press, 1956).

14. The argument is advanced in its most sophisticated form by J. L. Talmon, *The Origins of Totalitarian Democracy* (New York: Praeger, 1960), especially introduction and chapter 3.

15. As presented in the justly renowned essay, "Two Concepts of Liberty," by Isaiah Berlin in his *Four Essays on Liberty* (New York: Oxford University Press, 1969), pp. 118–72. For a pertinent critical comment on Berlin's buttressing argument concerning positive liberty, see Lawrence Crocker, "Marx, Liberty, and Democracy," chapter 2 in John P. Burke, Lawrence Crocker, and Lyman H. Legters, eds., *Marxism and the Good Society* (New York: Cambridge University Press, 1981), pp. 32–58.

16. It is widely understood that Marx was in his youth a radical democrat; it is less widely acknowledged that he remained such throughout his life. The evidence is scattered amongst his writings, but appears most plainly in his characterization of the Paris Commune. For a persuasive account of his participatory conceptions, especially pertinent to the present argument, see John P. Burke, "The Necessity of Revolution," chapter 4 in Burke, Crocker, and Legters, eds., *Marxism and the Good Society*, pp. 84–105.

17. This label covers a considerable variety of theories in a lineage that would usually be taken as beginning with Joseph A. Schumpeter, *Capitalism, Socialism and Democracy* (New York: Harper and Row, 1950), especially chapters 22 and 23. See also J. Roland Pennock, *Democratic Political Theory* (Princeton, N.J.: Princeton University Press, 1979).

18. The usual procedure is to erect a model based on study of the structure and workings of self-styled democracies and then to show either how other systems fail to measure up or how elements of the "democracy" under consideration deviate from self-proclaimed rules or goals.

19. For a detailed examination and defense of majoritarianism, see Elaine Spitz, *Majority Rule* (Chatham, N.J.: Chatham House, 1984), especially chapter 10. The most significant objections are found, along with a spirited defense of political equality, in Robert A. Dahl, *Democracy and its Critics* (New Haven, Conn.: Yale University Press, 1989). See also the discussion in Jack Lively, *Democracy* (New York: St. Martin's Press, 1975), chapter 2.

20. On the notion of recommendation, see Thomas Landon Thorson, *The Logic of Democracy* (New York: Holt, Rinehart and Winston, 1962), chapter 6.

21. Obviously it is not objectionable per se to defend property rights; it is merely questionable whether that can be done cogently in the name of democracy.

22. Notwithstanding the contention that majorities have a better chance than minorities of being right; see Brian Barry, "The Public Interest," in A. Quinton, ed. *Political Philosophy* (New York: Oxford University Press, 1976), p. 122.

23. For an incisive consideration of equality within the context of the present topic, see Thomas Nagel, "Equal Treatment and Compensatory Discrimination" in Marshall Cohen, Thomas Nagel, and Thomas Scanlon, eds., *Equality and Preferential Treatment* (Princeton, N.J.: Princeton University Press, 1977), pp. 3–18..

24. This is not the place for an extended foray into empirical questions, but it seems plain that the chief gain from the civil rights struggle was the increased sensitivity accorded the problems of racial discrimination that comes when a society's laws and institutions come down á la Myrdal on the side of racial equality. The deeper and less encouraging result, apropos my remarks above about private property and advanced capitalism, is that the benefits of racial inequality accrue to wealthy whites and have continued to do so despite the civil rights movement. See Michael Reich, *Racial Inequality* (Princeton, N.J.: Princeton University Press, 1981), pp. 305–13. I am not aware of empirical evidence that would support unambiguously the expectation that a greater adherence to democratic norms and procedures would improve racial equality, though that outcome seems implicit in the egalitarian corollary of democracy. The problem may lie in a paucity of instances of movement toward greater democracy.

25. Notably pertinent in this connection is the argument for "interracial coalitions" as instruments for building effective forces in behalf of racial equality and, therewith, democracy, advanced by Mark A. Chesler, "Creating and Maintaining Interracial Coalitions," in Benjamin P. Bowser and Raymond G. Hunt, eds., *Impacts of Racism on White Americans*, (Beverly Hills, Calif.: Sage Publications, 1981), a book with several relevant contributions.

26. This aspect of the democratic problematic is cogently discussed in Peter Singer, *Democracy and Disobedience* (New York: Oxford University Press, 1974), Part II.

Chapter 5

Democracy and the Majority Principle

Iring Fetscher

In contrast to the rhetorically appealing formula, "democracy is the rule of the people, by the people, and for the people," the characterization of democracy as majority rule has the apparent advantage of being workable and controllable. To be sure, no one will deny the necessary qualifications: The voters must be truly free to choose among several competing candidates, the outvoted minority must have the right (and the means that enable it) to seek to become the majority, etc. With the addition of these conditions, most contemporaries would agree to the definition: Where majority decisions prevail in free elections, democracy rules. I want to put this formula in question.

Every discussion of the limits of the majority principle in a democracy can refer back to Jean-Jacques Rousseau's distinction between *volonté générale* and *volonté de tous* (or *de la majorité*). Under volonté générale Rousseau understands that will—in the form of laws—that aims at the common weal, meaning the preservation of the republic. So long as the majority of the population wills the common weal, there is no difference between volonté générale and volonté de tous (or majority). But there is no guarantee that this will always be so. Apart from the somewhat questionable arithmetical example that Rousseau uses in the *Contrat Social*, his thesis leads toward the claim that democracy (which he calls "republic") is possible only so long as the majority of the citizenry is virtuous (*vertueux*), willing, that is, to favor the common will, and therewith the common weal, over private advantage. Rousseau is enough of a realist to acknowledge that this agreement between individual will and volonté générale has a chance to prevail only when the particular differences of interest within the population are small and when the weight of similarity of social circumstance is great. Like Aristotle, he thus idealizes the médiocrité (the middle stratum) as the optimal foundation for a viable democracy (republic). Even under such circumstances, "virtue" is still necessary, but in no greater measure than the average person is capable of. But when differences in the social conditions of the citizens increase, then they require ever greater ethical struggle to prefer the common weal over their direct private advantage.

When a society has a substantial minority of very rich and a corresponding group of very poor citizens, then, so Rousseau maintains, freedom can no longer be preserved. One must then expect that the rich will "buy" the votes of the poor or that demagogues will stir the poor to initiate willful political ventures. In either case, the general will falls victim to the will (or interest) of one fraction of society prevailing against that of another. The only choice remaining is that between anarchy and dictatorship. Rousseau disapproved as much of the minority rule of the rich, who deny the poor majority their voting rights, as he did of the dictatorship of the poor majority, agreeing also on this score with Aristotle.

The "classical" bourgeois democratic theory—that of Locke and Kant, as well as of Rousseau—recognized only the property-holding person as citizen. Kant is very precise that only the person who produces for the market with his own equipment could be a citizen; whoever "hires out" (Kant meant this though he did not know the term) to an owner of the means of production (i.e., one who has only his labor to sell) cannot be an active citizen. There is some confusion here, for Kant includes also those who offer a service for sale (the independent hairdresser, bathkeeper, etc.), among the dependent, though he clearly had in mind the economically dependent citizen who has nothing else than his work (in Marxian terms, his labor power) to hire out to an owner of means of production. Should voting rights be given to dependents (farm workers, apprentices, journeymen, shop assistants, etc), that would increase, unjustly and uncontrollably, the influence of those on whom these groups depend, for it was not to be expected, expecially when voting is done openly, that the socially dependent groups could express themselves freely in political matters or vote accordingly.

But there is something more than a "narrow class standpoint" behind this restriction of voting rights to "independent" persons. (In typical German fashion, Kant makes an exception for the state officialdom, because Germany's bourgeoisie consisted predominantly of officials from the educated middle class.) It is assumed that this sector of the populace has more or less the same interests and the same conception of the functions of the state, and can, therefore, by means of free discussion (publications, newspaper articles, speeches, etc.) arrive at a common will. Even when partial deviations occur, in all of the great decisions there will be a largely shared viewpoint that can be articulated then in the form of generally acceptable laws.

The image of society that underlay this classical bourgeois conception of democracy plainly did not correspond to reality. It overlooked the considerable differences in property and interest, visible in England already in the seventeenth century, and assumed—generally incorrectly—the predominance of common interests. These illusions are understandable, to be sure, so long as the democratic rule of the third estate or the delegates of the commercial class had not yet prevailed in the British House of Commons, in that there was an overriding interest in a united front against the monarchy and aristocracy. Later—after the bourgeois revolution—the need for a demarcation against the majority of propertyless supplied a new motive for the minimizing of substantial differences in interest for the sake of the struggle against the crown. The emphasis on virtue corresponded to the self-image of the rising bourgeoisie in its (puritanical or rational) way of life, its attitude toward industry, frugality, discipline, for example, as morally superior to the immoral conduct of the older dominant strata.

The classical economics of Adam Smith (anticipated ironically in this regard by Bernard Mandeville) further enabled the middle class to extol its own orientation to sober interest over the irrational passions of the nobility and the quarrelsomeness of the priests with their unreal and irrational arguments. "Look here; even when we calculate only our private advantage, we serve the common weal, whereas the wild passions of the belligerent nobility and the argumentative clerisy bring nothing but harm!"

The classical theories of democracy—in British and continental variants—presuppose a relatively homogeneous society of independent citizens, one that excludes those dependent on wages (servants, dayworkers, apprentices, etc.) politically. But in the roughly one hundred years from 1815 to 1918, the general and equal suffrage had prevailed throughout Europe and in its overseas settlements in Canada, Australia, and New Zealand, as in the United States. The great majority of voters in all those lands were no longer independent, but lived from the sale of their labor power. And within these societies there was not only the basic cleavage between the small minority of independent citizens and the great majority of dependent citizens; there were also very significant differences in property and influence inside both of those great classes. The common will could thus scarcely prevail so readily and with such modest application of 'virtue' as in the small, relatively homogeneous republic of Rousseau's dream or in Locke's bourgeois society of rank.

In the face of this social point of departure, systematically and historically, two contrasting strategies are available. The institutions of the state can be so arranged that the majority's interest in dispossessing the property-holding minority finds no outlet. That was the concern, successfully implemented, of the constitutional authors in the United States and of the authors of *The Federalist Papers*. Or an attempt can be made, in the manner of the democratic socialists, to remove the extreme differences of wealth and social power by means of a transformation of society. So far this second option has registered only very limited successes. Even in places where there is not such a meticulously developed constitutional order as in the United States, the rise of modern parties and the appearance of the mass media have led to a mediation and a channeling of popular opinion that prevents the victory, in all the developed industrial states, of a sufficiently strong democratic–socialist majority. This result has been favored of course by the perversion of socialism in Communist-controlled lands as well as by the development of a "social net" that ensures the relatively comfortable existence of those dependent on wages in the capitalist countries.

The modern democratic welfare state, with its two or more competing political parties, seemed in the period following World War II to have fashioned a variant of classical democracy that was definitely acceptable to the popular majority. Reality had less resemblance to traditional forms than to the pragmatic concept of an economic theory of democracy associated first with Joseph Schumpeter and then with Anthony Downs, but what was achieved represented an improvement—in contrast to so-called people's democracy and the fascist Führer-democracy. To be able to talk about democracy, it is enough, according to the economic theory of democracy, to have two groups of professional politicians in any country competing for a voting majority in free elections, then assuming the tasks of governing and legislating for a set period of time. One could say, in short, that democracy prevails where the majority principle is joined to the legal activity of an opposition.

That would exclude plebiscitary dictatorship. The fact that the Labour government in England, for example, stopped short of general socialization and, similarly, that the Conservatives, when they returned to power, chose not to abolish the national health service or reverse certain of the nationalizations suggests that majority factions in some degree respect the interests of the defeated minority (which could of course in that electoral system actually become the majority). There were tensions, but consensus prevailed (and apparently still does, even though the conduct of the Thatcher government hardly matched that of earlier Conservative governments).

The problems that arise from an uncompromising implementation of the majority principle have to do, now as before, with the heterogeneity of the population. They no longer reside solely in differences in wealth, but increasingly in regional differences and, further, in the fact that decisions of the central government intrude ever more deeply into the affairs of communities and provinces. The acceptance by the defeated minority of the decisions of the majority has rested and still does on the genuine possibility of correcting a decision as soon as today's minority becomes tomorrow's majority. But it rests also on the fact that fundamental laws and measures can usually be accomplished only by large majorities—even when, as in England, that is not expressly required in the constitution. However, the hope of later correction is nullified when a decision is irreversible or when it is not a general law but a particular determination with irreversible long-term consequences (e.g., the approval for building a waste disposal plant, or a nuclear plant). In such cases the defeated minority can scarcely take comfort in the notion that it can tomorrow, having become the majority, reverse the decision.

In such a case it is not just majority opinion against minority opinion but rather a majority of the entire society against a majority, probably even a very large one, of the locality. The democratic majority principle encounters new federal limitations. But in modern industrial states, competence is increasingly situated with the central government. A disquieting example was the struggle over the expansion of Frankfurt's Rhein-Main airport. For years the residents of the areas neighboring the airport fought the decision to expand; eventually they assembled a petition from the whole populace of the *Land* (Hesse); and they had numerous conflicts with the *Land* police. And then it was realized that the competence for airport matters rested not with the *Land* government but with the federal government. The petition, gathered in conformity with the constitution of Hesse, was therefore pointless. This aroused understandable agitation among those affected, especially because they had been left for all those years in ignorance of the jurisdictional issue. The decision struck them as a denial of their democratic rights, in reliance on which they had gathered the signatures on their petition.

Another similar case concerns the plan for a nuclear waste disposal facility in a community in North Hesse. At first a large majority of citizens of the area favored the plan. During construction the project would provide numerous jobs; it would bring people and money to the relatively undeveloped region; and, besides the prospect for additional public funds, it would assure income that could be used for public facilities. But after a few months the majority of the population had informed itself about the great risks of the planned facility and taken up a negative stance toward the project. Elected representatives addressing the populace were no longer able to satisfy their questioners with general formulations and reference to "competent authorities" but had to make themselves knowledgeable too, and thus had considerable difficulty justifying their decision. The jurisdictional distribution among *Land* government, legislature, and local administration and councils placed the decision about such a project in the hands of the central government, which could cite the majority vote of the *Land* legislature. Against that stood only the majority vote of a locality. Which majority should be decisive? Can one expect that all the representatives not personally affected by the construction would be as diligent in informing themselves as the affected residents? Mancur Olson's theory (*The Logic of Collective Action*, Cambridge, Mass.: Harvard University Press, 1965) suggests strongly that they would not. As Olson demonstrates, the particular interests of entrepreneurs are much easier to organize than are those of broad masses of workers, employees, members of health insurance plans, for example; and this seems to be true here also in the representation of a locally concentrated and locally mobilized understanding. Although it is taken to be self-evident in most Western democracies that interested entrepreneurs and their organizations will be called upon as experts (and also of course as representatives of their interests) in the preparation of legislation and their wishes usually taken up noisily by portions of the media, the same thing does not happen—at least not yet or in sufficient degree—when whole local populations are affected by state decisions on such things as nuclear plants and airports.

Against the demand for a veto right of informed, directly affected populations, it is generally argued that such a group operates according to St. Florian's Principle ("spare my house—set the other's afire"). But in fact that argument can easily be disarmed. It is not the informed local citizens but rather the voters and legislators in other districts—who have not troubled to inform themselves as well because they are not directly affected—who follow St. Florian's Principle. Disapproval of the construction of a waste disposal plant does not—at least not necessarily—imply approval of the construction at some other place. In any case, the question remains whether society has an overriding need for such an installation. Only if that question could be answered positively and without qualification would it be possible to reach the decision in a manner that was fair and responsive to the concerns of those affected. If no community should be prepared voluntarily to accept the facility (even despite the assurance of compensation), then the plan would have to be abandoned. As for compensation, the equivalent of buying the votes, the main objection would be that something was being imposed on the poorest communities and the poorest segment of the population, an outcome that could be comfortably avoided by more prosperous sectors. The fears of the poor communities would be more easily and cheaply bought-off, as it were. Such cases have already occurred in the Federal Republic of Germany and often in the United States. Nevertheless, buying agreement would already be an improvement over simple imposition.

Objections to the consideration of the claims of local majorities against general majority decisions taken at the center frequently take the form of insistence that the general majority should in principle prevail. It is only strange that these same critics are usually strong defenders of representative democracy and of the independent mandate for legislative representatives (against the binding mandate).   In this case, they argue for the necessity of quiet understanding, free discussion, and the absence of passion, qualities that would be endangered by plebiscite and the binding mandate. It even appears to them to be an achievement of representative democracy that in certain instances more balanced and enlightened majorities appear in parliaments than in the unenlightened population at large. A favorite argument concerns the death penalty often demanded by popular majorities (e.g., at the time of the "terrorist" proceedings in the Federal Republic) and resisted by liberal majorities in parliaments. But when enlightened parliamentarians can oppose their majority to the larger, popular one, why not also the informed majority of the affected persons in a community or locality?   Behind this uneven reasoning lurks an elitism that is seldom justified in general by the assumption of competence by legislators.

There is another reason for believing that the universal applicability of the principle of societywide majority, which is in actuality only a relative majority, is in need of correction. To be sure, voter participation in the Federal Republic occurs (except in European elections) in inverse proportion to the remoteness of the elective body: The lowest level of participation appears in local elections, the highest in elections for the federal parliament. Yet the competence of voters might (or could) be much greater on local issues than on federal ones.   A reason for election apathy is the diminution of the capabilities and financial capacities of local and provincial assemblies.

On the other hand, the past twenty years have seen a growing interest in home, neighborhood, environment, recreational areas, and the like, concerns that surface far more in civic initiative than in increased participation in local elections.   When one believes that political participation is not only a means of controlling the government but also a reasonable expression of genuine individual capabilities, then one might wish for the encouragement of local and regional (also workplace) forms of participation instead of the discouragement that follows from the denial of competence.   Just as the workplace engagement in decision-making has (or could have) the function of providing those dependent on wages with a substitute for their lack of economic independence and self-determination, so could active participation in local government and its increased capability contribute to making democracy more real, more accessible, and more convincing.   Nothing appears to me more dangerous for the preservation of democracy than an increasing number of engaged citizens coming to feel (and correctly) that their activity is without result and that the higher authorities just do as they wish.

S. M. Lipset (*Political Man*, New York: Doubleday, 1960) and others offered a thesis many years ago to the effect that a modern mass democracy is stable only so long as voter participation remains relatively low.   A high level of participation, according to his argument, will necessarily bring irrational and emotional extremism to the surface and endanger or even destroy institutions. This claim assumes an invincible lack of enlightenment and an emotional instability in large segments of the population.   But this is by no means a necessary fate.   It bases the stability of democracy on the apathy of the masses, but it strikes me that a democracy would be much more stable when it had no frustrated and apathetic masses to keep under control but could count on a large majority of enlightened, informed, and engaged citizens.   A precondition for that, along with better education, would be the strengthening of local, regional, sectoral, and workplace forms of participatory democratic decision-making and the enlargement of those competences that allow informed local groups to influence their own destiny.

The demand for agreement between local (affected and therefore informed) majorities and societywide majorities would of course have to hold in general and not just in cases of active local citizen initiative.   But so long as no constitutional provision covers this demand, the danger exists that localities with a high proportion of educationally privileged citizens will, through clamorous protest, succeed sooner than the less privileged residents of another area in averting the installation in their neighborhood of nuclear plants, chemical factories, airports, and the like.   A legal barrier to the easy approval of certain construction dangerous to persons and the environment would in any case represent no weakening but rather a strengthening (in effect and repute) of democracy. The implementation of the majority principle that is completely abstracted from the appearance and composition of a majority should already have become reprehensible through the abuse of one-party rule. And it has long been known that majorities only reflect the intentions of the population with some accuracy when they are sufficiently and objectively informed and when they are interested in the information. Both factors are likely to be missing from the aforementioned decisions of central governments and parliaments in the name of the majority of unaffected citizens (who are therefore too little interested in enlightenment and information). Thus, the suggested amplification of institutional provisions can be seen as a means of improving the quality of the democratic decision-making process. Because it cannot be assumed that the residents of all localities will inform themselves equally with those directly affected, it is clearly possible to legitimate giving those directly affected a sort of veto right. Mancur Olson deals convincingly with this situation, empirically and theoretically, when he asserts that the "costs" of additional information will only be assumed when the information in question has great importance directly for the representation of the pertinent interests. The connection between a societywide majority and a local one would thus be actuated in this form: Plans approved by a societywide majority or by a government responsible to a majority would be subject to an additional authorization by the informed citizens directly affected. This would not rescind the principle of a formal majority, but would only restrict it in its application, doing so in the name of a normative conception of democracy in no way contrary to democratic traditions.

A final example may help to show that such a combination of different majorities is not altogether unusual or new. One may regard the reform of self-government in West German higher education in the 1970s as problematical in several ways, yet precisely the more conservative provisions of the laws governing universities apply a procedure similar to what I have suggested. In most of the *Länder* it is required, in all decisions of a faculty department or commission (for instance, those concerning appointment lists), that any majority of the faculty department incorporate a majority of the professoriate. One can justify this requirement because the professors, who typically remain associated with their university for a longer time than students and lecturers, are the most affected by new appointments, and because they, for the same reason and even when appointment is in a discipline that is alien to them, will try harder to become informed. Even when these assumptions are not borne out in all cases, they do reflect a legitimate hypothesis. And the same can be said of the voting poplation of a locality in which a chemical plant is to be constructed. The differential assessment of these combined majority processes by conservative politicians cannot be maintained logically, unless one wants to make the habilitation or appointment to a professorial chair more important than the combination of being affected and trying to become better informed.

[translated by Lyman H. Legters]

Chapter 6

Democratic Solidarity and the Crisis of the Welfare State

Joseph M. Schwartz

Democratic Community and the Welfare State

How might contemporary democratic theory reconstruct a moral and political defense of public provision that persuasively responds to right-wing libertarian[1] and communitarian critiques of the welfare state? Both libertarians and communitarians criticize the welfare state as bureaucratic and paternalistic. The libertarian critique of the welfare state contends that its "coercive" redistribution violates the liberty of market freedom and inhibits individual initiative and economic productivity. Communitarians hold that liberalism's grounding of rights in the concept of individual autonomy morally undermines popular support for public goods because such a justification does not promote the "constitutive" communal identity necessary for shared provision.[2] Yet neither a liberal defense of rights as promoting moral autonomy nor a communitarian defense of public goods as promoting unspecified and narrowly localized communal virtues adequately explicates the shared understandings that have historically motivated American support for public provision. Support for public goods has been strongest when these goods, such as public education, have been popularly perceived as fostering the equal ability of each member to contribute to democratic public life. A moral theory of democratic community, which "situates" support for rights in a democratic community's commitment to the equal value of membership, better explicates the social solidarity underpinning stable forms of public provision than do appeals to the rights of autonomous individuals or the practices of constitutive communities.[3]

Communitarians correctly note that public provision can only be morally and politically sustained if it is in accord with societal values. But the communitarian depiction of the moral bonds of tightly knit, "constitutive" communities (implicitly modeled on an idealized family) cannot explain the broader but less comprehensive identity of shared citizenship and economic risk that morally girded the social programs of the New Deal. Nor can communitarianism explain how previously excluded minority communities with cultural identities radically divergent from those of the majority could successfully make moral claims in the 1960s to be treated as equal citizens. In their moments of political success, the labor movement of the 1930s and the civil rights movement of the 1960s spoke beyond the immediate needs of their particular communities, using the political and social discourse of a universal class whose specific grievances embodied the rights of all democratic *citizens* ("an injury to one is an injury to all"; "injustice anywhere is a threat to justice everywhere"). Any investigation of the decline in support for public provision must consider the decreasing purchase of the two visions of social solidarity advanced by the social movements of the New Deal and the Great Society.

Hubristic political theorists are tempted to ascribe declining support for public provision solely to the inadequacies of liberal political thought. But the primary causes for this sea change in moral values and ideology are more sociological and political than theoretical. As the workforce of late capitalism is increasingly segmented along lines of race, gender, and skill, the social solidarity of industrial trade unionism has precipitously declined. With the slowdown in postwar growth in the 1970s and 1980s, conservative political elites reconstructed working-class and middle-class ambivalence towards means-tested programs (Aid to Families with Dependent Children, Food Stamps) benefiting the poor into broader opposition to taxation and public spending. Although the majority of means-tested program beneficiaries are white, minority women and children are disproportionately represented (the legacy of racism being that African-American and Latino poverty rates are three times that of whites). Utilizing a calculated racial politics that played on "work ethic" hostility toward means-tested programs, the new right succeeded in identifying public provision with hand-outs to the minority poor, even though more than two-thirds of federal government social welfare spending goes to exceedingly popular, universal programs like Social Security and Medicare.

In addition to the vulnerability of means-tested programs to populist hostility, the greater individual security provided by the welfare state has ironically eroded the collective solidarity that helped create public provision.[4] Post–World War II beneficiaries of Social Security came to see these programs as individual entitlements rather than a product of the collective struggle of the depression. This erosion of social solidarity takes particularly acute forms in America, where the ideology of individualism led architects of Social Security to depict these mutual insurance programs as individual entitlements "earned" by individual, targeted tax investment (witness the targeted FICA tax and the government-sponsored myth of the individual Social Security account).[5]

Whether the democratic value of social solidarity central to a strong welfare society can be reconstructed in America is the issue this essay explores theoretically and sociologically.   This inquiry acknowledges that part of American popular mistrust of social "rights" derives from a belief that "liberals" are hostile to notions of communal obligation. Whereas the more generous universal benefits of social democratic welfare states are predicated on a strong work ethic,[6] American means-tested programs build in perverse work disincentives because benefits (Medicaid and Food Stamps) are often surrendered when a recipient accepts a low-paying job.

In this essay I explore the crisis of the welfare state in four steps. First, I examine the American welfare state in a comparative perspective and contend that liberal defenses of means-tested programs as providing a "safety net" for those failing to provide for themselves in the market facilitates libertarian criticisms of welfare provision.   Such a defense pejoratively identifies beneficiaries as failing to find jobs that would render them "self-sufficient" and degrades the productive social contribution of child-rearing. Public provision can best be defended in a democratic polity when tied to conceptions of mutual aid and common contribution (e.g., social insurance programs) or the social provision of universally recognized needs (e.g., public health care and child care).

Second, I explore whether "communitarianism" offers a coherent alternative to rights-based liberalism as a moral concept of the social solidarity essential for strong public provision. I hold that the communitarian's vague incantation of "community" does not adequately specify the membership rights and obligations that constitute a democratic community. On the other hand, the communitarians advance a sound, if overly formal, conception of the integral connection between concrete conceptions of the good, grounded in social practices, and convincing arguments about social justice. In American practices, the right to public provision has been closely tied to the obligation to contribute socially meaningful labor to the community.

Third, I examine the two-tiered American welfare state, divided (along lines of race and gender) between universal social insurance programs tied to long-term formal employment and minimally funded means-tested programs providing temporary relief to indigent children and women (in the absence of a male breadwinner). In the 1960s many liberal legal theorists defended welfare benefits as a "new property" entitlement providing the minimum economic means for citizenship.[7] But the failure of liberal theorists to join this theory of entitlement to a theory of social contribution (including the contribution of child-rearing) rendered the rationale for these programs particularly vulnerable during the economically stagnant 1970s and 1980s.

This is not to argue that targeted public provision has no future. Majority support may already exist for expanded Head Start, prenatal care for indigent pregnant women, and earned-income tax credits for low-income working parents (perhaps because few blame children for their social circumstances). But as the vicious AFDC and Medicaid cuts of the past twenty years demonstrate, public provision is unlikely to garner broad support unless it is based on universal principles of provision (though such universal programs could provide differential benefits according to need). The partial rollback of the welfare state over the past twenty years demonstrates that there can be no liberal a priori deduction of minimal welfare rights. Rather these rights can only be established through continuous political struggle over the rights and obligations of members of a democratic community.[8] Although one would hope that the rapidly deteriorating quality of life for poor Americans would generate a considered public policy response, it is more likely that growing working- and middle-class concern with the quality of education, health care, and child care will be the terrain upon which renewed contestation over public provision occurs.[9]

I conclude by examining the viability of reconceptualizing social rights as deriving from membership in a democratic community. Can such a concept of rights avoid the pitfalls of a vague communitarianism, on the one hand, and of an overly market-oriented liberalism, on the other? While criticizing racist and patriarchal myths used to undermine welfare provision, I contend that new social welfare initiatives should be based on universal, inclusionary principles (even while disproportionately benefiting the needy).

The "Liberal" American Welfare State: Blaming the Victims of Market Failure

Liberal democracies are characterized by a profound tension between the principles of democratic social equality and equality of economic opportunity.[10] Nowhere is this tension more evident than in attitudes toward the American welfare state, whose means-tested programs are often ideologically justified as protection for the unfortunately dependent and a means to enable the able-bodied excluded from the market to return to full participation in the equal opportunity of marketplace competition.[11]

To justify "the welfare state" is to ignore the distinct moral principles that inform different types of social programs and welfare states. In the United States, welfare provision is frequently justified as providing a "residual" safety net for the poor and the disabled. Yet more than two-thirds of social welfare expenditure in the United States goes to Social Security and Medicare (universal programs based on mutual insurance principles). In a comparative analysis, however, the United States best fits Albert Weale's definition of "residual" welfare states, whose programs focus upon improving the relative standing of the poor. In contrast, most European welfare states approximate Weale's "institutional" welfare states, which provide all members of society with specific stocks of goods and services deemed essential to full citizenship.[12] In the United States, this "residual" welfare state ideology sees public provision as enabling the able-bodied poor to reintegrate into the "mainstream" (i.e., the market economy). This ideology serves as a powerful political barrier to expanding universal programs and as a source of resentment against those who receive aid but do not shortly thereafter reenter the formal labor market. This resentment often blames the victim, as the absence of universal health care, child care, and job training programs engenders a "poverty trap" that makes it economically irrational for most adult AFDC recipients to enter the workforce.

Gosta Esping-Anderson distinguishes among three ideal types of capitalist welfare states: the liberal, the conservative (or corporatist–paternal), and the social democratic.[13] In reality, each particular welfare state combines certain of these elements.[14] The social provision of liberal welfare states is characterized primarily by means-tested antipoverty programs and modest social insurance programs. This gives rise to a market-differentiated dualism between welfare recipients and non-welfare recipients and further extension of the welfare state is made difficult by liberal work ethic norms. The Anglo-Saxon nations predominate under this rubric, with Great Britain having the most advanced—if underfinanced—social insurance programs and every nation except the United States having universal forms of health care provision.

Corporatist–paternal welfare states (characteristic of European regimes with a Catholic or authoritarian past) provide fairly generous social insurance benefits that maintain status differentiation through earnings-related insurance programs. These social insurance programs generally tie nonworking wives' benefits to the earnings records of their husbands. Generous child benefits (combined with underdeveloped day care) discourage female workforce participation. France, Italy, the Federal Republic of Germany, and Austria predominate in this group.

Social democratic welfare states are characterized by high-quality universal social rights that "decommodify" services such as health, child care, and parts of the housing market. Social insurance benefits have a high minimal floor, but also a supplementary earnings-related tier. Child care provision is heavily socialized, thus freeing women to choose between work at home and wage-work. Earnings-related benefits and high-quality (though expensive) social services maintain middle-class loyalty to a high-tax welfare system. The Scandinavian countries predominate in this category.

Although "only" 20 percent of American welfare provision is means-tested—as compared with no more than 5 percent in Europe—the gender and racial composition of its recipients has made it a lightning rod for conservative attacks on the welfare state. In a recent essay, Brian Barry regrets that many American liberal moral philosophers in justifying welfare provision still rely on "Poor Law" arguments about protecting the dependent and those excluded from the market from abject poverty. Barry correctly notes that even in the United

States the bulk of social provision is provided on grounds of mutual insurance against the hazards of unemployment, old age, and disability.[15] In a comparative perspective, however, American public policy has been strikingly reluctant to decommodify basic needs (e.g., health care and child care) and remove them from differential, competitive purchase in the private market. Thus, from a crude "sociology of knowledge" perspective, it is not surprising that American moral philosophers often conceive of the welfare state as primarily providing goods that the poor cannot secure in the market.

Although Barry decries the analytical work of Robert Goodin and Carl Wellman, their minimalist conception of welfare rights is in accord with the ideology of the American "liberal" welfare state.[16] (Though the American welfare state's practices are predominantly social insurance based.) Goodin describes "the minimalist essence" of the welfare state as protecting victims of the market from abject dependency and exploitation with the hope that the able among them will return as independent agents in that market.[17] Wellman contends that "welfare rights are only those forms of governmental assistance to maintain personal well-being in those incapable of providing it for themselves."[18] Because individuals pay taxes for public education and compulsory government insurance programs (Social Security, unemployment insurance, Medicare), Wellman denies that these programs are "true" forms of welfare. Only AFDC, Medicaid, and Food Stamps qualify, in Wellman's definition, as "welfare."[19]

In construing the welfare state as a natural outgrowth of marketplace liberalism, Wellman fails to recognize that many social welfare programs remove certain goods from the market. In addition, Wellman denies the centrality of moral conceptions of mutual insurance and mutual aid to the origins of American social welfare. By failing to analyze the ways in which the moral logic of democratic public provision stands in tension with that of equality of marketplace competition, American liberal moral philosophers justify a "residual" welfare state whose only moral responsibility is to the "dependent" poor. Their ignoring of the egalitarian and solidaristic impulses underlying the social insurance and universal programs of the welfare state leads them to describe a welfare state for the "dependent," which inadvertently conforms to the neoconservative caricature.

Goodin and Wellman openly state that their project is to explain how liberal conceptions of market choice and of individual autonomy can morally justify aid to the needy. While they hope this justification will increase conservative support for welfare provision, their philosophical analysis obfuscates the actual origins of the welfare programs of the New Deal and Great Society. They did not arise from what Goodin calls "modern noblesse oblige" (policymakers' concern for the poor), but from the interaction among policymakers, corporate interests, and mass social movements. Neither the trade union movement nor the welfare rights and civil rights movements of the 1960s primarily appealed to the moral responsibility of the affluent.   The New Deal's popular "corporatist welfare state" programs of social insurance were a response to the demands of the movements of the unemployed and organized labor for a "social democratic" program of flat-rate benefits financed from general revenues.   In the 1960s, the civil rights and welfare rights movements did not demonstrate solely for expansion of "liberal" means-tested programs (raising AFDC levels and implementing Medicaid and Food Stamps), but also demanded universal health care, a guaranteed minimum income, ambitious job training programs, and full employment.

The widespread indignation against President Ronald Reagan's exploration of altering Social Security benefits demonstrates that welfare programs based on principles of "mutual insurance" and mutual contribution are conceived of as social rights by a broad segment of the polity.   The Reagan administration's success at cutting federal support for AFDC and Food Stamps, on the other hand, was dependent upon tacit middle-strata hostility toward "liberal" welfare programs that disproportionately benefit racial minorities and poor, single-parent mothers.   The Reagan administration's disqualification of more than 400,000 poor working women from AFDC illustrates the hypocritical and patriarchal nature of the political right's "work ethic" attack on "welfare queens."   As Christopher Jencks's and Kathryn Edin's studies have shown, most women on welfare work off-the-books jobs or take in children and boarders to survive.   It is not any debilitating culture of poverty that prevents the majority of welfare mothers from entering the formal labor force.   Rather, for single-parent mothers the absence of affordable child care and the loss of Medicaid benefits renders full-time entrance into the formal labor market an irrational market choice. Thus, the social meanness of the American welfare state violates even its own liberal, minimal moral norms of self-help.[20] But such meanness also reveals the political vulnerability in a democracy of "liberal, marketplace" justifications of social welfare as defending the rights of the dependent poor.

Democratic Community:
Deriving Rights from Community

Thus far, I have explored how a liberal conception of welfare as fulfilling needs not met through the market fails to comprehend the mutual risk and solidarity grounding support for common provision in a democratic community. Might contemporary communitarianism offer a better theory for comprehending the moral basis of such provision? If it does not, is it because public provision is inherently bureaucratic, instrumental, and anticommunal, as some communitarians charge? Or is it because communitarians' disdain for economic issues as individualist and instrumental precludes their ability to outline the specific forms of public provision essential to a democracy?[21]

While in the 1970s John Rawls's *A Theory of Justice* revived interest in social contract liberalism, in the 1980s "communitarian critics" of Rawls such as Michael Sandel, Alasdair MacIntyre, and Michael Walzer refocused debate on the alleged philosophical and political weaknesses of social contract liberalism. Communitarians criticized John Rawls's and other "deontological" social contract theorists' attempts to discern principles of justice that "free, rational, and autonomous" individuals would agree upon. Such a quest was bound to fail, the communitarians argued, because it did not recognize that conceptions of morality are discerned by individuals whose moral identities are constituted by their communal ties. According to the communitarians, a liberal, "neutral, Archimedean point" cannot exist, from which an individual can judge whether a social institution is "fair or just." As membership in a community determines our vision of what is just, the communitarians contend we must first define the good—the practices of a virtuous community—before we can know what is just.[22]

Although the communitarians may be correct that moral principles are derived from concrete social practices, their failure to advance any coherent moral or political criteria for judging among competing conceptions of community or "the good" leaves them vulnerable to charges of relativism or conventionalism. Michael Sandel has expressed sympathy for communities that in defense of their own "way of life" ban pornographic bookstores or prevent industries from moving out.[23] But would he also support a community's right to defend its own way of life through the exclusion of African-Americans from residence? If communitarians are to reject intolerant conceptions of community, they must incorporate a theory of rights into their allegedly "postliberal" or "nonliberal" conceptions of virtuous communities.

Nor does their methodological critique of deriving rights from a metaphysical conception of human beings as "unencumbered selves" prove that rights inherently serve as a barrier to community. If our moral identity is constituted by our social life, then could not a commitment to rights be derived from a "situated" conception of "reflective" selves who are members of a democratic community? As democratic communities value equally the public voice of each member, they are committed to institutional guarantees against discrimination and repression. As Will Kymlicka has argued, this democratic self is not so "radically situated" that it cannot discern the need for "rights" to guarantee individuals' ability to "self-reflexively" evaluate their political and moral beliefs.[24] Amy Gutmann has described how procedural constraints on democratic majorities need not be derived from a narrow conception of liberal individualism, but can stem from a democratic commitment to guarantees of individual political participation.[25]

The "democratic communitarian" aspects of Michael Walzer's work explore how social (or welfare) rights are morally and politically dependent upon the shared understandings of members of a democratic community.[26] Although

Walzer insists that justice is inherently particularist (dependent on the practices that members of a given community deem to be just), his commitment to democracy drives his theory of complex equality toward a universal commitment to social and political rights. For example, he condemns the existing political practices of democratic polities that exclude immigrant "guest workers" from full citizenship and criticizes the American practice of providing health care on the basis of need for some (the indigent and elderly) but not others—the working uninsured.[27] This vision of political and social rights as integral to the shared meanings of a democratic community offers a more political version of Rawls's "idea of an overlapping consensus." Rawls's "idea of an overlapping consensus" contends that political justice is not a comprehensive theory of the good, but a moral concept developed when groups holding different and even conflicting views of the good affirm "the publicly shared basis of [democratic] political arrangements." The "overlapping consensus" of political justice is not a theory of the good, Rawls contends, but a moral concept of those cooperative virtues—tolerance, compromise—by which the plural communities of a democratic society are able to coexist and cooperate in the life of the "supracommunity of communities," a liberal democratic society.[28]

Rawls's concept of the overlapping consensus (in part a response to communitarian criticisms) represents a distancing from the metaphysical grounding of "justice as fairness" in the unencumbered view of the self. However, it places greater weight on liberal procedural virtues, such as tolerance and compromise, than on those social rights necessary for equally valuable citizenship. If democracy believes in the capacity of the individual to make informed decisions, then it must be committed to freedom of association and to the provision of those social and economic goods (e.g., education, health care, child care, job training) necessary to ensure individuals the possibility of an "enlightened understanding" of their own interests.[29] The contemporary crisis confronting democratic polities does not result from the breakdown of procedural guarantees of liberty, but from an eviscerated public sphere that precludes citizens from establishing the mutual identification necessary to sustain those public goods necessary for "enlightened understanding."

The absence of shared experience across barriers of race, class, and gender (in America, particularly race) has almost eliminated the concept of social solidarity from popular consciousness. The racially constructed perception that many white Americans have of the inner city as one homogenous drug-infested "underclass," combined with the means-tested nature of public health care and child care, has severely weakened popular support for democratic public provision. In a healthy democracy, democratic life includes not only participation in formal politics (currently at historic lows), but also involvement in public spaces and institutions in civil society that promote interaction among diverse communities (e.g., schools, unions, neighborhood associations, day care centers). The paucity of such interaction is central to the weakening of social solidarity in America. Ours is an increasingly passive, fragmented, media-oriented, consumer society in which a majority moves every two years and cannot name more than two nonrelated persons living on their block or in their apartment building.[30]   Although these demographics may change as mobile baby-boomers settle down to raise children, advocates of democracy need to consider seriously proposals for creating a more "republican" sense of citizenship. Universal public-service programs (structured so as not to undercut union wages) might promote working relationships among young and old Americans across lines of race, region, and class.

Communitarian critics of the anomic nature of mass society share with radical democrats a belief that participation in associational life in civil society is central to the development of self-motivated, self-governing citizens. But strikingly absent from communitarian analyses (except that of Walzer) is any grappling with how political economy—the structure of a capitalist or state socialist economy—thwarts the possibility of democratic politics by engendering huge disparities in power among competing societal and state interests. In their preference for small, tightly bonded communities, communitarians fail to discuss the national (or even international) government policies needed to control those undemocratically structured private institutions, such as transnational corporations, which frequently limit community control. Without significant economic redistribution, community empowerment often means community control of poverty.

Social movement theory has made democratic theorists increasingly sensitive to the distinct concepts of community and morality that various ethnic, racial, and social groups hold in modern societies. Without guaranteed rights for particular communities, the communitarian search for a "politics of the common good" could lead to an authoritarian imposition of one idea of the good upon all arenas of life. In a modern world of plural identities, the communitarian longing for a premodern universal and teleological concept of the good life offers no feasible political alternative to liberalism's failure to generate a compelling vision of the common good. What may promote solidarity among the plural communities of a democratic society, however, is the common commitment to the limited but substantive end of democratic participation. Members of a vibrant, pluralist democracy would share those constitutional and social resources that enable distinct communities in common to work out, reshape, and learn to live with the differences of pluralism. Diversity can only be truly empowering if it is achieved in the context of a shared commitment to the commonality of democratic citizenship.

Perhaps as a result of the depoliticization of the 1970s and 1980s, political theory has increasingly substituted metaethical argument for theoretical reflection upon concrete political problems. But whether we philosophically treat "equal respect" as a foundational principle (as Dworkin does)[31] or as an empirical reality of our culture (in Rorty's pragmatic, nonmetaphysical rendition of Rawls),[32] if such a value is not latent in our society then attempts to revive communal sentiments will come to naught. If there cannot be a political revival of a shared commitment to democratic equality, then purely philosophical arguments as to what rights free and rational persons would choose in an original position of equality will not aid us; that is, Rawls's philosophical concept of our latent understandings needs to be tested politically. Walzer is correct to argue that rights are not historically established by abstract arguments about the social contract. Rather, the nature of the contract is established through a community's shared understandings of what it means to be a member of that community and of what needs must be satisfied if one is to function as a member (as Walzer puts it, "membership for common provision, common provision for membership").[33] Walzer may underestimate, however, how readily a privileged majority within a political democracy can exclude others from its shared conception of membership (Athens' slaves and metics are today's guest workers and new immigrants). Only if the racial, political, and geographic divisions between middle-class suburbia and the inner city are attenuated will this sense of membership become more inclusive.

The communitarians offer a compelling critique of how the instrumental and bureaucratic nature of mass liberal societies precludes a shared sense of community. Alasdair MacIntyre provides a provocative account of how market-place values erode the integrity and internal coherence of socially cooperative practices[34] (an account similar to Walzer's theory of the dominance of money in liberal marketplace societies over other goods).[35] But MacIntyre's and Sandel's aloofness from issues of representative democracy, public provision, and democratic control of the economy leaves them with little to say about how to revitalize a popular commitment to democratic community. Whether growing middle-strata awareness of the inadequacies of public education, child care, and health care in their own communities provides an initial basis for the reconstruction of a politics of social solidarity is an issue for further exploration. Liberal democrats and democratic communitarians need not concur on the metaphysical nature of the self to draw up political articles of reconciliation focusing on the centrality of democratic public provision to equal membership in a democratic community (social rights, if one prefers the discourse of rights). Such a reconciliation might enable political theory to move from abstract ontological and metaphysical debates to the more pressing exploration of the cultural erosion of social solidarity and the prospects for (and barriers to) a renewed politics of social solidarity.

The Two-Tiered American Welfare State
and the Prospects for Social Solidarity[36]

Despite growing recognition that many Americans cannot by private means afford decent health care, education, housing, and child care, expansion of social policy in the United States is not yet seriously on the political agenda. The immediate obstacle is Democratic timidity before a federal budget deficit bequeathed by the perverse military Keynesian "recovery" of the Reagan years (a deficit that could readily be eased by instituting progressive taxation and a rational defense budget). Although the triumphalism over the "victory" in the Gulf War may have been a temporary collective psychological displacement of anxiety about social deterioration at home, so far President Clinton's fear of being labeled weak on defense has led him to propose only modest defense cuts. The inability to expand public provision in the face of growing public squalor partly arises, however, from a deeper ideological crisis in American life. Many citizens have grown suspicious of social expenditure and cynical about the possibility of quality public provision.

The sources of this erosion in a popular commitment to social solidarity are myriad: growing middle class dissatisfaction with public education and other public services; the increased isolation of the poor, particularly the African-American poor, from the rest of society; the popular misperception that most social welfare expenditure is for the indolent, "undeserving poor"; and the prevailing economic wisdom that we cannot afford generous social policies in an internationally competitive economy.

Political support for public provision depends on popular recognition that an unrestrained market economy will neither adequately provide "public goods" (infrastructure, police, schools, clean air) nor distribute income and resources so that all can fairly participate in economic and public life. As Richard Cloward and Frances Fox Piven have argued, a corporate ideological offensive against government regulation and the welfare state contributed to the decline in popular support for public provision in the 1980s.[37] But already-existing suspicion of taxation and the quality of public provision among blue-collar and middle-class constituencies provided a receptive audience for this orchestrated offensive. As with most ideological beliefs, these suspicions were not completely irrational. When American federal, state, and local taxes are taken together, our tax structure is at best "proportional"; and increasing reliance on "capped" Social Security payroll taxes threatens to render the overall tax system regressive. Periodic "tax reforms" have never fulfilled their promises of progressivity. (Although no tax reform has ever been as blatantly regressive as Reagan's.) Public provision is sometimes bureaucratic and inefficient, particularly in large cities. Metropolitan government, however, would obviously help secure the financial resources for inner cities that today facilitate higher quality suburban public provision. American federalism produces social democratic levels of public provision for the most affluent suburbs and inner-city conditions comparable to Third World metropolises. Unfortunately, we will be living with the fiscal and political constraints of federalism for some time to come.

There is evidence, however, that popular belief in the neoconservative nostrums of the 1980s are receding as the costs of the Reaganite "free market" become increasingly evident (e.g., the savings and loan crises, rampant financial speculation, homelessness). Enlightened sectors of corporate capital publicly acknowledge (most often in the pages of *Business Week*) that the erosion of public education and job training weakens productivity and international competitiveness. Yet because the majority of congressional Democrats now represent white suburban districts, there is a danger that renewed concern about public provision could yield neoliberal policies of socio-economic triage. Such policies might increase tax credits to subsidize private middle-class child care, health care and educational expenditures, while the bottom third of society is consigned to low-productivity jobs, poor social services, and chronic unemployment. If growing concern for the "health" of our society does not engender solidaristic politics that enhance opportunities for all, the United States will evolve into a nation more divided along lines of race, gender and class than when the Kerner Commission issued its warning in 1968 about worsening civil disorders.

Most industrial welfare states witnessed "populist" revolts in the 1970s and 1980s of the middle class (including skilled sectors of the working class) against high levels of taxation and public spending, with the wrath of the revolt focused on increasingly marginalized poor populations. (These populations are increasingly minority—West Indians and subcontinent Asians in Britain; North Africans in France; Turks in the Federal Republic of Germany). Yet most welfare states weathered the conservative attack better than did the United States. While Social Security and Medicare were unscathed, the Reagan period witnessed 15 percent real cuts in AFDC, 11 percent in food stamps, 90 percent in public housing expenditures, and a serious erosion of the purchasing power of the working poor.

This vulnerability of the American welfare state is largely due to two unique features of American social policy—its absence of universal principles for organizing public provision and the sharp disjuncture between social and economic policy. To comprehend this uniqueness, it is necessary to abandon the traditional left's concept of the welfare state as a uniform institution shaped by the functional needs of capitalism for steady economic demand and social stability. The nature of a given welfare state results, instead, from a complex history of political struggle, economic development, and state policy.

Since the New Deal, U.S. social policy has equivocated between a top tier of social insurance (Social Security, unemployment insurance) for those regularly employed (and their spouses) and a bottom tier of less generous, means-tested public assistance programs for those whose participation in the labor force is more sporadic (mostly single-parent women). These public policies have been supplemented by employer provision of private benefits, such as medical insurance, for those with "good" jobs.

This pattern of public and private policy has promoted a sharp societal division that, not surprisingly, has fallen along lines of race and gender. The jobs and employment patterns that qualify citizens for upper-tier programs and private insurance have traditionally been the prerogatives of white males. The core of the American welfare state, the Social Security Act of 1935, which created unemployment insurance, old age pensions, and aid to dependent children, largely excluded African-Americans (because it did not cover agricultural and domestic workers) and single-parent mothers who were not widows. The programs were founded on the model of a traditional nuclear family, with the father having steady employment and insurance programs stepping in to help with emergencies, such as unemployment, old age, and widowhood.[38] Even though the overt discrimination that kept members of minorities and women in inferior labor market positions has eased in the past two decades, these groups remain at a disadvantage in this divided world of social policy and segmented labor markets.

The second key feature of American social provision that has stunted programs and undermined public support has been the disjuncture between economic and social policy. In Western Europe social democrats have tried (though not always successfully) to integrate social welfare policy with broader labor market and economic strategies (aiming to tighten labor markets and upgrade low-wage jobs). The failure of the progressive economists around Franklin Roosevelt to make social policy an important complement to economic goals meant that the United States has never coherently linked employment policy to social welfare policy. Instead, in traditional American political discourse, the two arenas are conceived to be separate and often competing.[39] Thus, social policy can only be expanded when it can be "afforded." In the prosperous 1960s such reasoning facilitated a limited "war on poverty"; by the late 1970s, however, social policy was seen as an unaffordable luxury.

This historic failure to link social policy to broader economic policy has contributed to unemployment and poverty being popularly viewed as a problem of individual character and culture rather than of economic structure and policy. The antipoverty programs of the 1960s were created as separate, remedial programs, targeted on the poor (particularly African-American poor). Most job training programs did not teach marketable skills for jobs with career track potential, but rather taught "good work habits" for make-work jobs. Although these limited policies (AFDC liberalization, Medicaid, Food Stamps) improved the lives of the poor, their public support largely rested on the moral claim the civil rights movement made on the conscience of the majority in the affluent 1960s. The failure to invest these programs with a collective rationale (based on universal entitlements to job training and an economic minimum) rendered them vulnerable to the racial backlash of the economically stagnant 1970s.

Three key factors contributed to the peculiarly attenuated United States welfare state—the fragmented and localized nature of the American state, a relatively weak labor movement, and severe racial division. These factors interacted historically to make it difficult to construct an American counterpart to the much more centralized, solidaristic welfare states of Northern Europe. Strengthening institutions of collective solidarity, such as unions and neighborhood associations, will be integral to revitalizing popular belief in social solidarity. As mentioned earlier, the transient nature of American society poses obstacles to such organizing. Thus, a consumer-based (rather than strictly community-based) appeal to middle- and working-class voters' concerns with quality health care, education, and child care will also be central to a strategy of expanded social provision. The growing emphasis of the women's movement on issues of economic equality and child care has already stimulated moderate congressional proposals for federally subsidized child care, as well as legally guaranteed (but unpaid) parental leave. Increasing numbers of Americans personally experience how the transformation of the American family necessitates greater community and public support for childrearing.

The divided and limited character of the "liberal" American welfare state—if it can be called that—has meant that liberals have had neither the political nor the programmatic base to defend, much less to extend, social policy. The organization of American social policy has done little to promote the commonality necessary for generous social provision. Instead, it has exacerbated the division between the poor and the rest of society. The consequences have been particularly devastating for the African-American poor, who are now seen as alien "others" by white America. Thus in current mainstream policy debates, the problem of the African-American poor is "the behavior" of "the underclass"; and the solution consists of coercive programs that change their behavior, without radically altering social opportunities. *Underclass* is a woefully undefined term used to characterize a diverse group of poor people. William Julius Wilson now uses the broader term "urban poor," arguing that only one-third of poor African-American inner-city adults (and less than half of the inner city is poor) actually fit his technical definition of the underclass as individuals with no history of long-term employment. By this definition, the underclass constitutes, at a maximum, only 10 percent of the nation's poor adults.[40]

Current policy debates pay little attention to changing the structures of employment and social opportunities that would improve the lives of most low-income Americans (60 percent of whom are white). For low-income women, policy solutions have been narrowed to enforcing child support (from fathers who themselves are mostly poor) and work-fare programs, whose ability to prepare women for nonpoverty jobs is extremely doubtful. Job training for career ladder jobs, child care support for women across income lines, and income support for part-time workers with young children are all deemed "impractical."

As doubts about the "success" of Reaganism grow, progressives need to seize the opportunity to debunk popular myths about the welfare state. For example, one cannot reiterate too often that the major victims of Reagan's upwardly redistributive tax policies were the working poor (for whom he claimed to be specially concerned). Contrary to neoconservative econometric predictions that welfare rolls would shrink if benefit cuts rendered AFDC less attractive than work, welfare rolls expanded over the past twenty years despite benefit levels being slashed by 42 percent in real terms. The decline in job opportunities for the less skilled (particularly African-American men) was the main cause for the increase in poor, single-parent families. Yet the continued moral onus attached to welfare combined with restrictive eligibility requirements means that fewer than 75 percent of those economically eligible for AFDC actually receive benefits. (The take-up rate is even lower for Supplemental Security Income—55 percent—and Food Stamps—less than 50 percent.)[41]

Social welfare policy can no longer be predicated on the assumption that a typical family consists of a male breadwinner and a wife at home with children. Only 15 percent of American families conform to this picture, and 55 percent of women with children under the age of six work outside the home (though only half of these work full-time). Increased labor participation rates of women with young children may mean that a majority of Americans will not endorse levels of child support that would enable poor, single parents to stay home with their toddlers full-time. But if this be the case, then job-training, income maintenance, health care, and child care programs should render part-time work and humane child-rearing feasible for all adults. It is highly inequitable to require single women with preschool children to work full-time (as inadequately funded, punitive workfare programs propose), while the vast majority of two-parent families with infants do not have two income earners in full-time work.

Some feminists and "new social movement" advocates contend that a strong welfare society will inevitably enforce a paternalistic, bureaucratic model of citizenship and social organization upon its citizens. A compelling vision of social provision would emphasize democratic, decentralized forms of communal provision—neighborhood schools, child care co-ops, and community health clinics. Nonetheless, strong federal standards and funding will be necessary to avoid the severe regional, racial, and class inequalities that already afflict such public goods as education. State policy will profoundly affect the quality of provision available to citizens within decentralized caring institutions of civil society.

One can also affirm the culturally sustaining role of particular identities based on race, ethnicity, and gender without denigrating citizenship as a "homogenizing" category that reduces all to the pursuit of the same interests and needs. Although diversity is a central value of a pluralist democracy, so too is the social solidarity derived from a sense of common citizenship. If human beings and the particular communities to which they belong are to be accorded equal respect, they need to live in a society that guarantees those social rights necessary for each member to fulfill his or her human potential. The ending of the Cold War already has produced growing public recognition that economic strength is more central to a nation's well-being than military hardware. (We can hope that the Gulf War only temporarily slowed the growth of this consciousness.) If democratic theorists and activists can transform the elite discourse of "human capital" development into a cross-class concern for the development of each of our citizens, then the 1990s may well be a decade of social reform.

Conclusion: Democratic Community as a Defense of Welfare Rights

In this essay I have argued that a substantive concept of democratic community would serve as a more effective defense of public provision than a market-oriented liberal conception of social welfare as a "safety net" for individuals whose basic needs temporarily cannot be provided for by the market. One should not caricature liberalism as simply a defense of self-interested market behavior. There are many liberalisms, and egalitarian liberals also defend social rights as integral to individual freedom. But a defense of social rights that appeals to the professed values of American democracy is likely to be more politically efficacious than an abstract deduction of such rights from an a priori concept of individual autonomy.

In constructing a democratic defense of public provision three lessons are to be learned from America's experience as a less than fully democratic welfare society:

1. *New social welfare programs should be based on universal, inclusionary principles even if fiscal reality may preclude a uniform level of benefits.* Programs that provide some benefits to all will inevitably garner more support than strictly means-tested programs. Policies based on moral principles that speak to the needs of all people need not benefit each person uniformly. For example, while a new children's allowance policy (or earned-income tax credits) might provide a generous enough benefit level to facilitate humane childrearing by a single parent who worked part-time at a relatively low-wage job, such a program might also provide limited benefits to middle-income families. Similar principles could apply to the expansion of health care benefits (if we don't rationally opt for a universal system of provision in the near future). Christopher Jencks and Kathryn Edin propose that all Americans be given the option of purchasing (improved) Medicaid coverage for 5 percent of their total incomes.[42]

2. *Racist myths that create hostility to the welfare state must be directly confronted and cannot be avoided simply by a correct strategic emphasis on universal provision.* Although I share William Julius Wilson's and others' strategic emphasis on universal programs that would disproportionately benefit

the poor, that strategy may underestimate how racism functions as an ideological barrier to renewed support for all forms of public provision. Many middle-income taxpayers in New Jersey oppose Governor James Florio's tax reform proposals not only because they do not believe that cuts in property taxes will eventually offset (for 70 percent of taxpayers) increases in income taxes, but also because they believe that inner-city school districts could never effectively spend the increased funding (which will benefit two-thirds of school districts).

In defending public provision, advocates cannot underemphasize that whites remain the majority of beneficiaries of each and every social program. Of course, the reality of racism means that higher percentages of minority communities benefit from means-tested programs. Perhaps the most pernicious antiwelfare myth is that of the "welfare queen." Although 20 percent of AFDC beneficiaries are long-term recipients (more than four consecutive years on the rolls), numerous time-series studies demonstrate that the majority of female beneficiaries use AFDC as a form of temporary child support and subsequently return to the full-time labor market.

The query of many white Americans as to why African-Americans have not experienced mobility rates comparable to many other ethnic groups must also be answered head-on. Chattel slavery, sharecropping, and Jim Crow denied African-Americans access to cultural and economic resources available to other immigrant groups. Most white Americans do not realize the devastating effects that deindustrialization visited upon the political economy of the inner city nor the shattering of African-American communities caused by massive post–World War II migration and simultaneous urban renewal and gentrification. (Deindustrialization has had similar devastating effects on the economic performance of the Puerto Rican community in the Northeast.[43]) Nevertheless, the top third of the African-American community has experienced in just one generation extraordinary social mobility comparable to the most "successful" immigrant groups.

But greater public awareness of the specific oppression of the African-American community will not revive support for public provision. In a constrained economic environment, wide segments of Americans fear downward social mobility and are unsympathetic to programs that specifically benefit historically disadvantaged groups. Thus, Wilson is correct to contend that progressive social policy initiatives should promote a multiracial, cross-class coalition behind public policies that would benefit a majority of the population. The main barrier to such a coalition is not primarily, as some argue, narrow nationalist tendencies among African-American activists. Rather, the tragedy of American politics is the absence of a credible white liberal left, particularly among the political leadership of the Democratic Party. Only the African-American political class (the Congressional Black Caucus, Jesse Jackson) have had the courage to buck the dominant neoconservative climate and advocate a social democratic agenda speaking to the interests of all Americans.

3. *Perhaps most importantly, arguments for social rights must be tied to an acknowledgment of concurrent social obligations.* Support for such obligations does not mean accepting contemporary conceptions of "meaningful work," which often devalue forms of productive labor such as caring for children or the elderly (work often done by women outside the formal labor market). Despite the popularity of Social Security and Medicare, the right has convinced many citizens that social welfare programs inherently create dependency and preclude social reliance. A major task for democratic theorists is to demonstrate how public provision can enhance each member's ability to contribute to society. If the obligation of each citizen to contribute to the community is ignored and social programs are simply conceived of as automatic entitlements, then support for public provision will continue to erode among those who see themselves as contributing members of society. Whether such a contributory obligation on the part of adult citizens is met by full-time child-rearing of toddlers; or by part-time child-rearing and part-time work; or by full-time work and socialized forms of child care is an issue demanding democratic deliberation. But "workfare" proposals that would require poor, single parents on AFDC to accept low-wage, dead-end jobs without adequate child care and health care support are new forms of the poorhouse—without walls.

The struggle for civil rights and political rights of the 1930s and 1960s brought about a significant expansion of American democracy. The fight for universal social rights may be the next stage in the extension of our nation's conception of democracy. If an equal potential voice for each member in the political community is the vision of the good embraced by "communitarian democrats" and if attaining those social rights integral to democracy is the goal of "liberal democrats" then the political distance between the two camps may not be so great. Perhaps the philosophical distance might lessen as well. If this task is to be achieved, communitarians need to specify those rights necessary for the equal opportunity to participate in the good life of their envisioned "virtuous" (and hopefully democratic) community. Rights-based liberals, on their part, need to examine whether rights are not best defended and conceptualized by appealing to the notions of equal respect integral to our society's commitment to democracy. If we fail to achieve a more just *and* democratic society at least we will not have been divided by metaphysical debates that rarely get down to tackling tough political realities.

Notes

1. In the United States, right-wing libertarians such as Milton Friedman or Robert Nozick are popularly described as "conservative." This is partially due to the absence of an American feudal past that renders traditional American conservatism more hostile to the paternalist state than its European ideological equivalent. But the libertarian vision of

a minimalist state that bears no responsibility for the economic well-being of its members goes beyond traditional American conservatism's tolerance of modest welfare state arrangements (e.g., Social Security, unemployment insurance). Thus, in the parlance of continental European political thought libertarian theorists are best described as right-wing radicals rather than "conservatives." Hence, my use of the term libertarian rather than conservative in the main text.

The Reagan–Bush and Thatcher administrations relied upon libertarian ideology to justify their cuts in social welfare programs and regressive tax reforms. They also succeeded in moving traditional paternalist and corporatist conservatives to the margins of their respective nations' right-wing movements. Whether the social decay and radical inequalities resulting from the program of the radical right will engender a resurgence in traditional conservatism (perhaps John Major represents such a trend) remains to be seen. In this essay, to avoid confusion between statist–paternalist traditional conservatives and the "new conservatism" of Reaganism and Thatcherism I refer to the latter's ideology as libertarian.

2. The most influential libertarian theoretical critique of the welfare state is Robert Nozick, *Anarchy, State and Utopia* (New York: Basic Books, 1974). Two programmatic libertarian critiques that influenced Reagan administration policy were George Gilder, *Wealth and Poverty* (New York: Basic Books, 1981), and Charles Murray, *Losing Ground: American Social Policy 1950–80* (New York: Basic Books, 1984).

Michael Sandel advances a communitarian critique of welfare provision as bureaucratic and unsustainable because of its dependence on an anachronistic New Deal sense of a national community in "The Procedural Republic and the Unencumbered Self," *Political Theory* 12, no. 1 (February 1984):81–96, esp. pp. 90–96. Although Sandel appears sympathetic to forms of public provision based in local cooperative institutions, Alasdair MacIntyre disdains any politics of economic redistribution because this "civil war by other means" is another aspect of modernity's flawed attempt to achieve compromise among incommensurable conceptions of moral virtue. Instrumental, economic compromises cannot alleviate the need for a new moral consensus upon social virtues. See Alasdair MacIntyre, *After Virtue* (South Bend, Ind.: University of Notre Dame Press, 1981), esp. pp. 250–55.

3. While I will later take issue with the "particularist" aspect of Michael Walzer's conception of justice, the concept of public provision as integral to membership in a democratic community is obviously indebted to his work. He most explicitly works out the relationship between public provision and membership in a democratic community in *Spheres of Justice: A Defense of Pluralism and Equality* (New York: Basic Books, 1983), chapter 3, "Security and Welfare," pp. 64–83.

4. Claus Offe develops this insight in "Democracy Against the Welfare State" in Donald Moon, ed., *Responsibility, Rights and Welfare: The Theory of the Welfare State* (Boulder, Colo.: Westview Press, 1988), pp. 189–228.

5. Fred Siegal provocatively argues that middle-class support for Social Security and Medicare is no longer motivated by New Deal sentiments of social solidarity, but rather by a belief that such entitlements free them from burdensome social responsibilities to

family, parents, etc. See Fred Siegal, "Dependent Individualism," *Dissent* 35 (Fall 1988):437.

6. Critics of the Scandinavian welfare state allege that the decommodified provision of "basic needs" erodes the work ethic. Higher absentee rates among younger workers than among their parents' may be partly due to their less intense embrace of the social solidarity that enabled their parents' generation to implement generous vacation and sick leave provisions. But labor participation rates among the younger generation in Scandinavia remain among the highest in the industrial world, as is labor productivity. High labor participation rates partly derive from the decommodification of child care, which encourages mothers with young children to participate in the formal labor force.

7. The classic article outlining this position is Charles Reich, "The New Property," *Yale Law Journal* 73 (April 1964): 733–87.

8. Criticizing "abstract" conceptions of the social contract, Michael Walzer argues that a consensus upon what public goods are essential to membership in a democratic community develops out of political conflict and argument rather than from philosophical reflection. See Michael Walzer, *Spheres of Justice*, pp. 78–90.

9. A problem for the political sociology of my analysis is that social solidarity historically has intensified during periods of depression or war, when a broad range of citizens share collective risks. During these periods, public provision has grown most rapidly in democratic capitalist societies. Secondary periods of growth in public provision have occurred during economic booms when the majority feels generous enough to expand membership provisions to protesting, formerly excluded minorities. The unique period of relative stagnation of the past twenty years led beleaguered working- and middle-class persons to focus narrowly on their own private well-being. Growing sectors of the middle class may now recognize that they cannot afford to purchase human services in the private sector. But will renewed middle-class concern for improved public provision lead to social programs that benefit them and more disadvantaged sectors? The debate over "choice" in education may provide an initial answer to this question.

10. Jennifer Hochschild describes this tension as involving competing concepts of equal opportunity. "Prospect regarding" or marketplace concepts of equal opportunity involve the legal right to pursue a goal and to use whatever means one legally possesses to pursue that goal. "Means-regarding" or democratic equality of opportunity ensures that people have equal means or resources by which to pursue their chosen goal. See Jennifer Hochschild, "Race, Class, Power and the American Welfare State," in Amy Gutmann, ed., *Democracy and the Welfare State* (New York: Cambridge University Press, 1988), pp.157–84.

11. The most rigorous philosophical defense of the welfare state based on liberal marketplace principles that the dependent should not be subject to exploitative contracts of duress is Robert E. Goodin, *Reasons for Welfare: The Political Theory of the Welfare State* (Princeton, N.J.: Princeton University Press, 1988).

12. Albert Weale, "Equality, Social Solidarity and the Welfare State," *Ethics* 100, no. 3 (April 1990): 475.

13. Gosta Esping-Anderson, *The Three Worlds of Welfare Capitalism* (Princeton,

108   *Joseph M. Schwartz*

N.J.: Princeton University Press, 1989), chapter 1, "The Three Political Economies of the Welfare State," pp. 9–34.

14. I join Theda Skocpol, William Julius Wilson, and Margaret Weir in contending that the defense of the welfare state should highlight popular social insurance and universal programs (such as Social Security, Supplemental Security Income, unemployment insurance, and Medicare) while advocating new universal programs (national health care, child benefits, and meaningful job training) which, though benefiting all, would disproportionately aid the most disadvantaged. See William Julius Wilson, *The Truly Disadvantaged: The Inner City, the Underclass and Public Policy* (Chicago: University of Chicago Press, 1989), chapter 6, "The Hidden Agenda," pp. 140–64; Theda Skocpol, "Fighting Poverty without Poverty Programs," *The American Prospect* 2 (Summer 1990): 58–70; and Margaret Weir, Ann Shola Orloff, and Theda Skocpol, *The Politics of Social Policy in the United States* (Princeton, N.J.: Princeton University Press, 1988), introduction and conclusion.

15. Brian Barry, "The Welfare State Versus the Relief of Poverty," *Ethics* 100, no. 3 (April 1990): 503–29.

16. See Robert Goodin, *Reasons for Welfare,* and Carl Wellman, *Welfare Rights* (Totowa, N.J.: Rowman and Littlefield, 1982).

17. Goodin does not oppose arguments based on mutual dependence and risk-sharing that would "provide impetus for moving beyond minimal welfare state provision of social assistance to meet basic needs and towards programs of social insurance and of categorical assistance...." But he believes that "minimalist" welfare provision for the poor is most efficaciously defended by arguments that supporters of market economies can endorse. That is, "safety net" provision protects the inevitable victims of the market and enables some of them to return to "market independence." See chapter 13, "Conclusion" in *Reasons for Welfare,* pp. 361–69 and "Reasons for Welfare: Economic, Sociological and Political—but Ultimately Moral" in Moon, ed., *Responsibilities, Rights and Welfare,* pp. 19–54.

18. Wellman, *Welfare Rights,* p. 29.

19. See Wellman, *Welfare Rights,* chapter 1, "The Conception of a Welfare Right," pp. 22–29.

20. See Christopher Jencks and Kathryn Edin, "The Real Welfare Problem," *The American Prospect* 1 (Spring 1990):31–50.

21. MacIntyre rejects the compromises among competing interests integral to welfare state politics as instrumental and anticommunal. He might not oppose public provision if it were integral to a shared communal conception of virtue. But founding a political community on a universally shared conception of moral virtue violates the plurality of the modern world. See MacIntyre, *After Virtue,* pp. 250–54.

Hannah Arendt and Sheldon Wolin, two theorists who defy neat classification but who clearly influence contemporary communitarianism, share MacIntyre's and Sandel's belief that the interest-laden nature of issues of socio-economic distribution drive out from the public arena the truly political issues of "virtue" and collective "action." Wolin approvingly summarizes Arendt's view thus: "Public preoccupation with the redistribution of wealth and material goods, with the productivity of society, with levels of employment and with social security was indicative of a state of affairs in which anti-political forces and values had driven authentic politics from the public realm." See Sheldon Wolin, "Hannah Arendt and the Ordinance of Time," *Social Research* 44, no. 1 (Spring 1977):94.

22. Michael Sandel, *Liberalism and the Limits of Justice* (Cambridge: Cambridge University Press, 1982).

23. Michael Sandel, "Morality and the Liberal Ideal," *The New Republic*, May 7, 1984, pp. 15–17.

24. Will Kymlicka, "Liberalism and Communitarianism," *Canadian Journal of Philosophy* 18, no. 2 (June 1988):181–204.

25. Amy Gutmann, "How Liberal is Democracy?" in Douglas MacLean and Claudia Mills, eds., *Liberalism Reconsidered* (Totowa, N.J.: Rowman and Allanheld, 1983), pp. 25–50.

26. Michael Walzer, "Philosophy and Democracy," *Political Theory* 9, no. 3 (August 1981): 379–99, and Walzer, "Liberalism and the Art of Separation," *Political Theory* 12, no. 3 (August 1984): 315–30.

27. For a provocative exploration of Walzer's "universal" commitment to democracy and to the moral superiority of societies that allow the practice of social criticism, see William Galston, "Community, Democracy, Philosophy: The Political Thought of Michael Walzer," *Political Theory* 17, no. 1 (February 1989): 119–30. Walzer's critique of the existing practices of most democratic polities in regards to the political rights of "guest workers" is advanced in *Spheres of Justice*, pp. 52–63. His criticism of the existing practice of the United States as regards the distribution of health care is made in *Spheres of Justice*, pp. 86–91.

Walzer might claim that he does not impose a "universal" or "external" critique upon American cultural and political practices because there already exists—a morally and politically contested—internal contradiction in America between providing health care for the indigent and elderly based on need (Medicaid and Medicare) while leaving the working class and middle class to the vagaries of private insurance. But would not Walzer also criticize a society that had a stable political consensus behind distributing health care strictly by private market mechanisms (or by the American mixture of need-based and market mechanisms) as violating the moral principle of the good of health care—that it should be distributed according to need?

In his chapter on political power, Walzer appears to offer a universal defense of democracy as the only just way of distributing the good of political power: "Once we have located ownership, expertise, religious knowledge, and so on in their proper places and established their autonomy, there is no alternative to democracy in the political sphere.... Democracy is a way of allocating power and legitimating its use—or better, it is *the political way* of allocating power. Every extrinsic reason is ruled out. What counts is argument among the citizens...." *Spheres of Justice*, pp. 303–04. Walzer emphasizes that democracy is the only proper *political* way of distributing power. But would he defend other "nonpolitical" ways of distributing political power as just (even if they were the consensus practices of a given society)?

28. John Rawls, "The Idea of an Overlapping Consensus," *Oxford Journal of Legal Studies* 7, no. 1 (Spring 1987):10, fn. 17.

29. The concept of "enlightened understanding" is taken from Robert Dahl, *Democracy and Its Critics* (New Haven, Conn.: Yale University Press, 1989), pp. 111–12,307–8.

30. See Jim Shoch, "Communitarianism and the Limits of the Good", unpublished paper, M.I.T. Department of Political Science, 1989, Cambridge, Mass.

31. See Ronald Dworkin, "Why Liberals Should Care About Equality," in *A Matter of Principle* (Cambridge, Mass.: Harvard University Press, 1985), pp. 205–13, and Ronald Dworkin, "Justice and Rights," in *Taking Rights Seriously* (Cambridge, Mass.: Harvard University Press, 1977), pp. 150–83.

32. See Richard Rorty, "Postmodernist Bourgeois Liberalism," *The Journal of Philosophy* 80, no. 10 (October 1983): 583–89; and Rorty, "Thugs and Theorists: A Reply to Bernstein," *Political Theory* 15, no. 4 (November 1987):564–80.

33. Walzer, *Spheres of Justice*, p. 83.

34. See MacIntyre, *After Virtue*, pp. 202–3.

35. This comparison is insightfully noted by Ian Shapiro in *Political Criticism* (Berkeley: University of California Press, 1990), pp. 163–64.

36. Much of the analysis of this section is drawn from Joseph M. Schwartz and Margaret Weir, "Rebuilding Social Solidarity," *Democratic Left* 18, no. 2 (March–April 1990): 8–10; and Joseph M. Schwartz, "Coalition Politics in a 'Three Speed' Society," *Socialist Review* 90/2 (April–June 1990): 67–79, esp., pp. 70–73.

37. Richard Cloward and Frances Fox Piven, *The New Class War: Reagan's Attack on the Welfare State and Its Consequences* (New York: Pantheon Books, 1982).

38. The original Aid to Dependent Children did not recognize the existence of non-widowed single-parent mothers, although by the post–World War II era most states paid ADC to the children of divorced women. The children of unmarried women often did not become eligible for benefits until the 1960s.

39. See Margaret Weir, "The Federal Government and Unemployment: The Frustration of Policy Innovation from the New Deal to the Great Society," in Weir, Orloff, and Skocpol, *The Politics of Social Policy*, pp. 149–98.

40. For two illuminating articles on the "underclass" debate that argue that the term should be used with careful precision to refer to those (at maximum) two to three million adults who cannot be readily reincorporated into the workforce (a portion of the homeless, deinstitutionalized mental patients, and chronic drug addicts and alcoholics), see William Kornblum, "Who is the Underclass?" *Dissent* 38 (Spring 1991):202–11; and Bob Kuttner, "Notes from Underground," *Dissent* 38 (Spring 1991):212–17.

41. See Richard Cloward and Frances Fox Piven, chapter 2, "The Contemporary Relief Debate," in Fred Block, Barbara Ehrenreich, Richard Cloward and Frances Fox Piven, eds., *The Mean Season: The Attack on the Welfare State* (New York: Pantheon, 1987), pp. 61, 87.

42. Christopher Jencks and Kathryn Edin, "The Real Welfare Problem," *The American Prospect* 1 (Spring 1990): 48.

43. William Kornblum, "Who is the Underclass?" *Dissent* 38 (Spring 1991): 205–6.

Chapter 7

Trade Unions, Workers' Control, and Democracy

Philip Resnick

A rethinking and reappropriation of democratic theory are perhaps the most urgent task facing the left in Western societies. One could, of course, make an equally strong case for the societies where "actually existing socialisms" have given way to different types and degrees of political reform and capitalist restoration. Until the late 1980s, attempts to move in the direction of democratic theory and practice came to grief; and before that period only an inveterate optimist held out much hope for any relinquishing of party control or democratization of civil society in the foreseeable future.

Things have changed dramatically and the flux continues, but this is not to say that no important lessons can be drawn from past East European experience, where the relationship between trade unions and the state is concerned, or regarding the question of workers' control. The Yugoslav experience, in this regard, goes back more than thirty-five years and has been richly documented by Western social scientists as well as Yugoslavs.[1] An extensive literature touches on workers' councils not only in the Russian Revolutions at the beginning of this century, but again in Hungary in 1956, in Czechoslovakia in 1968–1969, and in Poland during the events of 1956, 1970, and 1976 and more recently, the early 1980s.[2]

The point of departure for this chapter is rather different. It is directed to the experience in Western societies that have been for many years of a predominantly capitalist kind, with important features of the mixed economy. It is written in a period that has seen the breakdown of the post–World War II consensus, a major crisis in the financing and objectives of the welfare state, and a decline in the membership and militancy of trade unions. It further reflects the sober, almost chastened, climate of debate in the English-speaking world, with neoconservatism in the ascendant in the United Kingdom, the United States, and to a slightly lesser degree, Canada.

The winds of conservatism are currently prevailing over the winds of radicalism in the Western part of the world. There are economic and structural reasons to explain this—stagflation, declining rates of growth and productivity, automation and the deindustrialization of traditional sectors, the new international division of labor, and mobility of capital. There are ideological reasons having to do with the increased backlash against the role of the state, middle-class angst, working-class disenchantment, and the strong dose of patriotism, religion, and old-fashioned virtues doled out by the high priests and practicing politicians of the new right. The heady days of the 1960s are far away. It is as though we are to collectively atone for the sins of those years—student insurrections, black militancy, antiwar fervor, participatory demands—by a wholesale cutting back in expectations and demands. This is the message that the Trilateral Commission preached in its manifesto of the mid-1970s, entitled *The Crisis of Democracy*.[3] It is the bitter medicine that the Margaret Thatchers and Ronald Reagans of this world, with their attacks on social services and tax breaks for the wealthy, have been administering since.

That the left has fallen on hard times is clear enough. Successive defeats of the British Labour Party, the demise of the Social Democratic-led coalition in the Federal Republic of Germany, ostensible setbacks in some of the Scandinavian countries, Reagan's two victories, the rapid waning of François Mitterrand's popularity in France, all serve to underline it. A pessimist with little faith in the cyclical pattern of events might think that the left were doomed for many a generation.

Beneath the surface, however, there are signs of renewal. And much of this renewal is taking place around the banner of democracy. The plethora of books and articles that have appeared in recent years—*Beyond Adversary Democracy, Democratic Theory and Practice, Strong Democracy, The Democratic Economy*[4]—attest to the rediscovery of democratic, especially participatory democratic, thought that has been occurring. The publications of the West German Greens with their emphasis on *Basis-demokratie*, the debates within the pages of *The New Socialist* and *Marxism Today* in the United Kingdom, the ongoing interest in community control and decentralized versions of economic democracy in North America confirm this. Whether the impetus comes from environmentalists, peace activists, women's groups, or trade unionists, the language of democracy has acquired a new luster on the left in Western societies.

As part of this democratic *aggiornamento*, there is a good deal less belief in state ownership and control as the preferred instrument for realizing collective objectives. It is not that the Western left has joined the marketeers on the right in vaunting the virtues of the unregulated private sphere. Rather, an anti-statism that had already surfaced in the student movements and New Left two decades before has become more explicit, with the crisis in which both social democracy and Keynesianism find themselves. State ownership does not in and of itself bring about a more participatory type of economy in which workers and ordinary citizens have any great say on key policy matters. Indeed, the technocratic character of much state enterprise in Western society, the authoritarian manner in which it is managed, and the lack of significant community involvement in setting its objectives, have greatly diminished the appeal of nationalization to broad sections of public opinion, middle class and working class.

Simultaneously, the negative image of "actually existing socialism" sundered belief in the state as the embodiment of the public sphere. Not only did the party–state run roughshod over civil society, over trade unions, over communal autonomy, but the very amalgamation of political with economic power seems to have fulfilled the worst prophecies of liberal critics of the socialist Leviathan. In the words of a Polish intellectual six months before the Gdansk occupation of August 1980, "We need a Montesquieu of socialism."[5] In other words, we, in the West no less than the East, need a more pluralistic model of socialism, one that postulates a separation of power between the apparatus of state and a socialized or collectivized economic sphere, and which retains the individual rights and freedoms we associate with the liberal democratic tradition.

This, I suggest, is the real reason that workers' control has, for more than two decades, enjoyed considerable support among broad sections of the left in Europe and beyond, and why economic democracy looms so large in contemporary left discourse. The mass strikes and factory occupations of May 1968 in France, often against the wishes of the union leadership, helped popularize the notion of *autogestion*, spawning not only a vast literature, but also a significant shift in the policies of the French trade union movement.[6] In West Germany, the codetermination legislation of 1951 was extended, in a modified form, to large corporations with 2,000 workers or more in the mid-1970s.[7] In the United Kingdom, the Bullock Commission of 1977, in its majority report, recommended an extensive system of industrial democracy with trade union directors equaling the number of directors appointed by management.[8] Workplace democracy has also loomed large in American and Canadian writings of recent years, embracing everything from worker-appointed directors to boards and worker-controlled enterprises, to more modest attempts at worker input under existing corporate ownership.[9]

It is not my purpose to review this literature, which is, in any case, reasonably familiar to the readers of this volume. I shall take it for granted that a more participatory economy is part and parcel of what a democratic left believes in and that, as Paul Blumberg argues, after examining seventeen experiments in worker participation, "generally acknowledged beneficial consequences accrue from a genuine increase in workers' decision-making power."[10] What I principally wish to explore then is the relationship between any system of workers' control that might be developed in Western societies and the trade union movement.

Workers' Control and Trade Unions—Some Questions

- Does a move towards greater economic democracy spell the enhancement of trade union power proper, or of other modes of worker–employee participation?
- To what degree is it in the interest of trade unions in the West, before any transition to socialism has occurred, to support greater worker participation in their plants or enterprises?
- How does the increased importance of the service sector, at the expense of the primary or secondary ones, in all Western societies affect the role of trade unions and of the traditional working class?
- Looking further ahead, on the assumption that at least a residual amount of economic planning exists under a market socialist economy, what functions ought trade unions to play?
- And what further function might they have if at least some of the directors of the worker-managed sector under such a system were appointed by the community and other groups from outside the existing workforce?

In posing such questions, I am perfectly aware of the fact that we in the West do not stand on the threshold of some sudden move to extend collective ownership over the means of production and with it to introduce some generalized form of workers' control. If anything, the current in recent years has been running in the direction of privatization of publicly owned enterprises, for example, in the United Kingdom. Where workers' control has been introduced, it has often been in the context of an inefficient or nearly bankrupt industry threatened with closure, or as a means of forcing a unionized workforce with a collective agreement into accepting steep cuts in pay.[11] Not surprisingly, the latter examples have helped give the concept of worker-controlled industries a negative image that more than balances out the positive one flowing from the Yugoslav example or the Mondragon experience in Northern Spain (the worker-owned and -controlled industrial cooperatives in the Basque country).

Still, it does no harm despite the continuing economic stagnation of traditional sectors of the economy and the difficulties that the trade union movement has been experiencing, to begin to talk about economic alternatives. Moreover, I hold at least some hope that once the current neoconservative wave has exhausted itself, the possibility of moving forward in the direction of greater economic, as well as political, democracy will arise. The questions I have just posed will be important to any decentralized and participatory model that the left can advance.

My first question is in many ways the most delicate and goes to the heart of the old left–new left cleavage. By economic democracy, those of a socialist persuasion mean a society where the distribution of the wealth is a good deal more egalitarian than it is today, where the power of large multinational corporations and banks has been tamed, and where an extensive network of employee- and worker-elected boards has become a central feature of the economy. Such a system often goes by the name of market socialism; and it differs from market capitalism as we know it today and from "actually existing socialism" through the existence of a large, collectively-owned sector of the economy not directly in the hands of the state. While certain monopolistic areas of the economy may continue under state tutelage (e.g., transportation, energy, or telecommunications), and while conversely the greater part of agriculture and small business will remain under private ownership, the bulk of the productive and distributive system will become part of a vastly expanded cooperative sector.[12]

In this cooperative sector, formal ownership of enterprises will be vested in the employees. For a shorter or longer transitional period, there may continue to be shareholders who are not employees of such enterprises (e.g., individuals, pension funds), but at best they would be limited to minority representation on boards of directors. Workers and employees under such a scheme would have the possibility of active and sustained participation in the decision-making of the firm through general meetings, elections, and service on the boards of directors and other specialized committees. In theory, at least, there would be much more extensive involvement by workers in such a system, particularly if care were taken to ensure frequent renewal of the membership of elected bodies.

The degree to which employees would participate actively in such a system is open to debate. Some, pointing to the Yugoslav experience and, to a certain degree, the Mondragon one as well, suggest that the worker-managed sector tends to fall prey to increased control by management, and by the better-educated and more organizationally astute members of the enterprise.[13] Others, without denying the inevitability of hierarchy even under a worker-managed system, would emphasize the educative consequences of participatory economic institutions.[14] Much as with any neighborhood assemblies or base-level units one might propose as part of a system of direct democracy,[15] the proof of such economic institutions could only come with their operation. With a generalized system of employee-controlled economic enterprises in existence, the motivation for participation could not but be vastly greater than is the case under existing corporate-dominated structures.

But where does this leave the trade unions? A central feature of the ill-fated Bullock Report in the United Kingdom was that trade unions themselves would appoint worker directors under the 2X + Y system (equal numbers of shareholder and worker directors, plus a certain number [Y] of independent directors beholden to neither group) proposed. This was not the only reason the report was torpedoed—British industry was strongly opposed to any dilution of management–shareholder control over decision-making within the firm. But the perception that trade unions were simply using industrial democracy as a means to enhance their own power was a further drawback.

In terms of democratic theory, there is no reason why trade unions should have a direct role to play in the appointment of the directors of worker-controlled industries. Nor does it even follow, if we are talking about a generalized model of a worker-managed economy, that the majority of enterprises involved will have been unionized in the first place. Whereas certain European countries have unionization rates approaching 90 percent, the figures are a good deal lower in countries such as the United Kingdom, Canada, Japan, or the United States.[16] This is even more true of the nongovernmental service sector than of the primary and secondary sectors. It seems absurd to tie the existence of a worker-managed economy to the existence of a trade union in any particular sector. To be sure, previous involvement in trade unions would be an important attribute for employee-elected directors of firms. However, one sharply reduces the appeal of the employee–worker-controlled model to sections of the middle class and even the working class in Western societies by organically associating it with trade unions. Greater economic democracy may well spell lesser, not greater, trade union influence over the economy.

There is evidence of this from Eastern Europe. In Yugoslavia, trade unions are reduced to a largely social and educational role in most worker-controlled enterprises with elected councils.[17] Unions clearly have a defensive role to play under these circumstances and strikes have not been uncommon; however, that role is not to be confused with the one played by elected councils. It is the latter that are vested with de facto control over the assets and direction of the enterprise. It is through these councils that workers have the greatest exposure to the economic and other problems facing the firm, and input into decision-making.[18]

The same situation would have arisen in Poland had the Solidarity experience flourished and the economy been restructured along the lines of greater worker control as opposed to party–state control. Solidarity called for such a system in the program approved at its October 1981 Congress:

> The present system that links political power to economic power, based on the permanent interference by the party in the operation of firms, is the principal cause of our present economic crisis.…The only solution to this situation is the creation of self-managing committees of workers which would give the real decision-making power to the employees of the firm.[19]

Quite clearly, vital decisions regarding investment, production, and distribution would have come to rest with worker-elected councils under such a system.

Inevitably, such worker-controlled enterprises would also have meant a diminution in the role of Solidarity as a trade union movement.[20] In terms of the democratization of Polish society this would, without any question, have been a price worth paying. Although admirable as a defensive weapon for workers against management, private owners, or the state itself, the trade union structure is not a logical instrument for democratic management and administration in its own right.

Russian and German revolutionary experience at the beginning of this century would seem to confirm this. Not trade unions, but an entirely new organization, the *Soviets*, based in the factories and elected by the working class, played a leading role in the events of 1905 and again 1917.[21] Similarly, the *Raete*, not the trade unions, emerged as the locus of proletarian power in November–December 1918, and as the putative basis for some alternative political and economic structure.[22] As an instrument of working-class democracy, such councils, directly responsible to their membership and elected by them, had a resonance that few trade unions, then or since, have been able to reproduce. As organs of economic administration, had they not succumbed to the monopoly of party power in the Soviet case, they would have constituted the embryo of a system of direct economic democracy.

They were rooted in a tradition of democracy going back to the Paris Commune, and before that to the Parisian sections during the French Revolution or the democratically elected army agitators or pamphleteers of the English Civil War. How often we forget that the left has its own variants of direct democracy that exist side by side with the versions we associate with Jean-Jacques Rousseau or with the Greeks.

> The communal regime once established in Paris and the secondary centres, the old centralized government would in the provinces, too, have to give way to the self-government of the producers.[23]

> Begone forever, abhorrent distinction between governors and governed.[24]

> O Parliament men + Soldiers! Necessity dissolves all laws and Government and Hunger will break through stone walls.[25]

I do not want to overstate my case. Insofar as trade unions over the past century have functioned as defenders of their members' interests, insofar as they too have aimed at radical changes in the capitalist system and at thoroughgoing democratic reforms, they clearly cannot be excluded from this discussion. Yet it seems to me that only the anarcho–syndicalists ever looked to the trade unions themselves as the privileged vehicle of working-class emancipation *and* self-government.[26] Does it make any sense to see them playing the central role in some market socialist system of the future?

One might ask, under these circumstances, whether it would be in the interest of unions to press for greater worker participation altogether. From a strictly organizational point of view, union leadership might stand to gain little from moving toward a system where union power, along with that of capital, stands to be gravely weakened. At the same time union leaders can argue, not always erroneously, that greater participation on terms dictated by corporations or the state does not bring economic democracy any closer. Whatever the possible merits of a fully worker-controlled economy under market socialism, it by no means follows that participation has the same virtues under capitalism. A minority of worker-elected directors on the boards of corporations is unlikely to change very much in their mode of organization or decision-making. Nor does increased worker input through quality of work circles and other consultative schemes transfer one iota of power from capital to labor, although it may make for more harmonious industrial relations. Why then should unions support the rather limited moves toward industrial democracy that seem at all plausible under existing conditions in the west?

Not all union leaderships, of course, have seen things in this way. In the Federal Republic of Germany and Scandinavia, much of the pressure for extending codetermination and other worker participation schemes has come from trade unions. Moreover, as Geoff Hodgson has argued, if one sees in participatory proposals the opening wedge toward a larger reform of the capitalist system, then criticism of industrial democracy is much weakened. After all, trade unions have also been denounced as reformist movements at various moments for seeking improvements for their members within an ongoing capitalist system. Why should one condemn moves toward greater participation as any less valid?[27]

This is no guarantee that trade unions, especially in English-speaking countries where workers' control is not a strong tradition, will subscribe to such policies. Yet here too self-interest would seem to suggest that they might. It is quite clear, for example, that investment decisions may have far greater consequences for long-term employment than salary or benefits agreed to through negotiations. For unions and workers to have any influence on the former would be greatly helped by worker representation on the board of directors. Similarly, regarding occupational safety or health issues, veto power in the hands of worker representatives can do far more to enhance worker interests than all the labor codes and grievance procedures in the world. Nor would such participation come at the expense of unions, where firms were unionized. The likelihood is great that representatives or directors chosen by the work force would be from among those who had been most active in defending their collective interests until then.

Clearly any quantum leap toward industrial democracy, let alone worker-controlled industries, would in Western societies require changes in the political arena. One would require a party or parties in power committed to such a scheme, and given the electoral composition of most Western societies, one(s) with support not only from the unionized working class, but from nonunionized workers and from the middle class. Such policies could not simply be sold in the name of traditional concepts of state ownership or public enterprise but, I am convinced, as part of a larger argument for democratization. It would mean that equality was restored to its rightful place as a core value of Western societies, that liberty ceased to be defined in exclusively individual terms and was given the collective dimension that liberal ideology so easily ignores. Clearly, such a transformation in political culture will not come easily, nor could it take place without the active support of the trade union movement. But it would have to involve a great many other social and community movements and class forces beyond those organized into unions.

Here, changes that are occurring in the political economy of late capitalism may prove significant. At the moment, two-thirds of the labor force in North America is in the service sector, the European figure is more than 50 percent.[28] While the rate of employment growth in this sector, as in all others, has slowed down dramatically in recent years, it is still slated to have the lion's share of any increased employment for the remainder of this century. Much of this employment, though by no means all, will be in the administrative and managerial categories, or in white-collar ones outside the public sector. These categories, at least in North America, do not tend to be highly unionized.

This poses all sorts of dilemmas for the trade union movement. On the one hand, there are attempts, not very successful, to organize such unorganized sectors as the restaurant trade, financial services, or retail trade. On the other, in countries such as the United States, the trade union movement as a percentage of the total labor force has shrunk to less than 20 percent, and is a declining political, no less than economic, force. In Europe, to be sure, the figures are much less alarming. Still, the concerns of white-collar and professional workers, as C. Wright Mills pointed out decades ago, weigh heavily in the political balance of Western societies.[29]

Workers and employees in this sector are faced with the threat of structural unemployment as the result of technological change, just like their colleagues in blue-collar positions. Issues of automation, job security, and job sharing loom ever larger, leading commentators to wonder: "Can we ever regain full employment in the sense in which we understood it in the past—or must we now question our concepts of employment and work, and their relation to leisure?"[30] Or as Andre Gorz, who earlier had bade farewell to the traditional proletariat, suggests in a more recent study, we may be approaching a stage where it will be technically possible for citizens in the advanced societies to work a 900-hour year or 20,000-hour lifetime, to meet necessary social needs.[31] In such a society, social organization, political and economic participation, and the allocation of surplus among the different members of society become all important.

Although it would be presumptuous of me to attempt to sketch the social contract that might thus become necessary, it is likely to be much more solidaristic than the one the new right currently offers. In such a society, the technical possibility for reducing the drudgery of necessary labor cannot be realized by the majority unless they have access to a great deal more economic decision-making than is currently the case. Automation, benefiting only the owners of the means of production or those in strategic occupations, would prove the solvent of existing social bonds and bring about a type of polarization between haves and have-nots that advanced capitalist societies have successfully avoided until now.

Where all this leaves the trade union movement, I do not know, although the recent experience of unions in declining industrial sectors, forced to choose between salary cuts or layoffs of members, may suggest the dilemmas that lie ahead. Their situation would be no different from the one that society as a whole would face, with work sharing becoming the norm along with socially relevant activities not directly tied to production.

Socialists and radical trade unionists with a reworked notion of solidarity and social justice might be in a good position to influence the agenda. For such a stage would entail a greater measure of redistribution than capitalism presently allows and would provide the basis for a move toward market socialism. The very logic of contemporary technological development, computerization, and information technology may lay the foundation for a radically different economic and social order, one in which demands for decentralization and citizen–worker control would probably grow. In the words of Gorz, "The socialism of the future will be post-industrial and anti-productivist or it will not be."[32]

Even were this to occur, were we to find a greater political will than is presently manifested in Western societies for collective(ist) solutions to our problems, the task of organizing the economy and reconciling a diversity of interests would remain. Under market socialism, we can assume there would be hundreds of thousands of discrete economic units, collectively owned by their work forces or privately owned. Market exchange would characterize much of the relationship among them, though an element of state economic planning would also exist.

We in the West, to be sure, would not for one moment embrace the centralized and command version of planning that characterized Soviet-type societies. Just as those societies fell remarkably short where grassroots consultation and input into decision-making were concerned, so in the economic sphere they came much closer to a version of "dictatorship over needs,"[33] than to a genuinely open and participatory economy. Planning under market socialism would certainly look to the different enterprises, regions, and communities for much of the input. It would be largely indicative in character, though if the state were to acquire control over the principal financial institutions, it would have important leverage over the discrete economic actors in the system. Still, that power would never be absolute, because the market would retain a key role where prices, salaries, and other factors were concerned.

Yet indicative planning can also connote a fair degree of state economic power, which when coupled to the fiscal, monetary, and regulative powers that the state would retain under market socialism, could potentially overwhelm individual enterprises and sectors. There would therefore be good reasons to retain an independent trade union organization, distinct from workers' councils, able to act as a defensive agent for its members.

Defense, in this case, could be directed against two targets. First, the state itself, in its capacity as overall organizer of the economy, is not immune from criticism and attack. One could hardly assume that financial, investment, tariff decisions, and the like might not have dire consequences for workers in particular industries, or that some degree of coordination and discussion among workers beyond that possible in workplace councils would not prove necessary. To be sure, a network grouping representatives of the worker councils might fulfill the role currently played by trade unions. Still, it seems logical to see trade unions, where these are already constituted, continuing to carry out such functions, at least in the initial stages of a market socialist economy. One does not move from a class-versus-class or interest-versus-interest mentality to one of harmony overnight. And as the Soviet example suggests, we may prefer to never reach the type of unbridled unity that can only be enforced by an all-powerful state.

There is a second reason why unions might exist in a worker–employee-managed economy. It is likely that the boards of directors of such enterprises, particularly those in vital economic sectors, with large numbers of employees and a key position in their local or regional economies, would be subject to many pressures other than from their employees. The managerial imperative, even with worker-elected directors formally in control, ensures that the broader interests of the firm, rather than the specific interests of individual employees, will prevail. There seems to be a natural division of labor here, as a study of worker-controlled enterprises in the United States suggests, with directors "attending to the ongoing health of the [firm] and leaders of the [union] concerning themselves with the material well-being of their members and the protection of their individual rights through the grievance process."[34]

Nor in a fully market socialist scheme would the directors all be worker-elected. The type of system I envisage would be one where at least a minority of directors were elected or appointed by community organizations. These directors would serve as public service advocates, ensuring that health, environmental, consumer, gender, and other issues were raised, and that the larger public interest was not lost in the pursuit of the sometimes narrow and particular interests of the enterprise. Ideally, such directors would themselves be drawn from the network of neighborhood assemblies or base-level units that a participatory political system would engender.[35] The mere existence of such directors, however, is a further reason to differentiate between worker-elected directors on a managing council and a trade union. The need for the latter would continue, although part of its function might be to demand "better management of 'the workers' company.' "[36]

In drawing this discussion to a conclusion, let me emphasize a few key points.

(1) Workers' control is rooted in a larger left tradition that goes beyond the limited measure of worker participation proposed under certain industrial consultation schemes. It requires a degree of worker participation that is effectively coupled with control.

> Worker participation at the firm level is the ability of workers to directly influence or form the management and work process in an enterprise. Inherent in this definition is the notion of power, that is, worker participation necessarily entails the wrestling of some prerogatives from management or capital by the workers. It follows that participation occurs at many levels and in many forms.[37]

Such a system is also distinct from and highly critical of the amalgam between public ownership and state ownership that characterizes most twentieth-century Marxist–Leninist regimes. Workers' control is an alternative to state ownership over the larger part of the economy, to the centralization of political and economic power in a single set of hands, to the abolition of all forms of market process and exchange in the name of socialism.

Although it rejects private ownership over the more concentrated means of production, a system of workers' control is not incompatible with small-scale private ownership. Nor is it incompatible with the political structures of liberal democracy, although it might well wish to extend participatory possibilities in the political and economic spheres.

In practice, workers' control would be based upon equal ownership—one worker, one vote—over all enterprises beyond a certain asset size. While some compensation would be paid to previous owners and, more especially, to pension funds and the like, there would be prescribed limits to the amount, and direct managerial control by the latter would be replaced.

Responsibility for all key decisions would rest with workers' councils or boards of directors predominantly chosen by the workers themselves. Provision might be made for frequent rotation of the membership of these bodies to ensure that many employees had exposure to the decision-making process, thereby acquiring the skills that make active participation possible. While the alienation that results from technology would not vanish under such an arrangement, the alienation resulting from the division of labor and the inequality of power would be greatly reduced.[38] This by itself is a telling justification for such a system.

(2) Trade unions have historically played a central role in advancing working-class concerns. In capitalist societies, they have functioned as a countervailing power to capital, wresting concessions on conditions, salaries, and benefits from

employers and from the state.

Collective bargaining, however, stops well short of workers' control. In an earlier period, when unions were more radical, there might have been criticism of worker-owned firms as simply a version of labor capitalism.[39] And indeed, critics on the left would advance similar arguments today. Yet it can be argued that trade unions have come up against the limitations of their position as defenders of workers' interests within the existing system, and that expanding economic democracy involves something more.

As I have argued, trade union appeal, especially to many employees in the service sector in Western economies, is limited and unlikely to increase sharply in the coming years. The central role, therefore, with which unions have been vested by socialists of Marxist and social democratic persuasions is open to challenge. This is not a matter of rejecting trade unions as one crucial component in any coalition for change; but it is to relativize the trade union movement as but one part of a larger political alliance or bloc.

Now I too remain sceptical that simply extending participatory structures will by itself bring an egalitarian or socialist society about. Codetermination has been a feature of the West German coal and steel industry since the early 1950s and of other large firms for the past decade, yet no one would argue that socialism is any closer to being on the agenda as a result.

The most one could claim is that extending industrial democracy under prevailing capitalist ownership provides somewhat greater possibilities for economic citizenship than is the case within existing hierarchical firms. And such experience may make it easier, further down the line, to make the transition to more collective and cooperative forms of ownership than capitalism allows.

The traditional role of trade unions may not prove very helpful here. While a transition of worker-controlled economy is unlikely without their support, their commitment to collective bargaining coupled with their own internal hierarchical structures may well prevent them from championing such a transition. Can it be that movements forged in an earlier stage of capitalism may not be ideally equipped to lead the salariat and working class of Western societies down such a road? Is it heresy to suggest that the connection between the trade union movement and socialism can no longer be the same at the end of the twentieth century as it was at the beginning?

(3) Democracy for socialists is an end and not just the means to an end. This is where the real divide lies between those inspired by post-1960 ideas of participatory democracy and those who hew to an older top-down model of socialism.

In making the argument so boldly, I do not ignore the fact that majority decisions in a more democratized political system will not always favor the left, that there is no guarantee that people will use the instruments of participation that we might devise—neighborhood assemblies, referenda, initiatives—in ways that we would like. Nor is it clear that egotistical interests would not prevail in the operation of market socialist enterprises.

Still, we in the West know full well how high a price has been paid for the dictatorial means by which "socialism" was introduced into East European societies. I am not simply referring to the price paid by the populations of those societies, or to the periodic and unsuccessful attempts to reform them, often initiated by a politically and economically repressed working class. I am referring just as much to the price socialists in the West have paid for the identification that our opponents in the center and on the right have made between socialism and the authoritarianism of the one-party state. Much of Cold War liberalism or of neoconservatism today rests precisely on such an identification.

It is no less true that social democracy in the West has been tarred with the brush of statism and bureaucracy. Not that the growth of the state as a powerful instrument of economic organization and social regulation is particularly due to socialists—two world wars and a Great Depression have had a great deal more effect. In the post–World War II period, however, the growth of social services and nationalization of a number of industries were associated with the left in countries such as the United Kingdom and France. The economic crisis of the 1970s helped to put these features of social democratic and socialist policy into question.[40]

In arguing for the revival of democratic theory, for a more participatory and less representative version thereof, for its extension into the economy and for that matter into the operation of social and community services, I am merely touching base with what many on the left in Western societies have come to realize. The ethical and political dimensions of socialism, its economic goals, cannot be divorced from the means by which it is to be attained. Nor can we envisage a particularly active or conscious citizenry, unless we begin to spell out the structures and develop the institutions within which the art of citizenship can be practiced.

Seen in this light, the arguments I have been making for workers' control and market socialism are not simply utopian striving after an impossible dream. They are, in fact, central components of any vision of economic democracy one could develop, and as such part of the larger democratization of Western societies (and perhaps Eastern ones) that one would hold out for the future. They provide powerful motives to continue to believe in socialism, as something profoundly liberating of human energies and of a dormant democratic vision.

Democracy has never been a key validating belief of the right. Ever since Plato, the right has looked to aristocracies and elites to provide legitimate rule. Even liberalism, as we know, was for long a hostile critic of democracy, which it identified with mob rule;[41] only in the twentieth century has it somewhat reluctantly come to terms with this concept, at least in the electoral arena. It is the left that believes in the primary value of what the Greeks called *isonomia*, equality; the left believes in the capacity of the population at large for political judgment and, by extension, for judgment in the economic arena as well; for the left, participation is a value without which democracy and socialism itself lose their very raison d'être.

Is it surprising, therefore, that a central part of left analysis today revolves around questions of democracy? The debate about workers' control, about how it intersects with and in part conflicts with traditional trade union interests, is part of this larger discussion. How we resolve it may well determine the fate of socialism in our time.

Notes

1. Among the numerous sources, I mention Howard Wachtel, *Workers' Management and Workers' Wages in Yugoslavia: The Theory and Practice of Participatory Socialism* (Ithaca, N.Y.: Cornell University Press, 1973); Branko Horvat, *The Political Economy of Socialism* (New York: M. E. Sharpe, 1982); Ellen T. Cosmisso, *Workers' Control under Plan and Market* (New Haven, Conn.: Yale University Press, 1979).

2. On the Russian Revolutions, see Oskar Anweiler, *The Soviets: The Russian Workers, Peasants and Soldiers Councils 1905–1921*(New York: Pantheon, 1975); on Hungary, Claude Lefort, *Elements d'une critique de la bureaucratie* (Paris: Gallimard, 1979), and F. Feher and A. Heller, *Hungary 1956 Revisited* (London: Allen and Unwin, 1983); on Czechoslovakia, Vladimir Fisera, ed., *Workers' Councils in Czechoslovakia: Documents and Essays, 1968–1969* (London: Allison and Busby, 1978); on Poland, *L'Alternative, le dossier de solidarite*, Special Number, Maspero, Paris, 1982, containing the texts of most of the important documents of the Solidarity period.

3. Michel Crozier et al., *The Crisis of Democracy* (New York: New York University Press, 1975).

4. Jane Mansbridge, *Beyond Adversary Democracy* (New York: Basic Books, 1980); Graeme Duncan, ed., *Democratic Theory and Practice* (New York: Cambridge University Press, 1983); Benjamin Barber, *Strong Democracy—Participatory Politics for a New Age* (Berkeley: University of California Press, 1984); Geoff Hodgson, *The Democratic Economy* (London: Pelican, 1984).

5. Cited by Bernard Gueta, *Le Monde*, February 10–11, 1980, p. 3.

6. On the May events themselves, Alain Schnapp and Pierre Vidal-Naquet, *Journal de la commune etudiante* (Paris: Seuil, 1969). On the French trade union movement and autogestion, see Pierre Ronsanvallon, *L'Age de l'autogestion* (Paris: Seuil, 1976); George Ross, *Workers and Communists in France: From Popular Front to Euro-communism* (Berkeley: University of California Press, 1982).

7. Cf. the discussion in Gerard Braunthal, *The West German Social Democrats, 1969–1982* (Boulder, Colo.: Westview, 1982).

8. See the discussion in Peter Brannen, *Authority and Participation in Industry* (London: Batsford Academie, 1983), chapter 6.

9. Martin Carnoy and Derek Shearer, *Economic Democracy: The Challenge of the 1980s* (New York: M. E. Sharpe, 1980); Daniel Zwerdling, ed., *Work Place Democracy*

(New York: Harper & Row, 1980); S. Bowles, D. Gordon, and T. Weisskopf, *Beyond the Waste Land* (New York: Anchor, 1983); George Sanderson, ed., *Industrial Democracy Today* (Toronto: McGraw-Hill, 1979).

10. P. Blumberg, *Industrial Democracy: The Sociology of Participation* (London: Constable, 1968), p. 123.

11. Cf. the discussion in Peter Jay, "The Workers Cooperative Economy," in his *The Crisis of Western Political Economy* (London: Andre Deutsch, 1984), p. 90; and in Christopher Eaton Gunn, *Workers' Self-Management in the United States* (Ithaca, N.Y.: Cornell University Press, 1984), pp. 136, 143.

12. Among the best studies of recent years that outline a market socialist economy of the type I have in mind are Alec Nove, *The Economics of Feasible Socialism* (London: Allen and Unwin, 1983), and Hodgson, *The Democratic Economy*.

13. Brannen, *Authority and Participation in Industry*, chapters 6–8.

14. Hodgson, *The Democratic Economy*, chapters 9–11.

15. Barber, *Strong Democracy*, chapter 10; Philip Resnick, *Parliament vs. People: An Essay on Democracy and Canadian Political Culture* (Vancouver: New Star Books, 1984), section 9.

16. See the tables in John D. Stephens, *The Transition from Capitalism to Socialism* (London: Macmillan, 1979), p. 116, reproduced in Stephen Bornstein et al., eds., *The State in Capitalist Europe* (London: Allen and Unwin, 1984), p. 84.

17. This is the argument in Patrick Kerans, Glenn Drover, and David Williams, *Welfare and Worker Participation: Eight Case Studies* (New York: St. Martin's Press, 1988).

18. Brannen, *Authority and Participation in Industry*, pp. 140–45; Saul Estrin, *Self-Management: Economic Theory and Yugoslav Practice* (New York: Cambridge University Press, 1983), chapter 3.

19. Section 6 of the Solidarity Programme, subtitled "The Self-governing Republic" in *L'Alternative, le dossier de solidarite*, p. 188.

20. There are hints of such a future cleavage in Jean-Yves Potel, "La revendication autogestionnaire dans la Pologne de Solidarite," *Sociologie du travail*, No. 3, 1982.

21. Cf. Anweiler, *The Soviets*; Maurice Brinton, *The Bolsheviks and Workers' Control, 1917-1921* (Montreal: Black Rose, 1975).

22. *Illustrierte Geschichte der deutschen Revolution* (Berlin: Internationaler Arbeiter-Verlag, 1929; reprinted Berlin: Junius Brucke, 1969); Hans Bock, *Syndikalismus und Linkskommunismus von 1918–1923* (Meissenheim am Glan, 1969).

23. Karl Marx, *The Civil War in France*, in Karl Marx and Frederick Engels, *Selected Works* (London: Lawrence and Wishart, 1968), p. 292.

24. *Le manifeste des egaux* in *La conspiration des egaux* (Paris: Editions Spartacus, no date).

25. *The Mournful Cries of Many Thousand Poor Tradesmen* (January 22, 1648) in *Leveller Manifestoes of the Puritan Revolution*, ed. Don M. Wolfe (New York: Nelson & Sons, 1944).

26. F. F. Ridley, *Revolutionary Syndicalism in France* (Cambridge: Cambridge

University Press, 1970); Melvyn Dubofsky, "The Radicalism of the Dispossessed: William Haywood and the IWW," in Alfred Young, ed., *Dissent: Explorations in the History of American Radicalism* (DeKalb: Northern Illinois University Press, 1968).

27. Hodgson, *The Democratic Economy*, pp. 195ff.

28. Organization for Economic Cooperation and Development, Paris, *Historical Statistics 1960–1981*, p. 37.

29. C. Wright Mills, *White Collar* (New York: Oxford University Press, 1951), part 4.

30. J. I. Gershunny and I. D. Miles, *The New Service Economy* (London: Frances Porter, 1983), p. 256.

31. Andre Gorz, *Les chemins du paradis* (Paris: Galilee, 1983), pp. 89–90.

32. Gorz, *Les chemins du paradis*, p. 23.

33. F. Feher, A. Heller, and G. Markus, *Dictatorship over Needs: An Analysis of Soviet Societies* (Oxford: Basil Blackwell, 1983).

34. Gunn, *Workers' Self-Management*, p. 161.

35. Cf. the references in note 14 above.

36. Gunn, *Workers' Self-Management*, p. 139.

37. J. G. Espinosa and A. S. Zimbalist, *Economic Democracy: Workers' Participation in Chilean Industry, 1970–1973* (Vancouver: Academic Press, 1978), pp. 2–3.

38. Cf. Brannen, *Authority and Participation in Industry*, p. 155.

39. Gunn, *Workers' Self-Management*, p. 202.

40. Cf. David Held and John Keane, "In a fit state," *New Socialist* (March–April 1984): 36–39; and my article, "The Ideology of Neo-conservatism," in W. Magnusson et al., eds., *The New Reality* (Vancouver: New Star Books, 1984), pp. 131–43.

41. Cf. Anthony Arblaster, *The Rise and Decline of Western Liberalism* (Oxford; Basil Blackwell, 1984); C. B. Macpherson, *The Life and Times of Liberal Democracy* (New York: Oxford University Press, 1977).

Chapter 8

Radical Democracy

Mihailo Marković

Radical democracy is a form of social organization that abolishes all existing relations of political, economic, and cultural domination and brings about conditions for full individual and group self-determination in all areas of social life.

Previously existing forms of socialism had been claiming historical legitimation by producing an accelerated industrialization and a higher level of social justice than was possible within the framework of classical capitalism. However, in these forms of socialism the industrial might of bourgeois society had not been achieved. In the meantime, the capitalist social system adapted to the situation and learned how to solve social problems. Although in some capitalist countries social welfare is still quite unsatisfactory or has been eroded recently by the pressure of neoconservative forces, some of them were ruled for extended periods of time by social-democratic governments, and they exceeded anything that had been achieved in the area of social security by the regimes of "really existing socialism."

On the other hand, socialism had not solved the problem of democracy. Basic socialist principles and claims opened the perspective of radical human emancipation. However, its forms of political organization (the only ones feasible in backward rural societies run by despotic elites) were hierarchical and repressive from the start. Political systems established after victorious revolutionary struggle were invariably authoritarian. To this fact, more than to anything else, we owe the present day legitimation crisis of socialism. It can truly overcome capitalism only if, on the basis of its humanist, emancipatory principles, it creates new forms of democracy that truly surpass those born in bourgeois society.

Consequently the starting point must be a critical analysis of the experiences of liberal bourgeois democracy. One should examine what in bourgeois democracy is of lasting, universal significance and constitutes a ground on which one might build further. At the same time, one should establish what are the essential limitations of liberal democracy, determined by the nature of the bourgeois world, that ought to be overcome.

Second, one should clarify the basic idea of the socialist theoretical tradition, the idea of the democracy of councils, explain its structure, and establish whether, as a conceptual model, it promises to remove the difficulties of bourgeois democracy.

Third, one should critically sum up the experience of past attempts at the realization of council democracy, especially the experience of Yugoslav self-government, and indicate the problems that await solution.

Fourth, a praxis-oriented theory must propose a strategy for the realization of council democracy.

Achievements and Limitations of Liberal Democracy

There are essential differences between, on the one hand, democratic political philosophy (of Locke, Rousseau, and Jefferson) that precedes the establishment of a liberal political system in the West and, on the other hand, political practice within the framework of that system. Great radical ideas—of the sovereignty of people, social contract, and the right of people to a violent overthrow of any government that pursues its selfish particular interest—were in reality reduced to the right of election of the people's representatives and to the right of (tacit) consent to the government's policies. If we leave aside that gap between ideology and reality, the fact still remains that some structural characteristics of the liberal political system constitute the lasting, universal, necessary conditions of any political democracy. Here belong:

(1) Freedom of speech, of the press, of political organization, manifestation, and demonstration; freedom of conscience (of moral, religious, and ideological views); freedom of movement. The implication of those civil liberties is a pluralism of ideas, interests, and political organizations, as well as full freedom of public opinion formation.

(2) Direct election of people's representatives by a universal secret vote and the limitation of the length and number of possible mandates.

(3) Separation of powers (into legislative, executive, and judicial power), mutual limitation and control (checks and balances) of political institutions.

(4) Rules that govern the conduct of citizen and state functionaries in the form of laws binding on all without privilege and without discrimination regarding any specific political, ethnic, racial, religious, or any other social difference.

(5) Those many areas and dimensions of social life that remain politically or legally unregulated and constitute "civil society." In the sphere of "political society," local and regional communities enjoy autonomy within the limits of the constitution and the law.

(6) Decision-making on all those issues where communal unanimity was not possible takes place by majority vote. One citizen or people's representative has one vote.

Basic limitations of liberal democracy are the following:

First, this form of democracy is purely political, not economic, nor even cultural. Individuals are reduced to citizens, their human rights to civil rights, their freedom to political liberties. They are denied the right to take part in decision-making in their working organizations, they have no say in the determination of cultural policies or in the actual running of educational and other cultural institutions. What is needed is a radical democratization of all spheres of public life.

Second, parliamentary democracy is predominantly representative. As Rousseau anticipated, in any large society representatives will become alienated from the people who elected them. They will be responsible to those centers of power that got them elected and on whose support their political future depends, rather than to the electorate that has no power over them once they are in office. There is a limited degree of direct democracy in local communities; they deal with local issues and only exceptionally (in Swiss referenda for example) are called to express a view or make a decision on national policies. There is no direct democracy in workplace or cultural organizations.

Third, being representative, parliamentary democracy is excessively centralistic. Centralism involves a considerable amount of domination, of heteronomy, of bureaucratic mediation, of wasteful, delayed, inadequate decision-making, taken from a great distance, in ignorance of specific local conditions and of important psychological factors.

Fourth, parliamentary democracy presupposes the existence of political *parties* to articulate and express particular interests and to assume ruling functions. Not all political organizations are parties, and political pluralism should not be reduced to a multiparty system. Parties are necessary political forms in a class society, and some of the functions performed by the parties must remain in any democratic society. However, we must be aware of some basic limitations of the party form of a political organization. A party struggles to win and keep power, to become a ruling party (or part of a ruling coalition). From this fact it follows that power relations are maintained within each party. There is a dominating center (an oligarchy or an individual leader), and there is a hierarchy of levels of power. Decision-making tends to be authoritarian and party decisions are transmitted from the top downward. Each party turns a political theory into an ideology (a rationalization of selfish group interests) needed to manipulate the masses.

Fifth, if the essence of political life in a parliamentary democracy is rule over people, exercise of dominating power, with the consent of ruled subjects, then two negative defining features of the state will be perpetuated. One is professional politics. Leaders of the parties tend to become *Berufs-*

politiker—professional cadres who merely move from one leadership position to the other. Another one is use of coercive means in order to implement governmental policies and to preserve the existing social order, no matter how justified and urgent might be the need to change it.

Sixth, it follows that parliamentary democracy involves the existence of dominating social groups. The bourgeoisie dominates owing to its economic power, ownership of mass media, powerful lobbies, and the ability to outspend other groups in a costly election process. Bureaucracy dominates because it controls the state apparatus.

To conclude, parliamentary democracy is a political form fully adapted to the needs of modern bourgeois society. A socialist economic structure requires a form of democracy without professional political leadership and ruling parties.

General Characteristics of Council Democracy

The democratic principle of classless society is the association of producer and citizen, excluding any monopoly of social power. In all working organizations and territorial communities, citizens immediately take part in decision-making on matters of general public importance. Coordination and rational direction of development at higher levels of social organization (regions, branches of work, society as a whole) are provided by elected delegates, responsible to their electorate, recallable, and devoid of any material privileges. The structure of self-governing councils and assemblies constituted in this way has a federal character: It permits maximum autonomy of the parts but also secures a rational coordination of the whole. Democracy of this type is in principle able to solve all the problems that plague bourgeois democracy.

Not only political but also economic and cultural life is now organized in a democratic way. The principle of equal self-determination is extended to all of public life. Everywhere the rule holds: one member of the community—one vote. This is incompatible with private ownership of large means of production, of mass media, of cultural institutions. All these means being the product of social work are truly socialized (rather than turned into state property). That does not exclude individual and cooperative property that is the product of past work of definite individuals and groups. The concept of human right is generalized in such a way as to embrace civil, socioeconomic, and cultural rights (e.g., the right to work, to remuneration according to work, to social security, to education and cultural goods). The basic principle of this generalized idea of democracy is that no one has any public power or dominates other persons on the basis of property.

Council democracy is a network of self-governing bodies at all levels of social organization from local to global levels; it embraces direct participatory and indirect representative democracy. All individual members of society take part in the decision-making on specific public issues where they live and where they work. Those issues that, according to their nature, require coordination and more holistic regulation are passed to the next higher level. Representatives are elected for the next higher level—self-governing council or assembly—and power is delegated to them to resolve such issues.

The structure of council democracy is federalistic in the broadest sense. In contrast to the centralism of parliamentary democracy, federal units have considerably greater political, economic, and cultural autonomy. Possible disorganization and instability of excessive decentralization are precluded through the constitutionally fixed consensus about areas of common values for which federal self-governing bodies are fully responsible.

In a fully developed council democracy, political organizations have a different role and different structure from those of traditional political parties. They cannot rule because decision-making authority is in the hands of self-governing councils and assemblies. They are supposed to be non-authoritarian, nonhierarchical, nonideological organizations. Now their only roles are raising political consciousness, formulating long-range goals and policies, mobilizing mass support for them, educating political activists, and building collective will.

Radical democratization of political life involves deep changes of the two basic features of the traditional state. One is deprofessionalization of political leadership. The only professional state apparatus that survives is a body of specialists that deal with technical aspects of decision-making. Basic (political) decision-making is in the hands of elected leaders who return to their occupations when their mandates expire. Another radical change lies in turning coercive institutions of the state into organs of self-defense that embrace all citizens and are run by elected nonprofessionals.

The building of self-government at all levels and in all spheres of social life eventually dismantles all monopoly of power. The authority of public institutions rests on the competence of leaders and on the quality of their decisions reached through democratic debate. The very structure of this kind of democracy excludes the possibility of any dominating group that alienates itself from the people and usurps public power.

The Structure of Council Democracy

The institutions of council democracy (of integral self-government) are a network of councils and assemblies constituted at different levels of social reality on territorial and productive principles. At least the following four levels should be distinguished:

- basic organs of self-management in small working organizations and in local communities;

- organs of self-management in larger working organizations and in communes;
- organs of self-management for entire branches of activity and regions; and
- central organs of self-government for the global society.

The basic level of self-government is characterized by direct democracy. Everyone has the right to take part directly in decision-making in the enterprise where one works and in the local community where one lives. In this way all persons get an opportunity to express and affirm themselves not only as citizens but also as producers and consumers of material and cultural goods. Workers' councils and other basic organs of self-management have the right to decide how much power they wish to transfer to higher level, self-managing organs, or more specifically, which coordinating, directing, and controlling functions they wish to delegate to their representatives at higher levels of social organization. It might seem that individuals and elementary social groups get too much power in this way. Assuming "possessive individualism" as the "natural" attitude of a person, a society in which the principle of popular sovereignty is fully realized could end up in chaos and disintegration. However, the philosophical premises of radical democracy are neither individualistic nor collectivist. Individuals tend to be and must be socially encouraged to be autonomous in their choices, but the framework of possibilities among which they autonomously choose has been determined by the social nature of their existence. An individual is born into a community and becomes a human being by learning a language, by appropriating a culture, a morality, a set of rules that govern everyday life, by developing a profound need to belong, to be recognized, to care for others. Thus there is a dialectic between society's shaping of individuals (through internalization of social values and projects) and individuals' shaping of society (through the exercise of autonomous will in self-governing bodies).

The next higher level in the model of self-government is constituted by the councils of large producers' associations and by the assemblies of large living communities (communes). Referenda in which all individuals take part remain the form of direct democracy. Yet elements of representative democracy also emerge at this level. Elected delegates in the worker's council of a large enterprise make basic (political) decisions on production plans, on election and control of executive managers, on work conditions, on distribution of revenue, investment contributions to the needs of local community and the entire society. Councils in educational, cultural, scientific, health, and other service institutions have similar functions. However, the assemblies of communes are responsible for policies of economic development, education, public transportation, and social security in their territories. Councils and assemblies are limited in their decision-making by the laws and political decisions of the higher level, self-governing organs. The point is, however, that in a true democracy laws and policies are not imposed by centers of alienated power. The center, the federal assembly, has delegated power to pass the laws to meet general interests and needs and those laws are obligatory. But in any case when power is used to pursue selfish particular interest, that power can be denied and the leaders recalled.

The next higher level comprises self-governing bodies for entire branches of work (industrial production, energy transportation, scientific research) or for entire regions.

The experience of Yugoslav self-governing communities in education, sciences, and culture from the 1960s is very relevant here. They were not part of the state apparatus and were not financed from the state budget. They consisted of elected representatives of corresponding institutions (universities, research institutes, theaters, publishing houses, etc.). They were responsible for basic policy decisions concerning science, education, and culture, A special law would determine the percentage of social product that would automatically go for further distribution to the assemblies of those self-governing communities. This institutional arrangement was responsible for remarkable freedom and creativity in Yugoslav science and culture during the 1960s and early 1970s. Yugoslav universities during that time were among the freest in the world. Later those communities were considerably bureaucratized (overstaffed with professional administrative employees and made increasingly dependent on the state), and therefore they declined in their relevance.

Self-government at the level of global society does not yet exist in any country, but some of its elements are present in the political theory and practice of most advanced countries. The central organ of self-government, a federal assembly, should integrate both networks of self-governing organs: the one that covers varied public activities, the other that embraces territorial communities (in the case of a multinational country such as the former Yugoslavia, various national republics). There are various possibilities of internal organizations of such an assembly, but three necessities must be taken into account:

The first is to reconcile the particular interests of various branches of activity among themselves and with the particular interests of various regions (or national republics).

The second necessity is to reconcile all of those (professional or regional–national) particular interests with the common interests of the entire society.

The third is to maintain unity of the political authority of the federal assembly, but at the same time separate powers to preclude any dangerous concentration of power in the hands of some oligarchy.

As to the first, two chambers are necessary. One is the chamber of associated labor constituted by the representatives of working organizations; the other is the chamber of federal units constituted by representatives of regions (or national republics), which are parts of the federation. Because conflicts among particular interests within each of these two chambers and between them are hardly avoidable, a third, mediating chamber is necessary, which would be constituted by the directly elected representatives of all citizens who are not bound by any particular interests and represent common interests of the entire society.

A common interest is constituted in a democratic way through dialogue in a free, public struggle of opinions. Once formulated and established through the constitution, the laws, the long-range project of development of the country as a whole, such a common interest becomes a limiting framework for the expression of legitimate particular interests.

The authority of the central self-government organ could be stronger or weaker, depending on the historical experience of a people: long suffering from disorder and instability prepares the ground psychologically for a widespread tendency toward greater concentration of power; on the contrary, people who are fed up with authoritarian rulers would favor decentralization and greater separation of power. No matter how much power is delegated to central institutions, in a democracy it would have to be separated according to its different basic functions. In traditional parliamentary or congressional democracy, legislative, executive, and judicial functions are distinguished. In a modern society, functions of planning, of overall control of the execution of adopted policies, and of information gathering are also sources of considerable power and ought to be separated. Separation of powers, abolition of all bureaucratic privileges, reduction of ruling parties to political–educational organizations, rotation of all elected representatives (after one or two mandates), recall of overambitious, incompetent, or corrupt leaders, the cultivation of a critical public opinion—these are some of the social arrangements that effectively prevent the emergence of any new bureaucratic power elite.

Practical Problems of Radical Democracy

Clarity about the concept of council democracy (or self-government) is obviously an essential part of a good contemporary socialist theory of democracy, because it provides a long-range perspective on the democratic process. However, several very difficult practical problems arise as soon as the first steps are undertaken toward this kind of democracy. It is significant for our discussion to specify at least the most important among them. Yugoslav experience of the past three decades is very valuable for this purpose.

First, one such problem is the tension between self-government and the political vanguard of the revolutionary movement. The vanguard identifies itself with the socialist cause and assumes full responsibility for the future of the movement. However, hegemony of the vanguard party is incompatible with full autonomy of self-governing bodies. It seems that we are facing the following dilemma: either the Party will be able to undergo radical democratization and turn into an essentially political–educational organization—this is what the Yugoslav Communist Party decided to do in 1958, practically explored in the subsequent years, and abandoned in 1972—or else one must go back to Karl

Marx's idea, from the *Communist Manifesto*, that communists should not create their own party, should not aspire to be a dominating vanguard organization. They should act as the vanguard of consciousness within the organization of the entire working class. Once council democracy is brought into being, the function of political organizations is not ruling, political tutorship, but creation of political culture.

A second problem is the contradiction between the professional apparatus of the state and the nonprofessional structure of self-governing councils and assemblies. In theory the way to resolve this contradiction is clear: The workers' state is supposed to wither away; gradually its institutions are replaced by self-governing organs composed of freely elected, rotatable, recallable delegates devoid of any lasting bureaucratic powers and privileges. In practice, the "worker's state" refused to wither away and to surrender its monopoly of power. In all past socialist revolutions, it grew alienated from the working class and turned into a dominating bureaucratic institution, determined to stay on the historical stage. In Yugoslavia after the 1948 conflict with the Soviet Union, the state apparatus was first greatly reduced, then allowed to grow beyond reasonable limits, and finally it presented a vast costly burden for the working class. The central or federal apparatus gave up most of its former functions, but they were transferred to professional cadres in the republics and the communes. Alienated power was not abolished but merely decentralized. Overall planning was not democratized but practically dismantled. Workers' councils were limited in their structure and their functioning. They lacked vertical organization on the production principle and were therefore unable to regulate and direct production within a whole branch and among branches of production. They still have no power over extended reproduction. And even in those local areas where their authority is recognized in principle, it is severely restricted by numerous laws and state decisions or by "informal," bureaucratic interference.

This kind of experience leads inevitably to the following blunt question: Is it reasonable to expect that a state, even a workers' state, would voluntarily "wither away," in other words, transfer its power to self-governing councils and assemblies? If the answer to this question is "No," then there are only three remaining alternatives. One is a cynical rationalization: Council democracy is only an ideological slogan, suitable to mobilize mass support in an early stage of socialist revolution. After that, "soviets" become a part of the state, which is what happened in the Soviet Union.

Another alternative is a realistic mental adjustment: Council democracy—in the sense of a federation of associations of producers—is a utopian vision that cannot be realized within the horizon of our epoch. Democratic socialism in our time is then a mixed society in which self-governing councils have an important role to play at the microlevel (in working organizations and local communities), while overall power at the macrolevel must remain in the hands of a preferably liberal and efficient state.

A third alternative is to reject the idea of the "dictatorship of the proletariat," or the "workers' state." That means the victorious socialist movement builds a council democracy from the start. New organs of social power that replace the bourgeois state must, from the very beginning, meet the conditions described by Marx in his analysis of the Paris Commune: free elections, rotation, recall, absence of professionalization and of bureaucratic privileges.

A third problem in the practical realization of council democracy is to prevent the growth of technocracy. Although profitability disappears in socialism as the basic motive of production, a reasonable degree of efficiency is still needed to meet various social needs; consequently, competent, skillful managers will still be in great demand. Their special skills, managerial competence, and full access to information clearly open the possibility of managers becoming a dominating, technocratic elite who might easily manipulate self-governing councils. The councils will be able to counteract such a threat successfully if they secure their independent access to data, if they make use of intellectual forces independent of management for critical analysis of the management's functioning, and if they preserve their right to make basic, political choices among alternatives proposed by specialists.

The fourth problem is how to prevent an intelligentsia from becoming a ruling elite. In any rational decision-making, knowledge plays a decisive role and increasingly becomes an outstanding power. With the growing gap between intellectuals and ordinary people, carriers of knowledge, master-thinkers, dominating ideologues, would increasingly gain in influence. Obviously knowledge, like any other power, has to be distributed more equally. This involves a true revolution in the entire area of education.

The fifth problem is different from all preceding ones. The basic purpose of radical democracy is to prevent domination and the emergence of any new monopoly of power. But if it goes too far in leveling and annulling the influence of individuals, even when that influence is based on nothing but competence, it would face the problem of the absence of any leadership. It is not difficult to conceive a democratic society that spends enormous time and energy to arrive at any decision, that exhausts itself in senseless debates, and is, therefore, unstable and disorganized. While resolutely resisting any political monopoly of power of individuals and groups, radical democracy need not fear powerful ideas that prevail in a free public debate. The stability and rationality of a democratic order depend on the existence of a political culture that brings to people's consciousness general and long-range needs of its development. What is needed is both spiritual leadership (without ideological indoctrination) and practical leadership (without domination). It is essential that leadership not be perpetuated and professionalized and that powers be separated. Different individuals are responsible for legislation, operative management, the judiciary, planning, control, personnel policies. It is important, however, that elected representatives, in the course of their mandates, do not depend on fluctuations of public opinion, that they not be merely executors of the general will but also its creators. In the service of truth and moral values, they must be able to advocate what is unpopular and what the majority does not yet understand. They may always preserve their integrity by resigning. On the other hand, the people can protect themselves from usurpers by recalling them. Between those two extreme situations, democracy must in its own interest tolerate a certain degree of tension between those who implement a policy and those who resist it. To the extent to which people learn to be prudent, they begin to be more concerned about continuity. Then they manage to find a reasonable way between the two extremes of uncritically following their leaders and of being so suspicious toward any leadership as to paralyze reasonable and imaginative long-term projects.

The sixth problem is how to create a truly independent, critical public opinion. If socialism is to go beyond the limits of the bourgeois form of democracy it must make sure that a symmetrical, democratic, critical discourse, without domination, goes on all the time and contributes to a better quality of decision-making in self-governing bodies. Some necessary preconditions seem to be the existence of independent, truly socialized mass media and a plurality of various social organizations.

The seventh problem is how to protect minorities. Yugoslav federalism until 1974 offered some reasonably effective institutional arrangements to safeguard the rights of smaller federal units and ethnic groups. The price paid, especially after the 1974 constitution, was a considerable loss of integrity and unity at the global level. While one-sided centralism allows a permanent out-voting of minorities, one-sided decentralization violates the basic social and political equality of all citizens and the democratic principle: "The vote of each citizen has equal weight." In a system in which all decisions are made by consensus of federal units, and in which the smallest units count as much as the biggest, the votes of citizens who live in the former obviously carry much more weight than the votes of those who live in the latter. The problem is finding the proper mean between two opposite approaches. The constitution should regulate those issues that are highly relevant and sensitive to the interests of minorities and therefore require full consensus for their solution. All other issues could be solved by customary democratic procedure (the majority vote). The problem of the protection of minorities cannot, however, be solved in a purely institutional way. A political culture is needed that reconciles autonomy with solidarity and pluralism with unanimity on basic issues.

The eighth problem is how to reduce gaps in the level of development among various parts of a federation. An a priori socialist answer to this kind of problem is, of course, that more developed parts of the federation must help the less developed ones catch up. The problem is, however, that the donors do not always see the justice of prolonged aid, and that the receivers do not always use aid in the most rational way. There is a lack of understanding that aid is hardly ever a merely humanitarian act but also a just return to the less developed areas for what was taken from them in terms of cheap food, energy, raw materials, and less expensive labor. However, more rational use of aid may be secured if the community (the federation) as a whole decides about the most rational use of funds. Federal programs must be federally conceived and controlled.

The ninth problem of radical democracy is the protection of individual civil and socio-economic rights. Although Marx stated already in the *Communist Manifesto* that in a new society "free development of each will be the condition for free development of all," regimes were produced, in the name of socialism, in which an individual was actually helpless facing the huge bureaucratic machine and omnipotent organs of public security. In liberal bourgeois societies, individual rights are legally guaranteed but justice turns out to be quite expensive. Defense of one's rights as well as defense of one's health may require financial means beyond one's reach. Socialism could secure a higher level protection of individual rights only by building special social institutions that offer the individual free protection from abuse. These would not only inform citizens about their rights and offer free legal advice, they would also—like Scandinavian ombudsmen—have the authority to investigate, to intervene directly in favor of the wronged individual, and to demand urgent solutions of important issues.

Strategy of Realization of Radical Democracy

The strategy of bringing to life radical democracy depends on historical conditions. The following types of historical situations could be distinguished: (1) a revolutionary situation that gives rise to a social movement strong enough to overthrow the power of the bourgeoisie; (2) a postrevolutionary situation after the establishment of power of socialist forces and after the socialization of the means of production; (3) a crisis of bourgeois society in which the institutions of liberal democracy still function. Whatever the differences among those various types of situations, the precondition for radical democracy is a deep structural transformation that presupposes the existence of many conditions and that provokes a powerful resistance of all privileged social groups.

A socialist revolutionary movement can realize council democracy only if it is constituted as a democratic pluralist movement from the start, and if it gives up the idea of a special transition period in which democracy is suspended, allegedly to preclude counter-revolution. A movement can realize the principle of self-determination only if that principle serves as the basis of its own organization. In a situation of deep crisis that is really revolutionary, in which there is a unity of purpose of different socialist forces, the unity of the movement is possible without hegemony of one vanguard party. When Marx spoke in the *Communist Manifesto* about communists as the vanguard of the labor movement, he stated explicitly that they should not organize their own party, that instead, they should constitute a vanguard of consciousness in the movement of the entire working class. In addition to communists, the movement must embrace other socialist forces as well (which was the case in the First International).

The new society must organize itself as a self-governing society from the beginning. Each social cell—in a factory or a hospital, in towns and villages—organizes self-governing councils and assemblies. Institutions of the old state are replaced by central self-governing organs of the new society.

Marx's greatest single error was his belief in the dictatorship of the proletariat, that is, his belief in the indispensability of a transition period in which the victorious proletariat "temporarily" organizes its own state. Once formed, the "workers' state" will never yield the basic levers of power. Its bureaucratic elite will not hesitate to use violence against democratic strivings of its people. It is a fatal blunder to believe that the revolutionary movement—once it has defeated the powerful bourgeois apparatus and destroyed its army and its police—ought to turn its self-governing organizations (a network of councils, a nonprofessional liberation army) into a state (with professional functionaries and the organs of coercion) allegedly to defend itself from counter revolution, which can no longer rely on any organized state force. As much as the possibilities of counter revolution were overestimated (in Yugoslavia it was defeated by the partisan army, although it had dozens of divisions of the regular German, Italian, Bulgarian, and Hungarian armies at its disposal), the possibilities of the self-governing organization of society were underestimated. A democratic order based on autonomous choice and conscious discipline can be stronger, more efficient, more successful than a hierarchical society that undergoes a process of fast bureaucratization.

In a postrevolutionary society that has already been organized as a state, the road to radical democracy is very long, if it is possible at all. Some initial forms of self-government could be introduced from "above" (as in Yugoslavia) before the process of bureaucratization is completed, in case of an imminent external danger. They could be forced from "below," in the conditions of a profound social crisis of the system. The regime could experiment with them to remove the shortcomings of state management. Historical experience has not so far confirmed that in this type of situation democratization can proceed very far or that the liberated space can be maintained for long. Societies of this type may preserve stability if they are able to maintain material growth in spite of political stagnation. The only alternative for progressive forces is engagement in steady, slow movement toward self-government and the liberation of the economy, science, culture, and mass media from excessive state control and bureaucratic arbitrariness. Real social factors that act in that direction are rejuvenation of leadership, better education of functionaries, erosion of official ideology, and higher competence of trusted specialists. Accelerated development and better use of material and human resources may be secured only by a greater participation of citizens and producers and by an increase in the initiative of individuals and collectives.

Marx's conviction that a new society can emerge only on the ground of material abundance, of civil liberties, and of a wealth of human needs has been demonstrated. Today, advanced liberal capitalism probably opens more real possibilities for an evolution toward council democracy than bureaucratic socialism. However, the road here is also long and uncertain. Resistance is offered by powerful and numerous forces: capital, state bureaucracy, technocracy, ruling oligarchies of political parties, apologetic and conformist intellectuals, trade union officials, and most of the middle class. Nevertheless, in this kind of historical situation, it is at least possible to identify some social forces that act in the right direction, and it is possible to envisage a scenario for this kind of evolution. The forces in question are those that oppose authoritarian institutions and practices, excessive social differences, the arms race, excessive expense of state management, an ongoing destruction of natural environment, abolition or reduction of already achieved forms of social security, increasing unemployment.

Under current circumstances the political system of liberal bourgeois democracy still enjoys the consensus of the majority of citizens and is able to function relatively successfully. However, if the present crisis of bourgeois society is perpetuated (because of wars and armament burdens, social consequences of the electronic revolution, a growing gap between production and consumption, almost universal indebtedness, and a breakdown of the world financial system), the revolt of a majority of people could assume the form of a search for alternative solutions. As numerous European examples demonstrate, under those conditions socialist forces could assume power using the existing institutions of parliamentary democracy. Until now those forces have quickly lost the confidence of the electorate, not only because world capital managed invariably to produce inner economic difficulties, but also because the same error was stubbornly repeated time and again: means of production were (partially) nationalized without introducing self-management at the same time. The French Socialist Party even introduced the idea of self-government into its party program—but did not even try to implement it when the party came to power.

The only truly revolutionary strategy in the West would be the rise of a movement of all left forces prepared to act for an evolution toward council democracy. This is the only form of the political organization of society that promises to solve the fundamental problems of our epoch: peace, ecological balance, full employment, participation in decision-making, a shift of consumption from material toward cultural goods, a drastic reduction of public expenses, and a reduction of social differences. The essential part of the preparation for such a movement and such a reorientation of social development is the articulation of the key idea of "integral self-government," or of council democracy.

The concept of radical democracy expounded in this essay can hardly be attacked for being unclear. To be sure it is a synthesis of various elements: it contains experiences of the ancient Greek participatory democracy, some radical implications of eighteenth-century liberal political philosophy, anarchist and Marxian ideas on transcendence of the state, the experience of early stages of socialist revolutions, the experience of Yugoslav self-management, and the record of direct democracy in Israeli kibbutzim. All those various forms of democratic theory and practice express similar aspirations for maximizing human autonomy and self-determination. Therefore, in spite of the inner tensions that are present in all that is alive, the elements of the model of radical democracy are not mutually incompatible. In suitable historical conditions the model could function in practice and could bring about a level of human emancipation higher than any other existing social system.

To be sure, the idea of radical democracy could be criticized as "utopian." Such a form of social organization has not been realized anywhere in its entirety (although many of its elements are indispensable parts of contemporary social reality). Radical democracy is a utopian idea if by the latter term is meant that it essentially transcends the actually existing social world, or that nothing guarantees its realization. It is *not* utopian in the sense of being beyond the realm of epochal historical possibilities, nor in the sense that historical conditions cannot be described under which it could be realized.

Radical democracy is certainly not probable in materially and culturally underdeveloped societies. The accelerated development in those societies will, in all probability, give rise to various hybrid forms, in which authoritarian power will be the price to be paid for liberation from material misery. In advanced industrial societies entering a profound economic and moral crisis, radical democratization may turn out to be the only or by far the best option for further development.

Chapter 9

Objective Interests

D. Goldstick

Marxists, of course, are most definitely concerned with *interests*. On the one hand, historical materialism traces major developments in any society's politics, law, religion, art, etc., largely to the clashing economic interests of ruling classes and of those they rule. On the other hand, as political activists themselves, Marxists base their own politics—as well as they are able—upon the class interests of the industrial and nonindustrial proletariat and, more generally still, on those of the working masses as a whole.

But the objective interests of a group of people—for instance, a class— and their felt desires can coincide to a greater or to a lesser degree. Only insofar as workers are *class-conscious* does the proletariat become, as Karl Marx put it, a "class for itself,"[1] knowing its interests and acting on them in a concerted way. Marxists and Leninists see it as their task to bring their fellow workers increasingly to such class consciousness, through propaganda and—es-pecially—through practical struggle, giving leadership to them and learning from them simultaneously. Already within capitalist society the developing vanguard of conscious revolutionaries can be in a practical position to lead their fellow workers—against the most ferocious opposition—because in a certain sense they do bring to the class struggle the objectively substantiated theory and practice (as they see it) of scientific Marxism–Leninism, which helps to give them a general orientation on the overall meaning and direction of the movement as a whole; but also because they sharpen and refine this science, and their own concrete strategy and tactics, through total immersion in the real-life struggles of all the workers, advanced and less advanced alike, who as a group share in any case the epistemological advantage of actual first-hand experience of class oppression and class struggle, however incompletely or completely they may have understood it. The Marxist–Leninists aspire to lead the proletariat, not so much on the basis of superior personal zeal and commitment, as on the basis of scientific understanding and organized practical involvement in the people's ongoing struggles. This means that they have to think they themselves know already, *not* perfectly but still better than most of the workers do, what the long-term interests of those same workers really are. Not only that, they also think they know what is in the historical interests of the development of society as a whole better than most of society's members currently do. Of course, it is by the criterion of these interests that they seek to govern their basic strategy. Lenin, for instance, felt entitled to write,

> From the standpoint of the basic ideas of Marxism, the interests of social development are higher than the interests of the proletariat—the interests of the working-class movement as a whole are higher than the interests of a separate section of the workers, or of separate phases of the movement....[2]

About fifty years ago, the following rightist joke was widely current in the English-speaking countries.

Socialist orator: When the Revolution comes, you will all eat strawberries and cream.

Voice from the back: But I don't *like* strawberries and cream.

Socialist orator: When the Revolution comes, you will eat strawberries and cream, *and* you will like it.

The jokester had obviously heard of the familiar boast of revolutionaries that under socialism and communism the reorganized social environment would in time give rise to a "new man" and a "new woman" with a personality makeup radically different from what has been normal in the old bourgeois society: cooperative rather than selfish, bold yet disciplined rather than docile or bossy, etc., etc. The rightist assumes that people in bourgeois society generally prefer themselves as they are now and are not going to be attracted to the prospect of changing by the allegation that their preferences on this score will change too, so that they will then be content with what they have become and even prefer that to their old prerevolutionary selves. In ideological opposition to the overthrow of bourgeois society, the suggestion is that, if the Revolution does fulfill its promise and produces a psychologically reconstructed "new man" and "new woman," that will be something objectionably antidemocratic, making people change against their will.

To this the Marxist rebuttal is, of course, that it is the masses of the people themselves, or at least the proletarian masses, who must be and are the prime movers of the revolutionary transformation of society. Insofar as the revolutionary vanguard succeeds in giving effective leadership in the process, it is their scientific understanding and ongoing involvement in the people's struggles that can equip the revolutionary party with an enhanced clarity and exactness in grasping and expressing in a plan of action what it is that the historical moment demands of the masses. But it is those masses who must collectively take the necessary action if the revolution is going to be successful. Unquestionably people do tend to experience a general upheaval in their values in a revolutionary situation. Naturally enough, it is a widely varied range of motivations that is going to be effective in spurring individuals to action in differing degrees. But people will surely be very apt to find in the psychological remaking of human nature, which is foreseen, a definite further point of attraction of the socialist revolution for them. Or at least they will regard this remodeling as an acceptable price for resorting to socialism as the one way of dealing permanently and tolerably with the generalized societal breakdown manifested in the crisis of the revolutionary situation. It is of course possible for people to be dissatisfied with themselves the way they currently are—the way they currently are in their motivational makeup as well as in other ways.[3] In many respects the cooperative spirit of comradely solidarity fostered and developed structurally under socialism and, even more so, under communism can be seen as the realization of the brotherly love that humankind's religions have preached continually over the ages with such little effect. It is indeed possible for people to choose social conditions that they foresee will radically alter them, even conditions that will do so forcibly. Insofar as democracy has to do with the people ruling themselves, in matters great and small, a socialist revolution is a profoundly democratic happening. "It is," said Frederick Engels, "humanity's leap from the realm of necessity into the realm of freedom."[4]

Pause. Before going on with this excursion into democratic theory, I must get technical long enough to explore what it means to attribute a "desire" to somebody. I want to explore this at least far enough to yield some results that I shall use later. What I wish to say is something like this. That which people "desire" is that to which they are inclined to take "means."[5] What, then, are "means"? Whatever else they are, "means" are the things that people do because they believe that doing them will increase the chances of realizing their desires. Furthermore, whenever people do anything as a "means" to something else, they do or would in turn take means (or at least try to take means) to that first thing in the event of such further means seeming to them available and effective and necessary and not-too-onerous.[6] And so, people may be said in general to "desire" something just in case they are inclined to do things as a result of believing (*if* they do believe) that doing them will increase its chances of realization—provided that they are themselves things of which it is true to say these people are or would be inclined to do *other* things as a result of believing (*if* they do or did believe) that doing the latter would increase the chances of the former.[7] So much for the concept of what it is to desire something.

Returning to our discussion of democratic theory. Within bourgeois polemics, we find the accusation of being *un*democratic commonly leveled against anyone who claims to know what the real interests of the majority are better than the majority do themselves. In general, this sort of accusation is also leveled against any minority position, even if the minority stress that their aim, as democrats, is not to impose their policies on the majority, but to have them implemented only after the majority has been won over by rational arguments. Even so, they do claim to know the objective interests of most people better than those people themselves do. And that, so the accusation goes, is something inherently undemocratic.[8] From this arises what has been called "the democratic paradox": whose preposterous upshot is that, if the voters are committed democrats, they could never vote for any specific policy, because no voter could cast a vote in conscience without first ascertaining how most of the others were voting. Voting for any particular policy would express a personal judgment that that policy ought to be implemented, but, if the majority were to vote against implementing it, respect for democracy would then demand rather that it *ought not* to be implemented. Put this way, the reasoning can easily be seen to be sophistical, although just where the fallacy lies is a technical problem for separate investigation.[9]

For our purposes what matters is that none of us can seriously object to the distinction in principle between what people currently desire and what is objectively in their interests, if we reflect personally on the desires we ourselves have had in the past: Have there not been cases, for each of us, where we have desired something but later concluded for good reasons that we had been mistaken to desire it, in fact it was not something that was in our best interests after all? "Live and learn," says the English proverb; and, indeed, life itself is a learning process where we progressively learn, as we individually and collectively grow in practical wisdom, what the best goals to pursue really are—in short, we progressively learn what to desire. At any rate, such progressive learning does go on in favorable cases, and goes on to some extent, surely, in all of us. But a process of learning what to desire presupposes the possibility that our desires at a given time are susceptible to criticism and improvement. It is this process of learning that education, rightly conceived, is concerned with furthering. This is certainly one major reason why Marxists, indeed socialists and democrats, have always stressed the importance of mass education.[10]

Elitists, on the other hand, have tended naturally to feel more reluctance on this score. "What you don't know won't hurt you," says another English proverb, and, to the same effect, "Ignorance is bliss." Why stuff the masses' heads full of knowledge, so the argument runs, when it will make them discontented and unhappy with their lot?[11] Or will it rather make them come to appreciate how unhappy their lot already has been, without their realizing it?

This brings us to the subject of "paternalism." The "paternalist," X, claims to know what is best for someone else, Y, and arranges things accordingly, without reference to the wishes of Y. Cases do arise where this is both desirable and inevitable—for example, in our treatment of children, especially very young children. But, as they grow older, children become more and more capable of deciding things for themselves. With this growth in maturity, and sometimes outpacing it, comes a decline in their psychological dependence on the adults who care for them, that is, their trust in the judgment of those adults about what is best for them.

Is it ever rational to trust somebody else's judgment about what is best for us? Obviously the answer to this question is yes. We do or ought to defer cheerfully to the judgment of experts on what is the best course for us to take on such matters as diet, crop rotation, or how to avoid offending our visiting aunt. The experts in each case are the people who (in terms of nutrition, agronomy, or our aunt) have relevant knowledge that we do not. Our own role in decision-making may extend no further than making the decision that those experts are to be trusted, on the matters concerning their expertise. The trust of children in the actions and commands of adults on their behalf can be seen as a more or less rational judgment of this sort. Normally children will have had ample opportunity to discover empirically that the adults to whom they defer deeply care about them and know many important things that they do not.

Formally, this is comparable to the attitude of loyal subjects toward an autocratic monarch. But, in real life, how much evidence do those subjects have that their monarch does know better than they do what their best interests are—or, for that matter, cares enough about their interests to make even a minor personal sacrifice for the sake of their interests, if need be? This question, of course, applies equally to the regime of an individual autocrat or that of a governing oligarchy.

The case is different, however, when experts are freely and intelligently chosen by us to manage some of our affairs for us because it is not possible or not convenient to acquire all the know-how requisite for managing them ourselves or because we are too apathetic, fearful, or lazy to take on their management ourselves. Stewardship is by no means always without justification. It can in some cases be perfectly rational for us individually or collectively to put chosen individuals in charge of managing some of our affairs—subject always to their potential removal by us from such special responsibilities, either in accordance with formally laid-down procedures, or by more informal means. Even democratic theory must allow a definite place to stewardship, to the conscious willingness of the governed to entrust to the hands of only a few certain governmental responsibilities and, accordingly, authority. However little we may appreciate it, the "cult of personality" must be seen in this light, as well as the corresponding phenomenon involving a governing group. When a populace, or even a ruling class, feels too weak, divided, and fearful to govern in a more direct way, recourse may be had to a "strong man," such as Oliver Cromwell representing the beleaguered revolutionary English bourgeoisie in the mid-seventeenth century, or, in entirely different circumstances, a rightist Latin American military junta representing its own monopoly or *comprador* bourgeoisie in the twentieth century.[12]

But this is taking us away from our topic. The point is that even democratic theory must allow that relatively unsophisticated, insecure, or apathetic populations are, up to a point, quite legitimately more apt to entrust their governmental affairs to a stewardship of wider or narrower de facto limits than are relatively more advanced populations with a higher level of knowledge and sophistication, a greater sense of security and a more intense and widely diffused public-spiritedness. Outsiders often exhibit a utopian naïveté and a repulsive moralistic smugness when they captiously find fault at every turn with progressively struggling and developing democracies, which fail to actualize some theoretical ideal of democracy, however laudable in the abstract. The role of insiders, of course, is necessarily different.

But, whatever the good or bad justifications for it, there are always two cardinal defects in governmental and any other paternalism. The first is that people learn to do things on their own, above all through the practical experience of trial and error. The theory of swimming or of playing the piano will only take you so far. You will never be able to swim or to play the piano without actually doing it, of necessity at first relatively *badly*. And the same goes for decision-making. The time sometimes comes in the development of young persons when it is necessary to force them, much against their will, to take actions on their own, without that direct supervision on which they have been dependent hitherto. Afterwards, they will be grateful for the experience (or else ungratefully forgetful of whom they owe it to). Nevertheless, it is a cardinal defect in all paternalism that it stands in the way of such growth experiences, so necessary to maturation. This point applies, I think, to classes and whole populations as well as to individuals.

The second cardinal defect in all paternalism is equally obvious. Although varying in degree, it appears to be a universal feature of human nature to value freedom as such. This is not just the tautologous point that whatever one desires one desires to be free to obtain. In addition, there is a manifest tendency for people to value freedom in general, to value mastery over their own lives in general. *Desiderata* delivered up on a silver platter are often strikingly less delightful than the same things won through independent effort and exertion. All the delights of the independent quest for the attainment of their hearts' desires are of necessity foregone and lost by the intended beneficiaries of paternalism, however justified it may be in the circumstances. It is true that, just as people do tend positively to value freedom as such, in one area of life or another, they can also on occasion positively disvalue it as such—not just because they are willing to give it up to others so as to save the time and trouble of making decisions for themselves or to take advantage of others' greater expertise; but rather, sometimes, because psychologically they feel so insecure, even if they know better, or ought to, that they do not dare to decide things for themselves. In those areas of decision-making at any rate, they have remained, or have again become, like children. The perpetuation of such stunted human development can indeed be the price paid for paternalism, however justified it may be in the particular circumstances.

And so, paternalism should be seen as an ineliminable element in human life, but not without very real dangers. In this respect it is like freedom. For our purposes, the paternalist, as well as the expert consultant and the advocate of a temporarily unpopular public policy option, are all committed to the claim that they know better than the majority of the people concerned what the objective interests of those people really are. But if people's objective interests then, rightly understood, are not quite identifiable with those people's actual desires, just what in fact are they? The distinction relied on in the preceding was the distinction between the uninformed desire and the informed desire, which makes it natural to think of defining what is in people's (objective) interests as what they *would* on balance desire *if* informed of all the relevant nonnormative truths (whether concerning empirical facts or the results of a priori calculations); the "relevant" truths here include all those truths and only those truths knowledge of which would make a difference in those people's desires, whether by creating new desires, by destroying old desires or by altering their different desires' relative strengths.[13]

But how, then, does such knowledge influence our desires? One obvious way is by informing us of means to what we desire, which we then may come to want also, and of unwanted effects resulting or capable of resulting from whatever it is we currently desire, which may make us stop desiring it. This last outcome can be seen as flowing from increased knowledge of means, because if we already wanted to avoid a certain effect, the discovery of its tendency to result from something that we have hitherto desired can be seen as influencing us toward a decision to avoid this hitherto desired thing, as a means towards the avoidance of that effect.

In certain cases, though, our failure to desire something, or to desire to avoid it, is due not merely to a lack of information about its effects, but to our having no idea whatsoever of it. John Locke maintained that nobody could ever know just the way a pineapple tastes without having tasted one.[14] And, without having the idea of pineapple taste, the hedonic desirability of experiencing that taste could not be known, so that before having that experience we could not specifically desire it or see it as in our interests. Of course, others could credibly inform us, speaking as relative experts, that we probably would be glad to have tasted a pineapple, even if they could not describe in words the precise experiential quality of the flavor in question, and so could not imbue us with a desire specifically for it. Less plausibly, it might be maintained that the specific experiential "flavor" of life in an authentically caring, unhierarchical community of comradely cooperation could never be truly known by people who have never actually lived in such a community, so that it is necessary, even logically necessary, that one actually get out of the bourgeois way of life in all of its facets, to appreciate fully how much in one's objective interests it is to do so. A more likely explanation for the sense of revelation that the actual experience of a new and more satisfying way of life can provide is the way it can bring home to us the practical feasibility of bringing together and intensifying some already cherished modes of interrelating personally. The point for our purposes is that, if having certain ideas or concepts is a necessary condition of desiring to secure—or to avoid—the things that they are the ideas or concepts of, then having any information about those things is a sufficient condition of possessing the necessary ideas or concepts. Thus, whenever the sole reason why we did not desire something—or did not desire to avoid it—was our failure to possess the specific idea or concept of it, then this lack would be made good, and our desires modified accordingly, if only information were to be added to our knowledge about the means of securing or avoiding it, or about how securing or avoiding it could serve as a means to other things. Here too, then, the modifications in our desires that would result from the acquisition of any new information would be produced by the acquisition specifically of information as to the means of accomplishing things.

However, there are also quite different ways in which the acquisition of new information can affect our desires. Not only is it not logically necessary, it is not even true, that all the ways in which knowledge can influence people are rational ways. If a person has a passion for X and then learns of some association between X and Y (other than X potentially resulting from Y), this may psychologically cause the person to start having a passion for Y—"by association," as we say. If a certain individual were to be fully conscious, for example, of the pain and suffering that go on in hospitals, then the individual might develop a phobia about hospitals, a passionate desire to stay away from them—and not merely, that is, a desire to stay out of them by staying healthy. With such a phobia, the individual would have a sufficient bona fide interest in staying out of hospitals that it would take a somewhat more serious need to justify going into a hospital than would be enough to justify it in the absence of the phobia: The mental anguish that would result just from entering the hospital would have to count as one consideration in favor of the individual's staying out. However, it surely does not follow at all from this example that, as the individual now is, without a full consciousness of the pain and suffering that go on in hospitals, and consequently without any specific hospital phobia, that the individual has already an objective interest now in staying away from any hospital (given that entering a hospital for a brief period would not be enough to make that individual become fully conscious of all the pain and suffering around and, as a result, become seriously hospital phobic).

In this example, the pain and suffering associated with hospitals does not really result, in the main, just from being in a hospital, and so an absence of pain and suffering is not for the most part a bona fide potential effect of not being there, despite the correlation that exists. We cannot consider something to be in any person's interests merely because that person would desire it if acquainted with any body of information extensive enough to include certain causally irrelevant facts that nonetheless could somehow psychologically influence the person to desire that thing. Presumably, all those things and only those things are actually in our (objective) interests, which we would on balance desire if apprised of so much information about their potential effects that no additional information about their potential effects would modify our desires further. This I propose as a definition of objective interests.[15] It is to be understood that information about the potential effects of any action we might take, such as the action of attempting to bring about a certain result, must include all the relevant facts about whether the action would or could succeed. By the same token, information about the potential effects of something's being brought about, or coming about, will likewise have to include the relevant facts regarding whatever this would in the circumstances obtaining effectively prevent from being brought about, or from coming about, and all of the potential effects of that.

From what I have said, you will have gathered that I do not accept the idea that the attractiveness of the socialist, or anyway the communist, way of life is capable of being appreciated only by the "new man" or "new woman" that the new social order produces. For the most part people in bourgeois society do not so much actively dislike the idea of a thoroughly cooperative style of life, as consider it, rather, to be a utopian dream. If working people are sometimes slow to experience a sense of solidarity with their fellow workers, it is not because of any personal commitment to selfishness in principle. Rather, their daily conditions of life and work have concealed what they have in common, in the way of objective interests especially, with these fellow workers of theirs. Indeed, they may have short-term interests, which really are at variance with the interests of others. Craft divisions and privileges, racism, sexism, and national chauvinism can all effectively block off a clear perception of common exploitation and common class interests. But life itself can teach the interconnection of different struggles, and few will be even tempted to make any conscious sacrifice of their own objective interests, once they see them distinctly, merely for the sake of preserving selfish divisions. If people do tend to be selfish in bourgeois society, it is not because they profoundly like being that way. Most people, even in bourgeois society, I think, would prefer to be unselfish people in a largely unselfish society rather than be just the way they are.

It is an empirical fact of cardinal importance, however, that radical self-change is not, in general, achievable by sheer will power alone but requires a changed social environment, perhaps over several generations. Even the most ardent socialists living in bourgeois society might have to admit that they themselves would be unable to reform their own characters completely if they awoke one morning to find that communism had finally arrived. It is one thing to desire an unselfish motivational makeup, no matter how sincerely; it is a different thing actually to have it. Other persons, less committed to socialism, might sincerely value unselfishness in the abstract, but timidly turn away from the protracted inner stress and turmoil that self-change would undoubtedly necessitate. Still others might be so inveterately bourgeois as actually to prefer a selfish and competitive personality and a way of social life to match. Certainly, theorists exist who do verbalize such a preference. Such persons, in short, really do dislike "strawberries and cream," even though changed environmental conditions will in time predictably make most of them at least start instead to like it. Is "strawberries and cream" (i.e., the cooperative socialistic or communistic way of life) really in their objective interests? No, I think we must answer. But their interests are outweighed by the interests of the majority. In any case, I am thinking here merely of a segment of that well-fed minority living in the partly developed and partly under developed capitalist world who themselves do not seem set to gain anything, from a personally selfish point of view, through a socialist social revolution. Even many of them will eventually be in danger of losing the security of their present comfortable position in society as a result of the all-encompassing crisis situation that precedes a social revolution. And, presumedly, nearly everyone, even from a purely selfish point of view, has an objective and subjective interest in personal survival, which is severely threatened now by the possibility of worldwide nuclear war, a possibility scarcely capable of persisting indefinitely: for clearly the ever-present possibility of thermonuclear war must eventually come to an end, either in consequence of real Armageddon or in consequence of worldwide socialism.

I have proposed that we should consider something to be in a person's objective interests just in case that person would on balance desire it if sufficiently informed about its potential effects. I believe this formula is able to handle the sorts of cases brought up in the literature. For example, James Griffin writes:

> If I knew all the discriminations of flavors *premier cru* clarets allow, I might then prefer them to the soda pop I now love. But you do me no favour by giving me grand clarets now, unless it is part of some well conceived education.[16]

Whether a protracted process of wine-tasting "education" would really be worth all the necessary trouble and expense or not, Griffin's point here presumedly is that the kind of taste experience—let us call it "E_2"—that Griffin would be able to get from *premier cru* clarets might be more satisfying than the kind of taste-experience—call it "E_1"—which he would derive if he drank such clarets today, and that the kind of taste experience that he gets from soda pop (for simplicity, let's assume it constant) is a kind of experience more satisfying than E_1, but less satisfying than E_2. Given the alternative between (I) drinking grand clarets with a palate "uneducated" in wine-tasting and (II) drinking soda pop with a palate "uneducated" in wine-tasting, even an "educated" Griffin (sufficiently informed as to the taste-effects on him of drinking grand clarets with the "education" and without it) presumedly would prefer option (II)—that is, in abstraction, of course, from any "educational" benefit foreseeable as maybe resulting eventually from option (I).[17] And so, by our criterion, it is the soda pop, and not the clarets, which it is in Griffin's objective interests to drink, the way he is now (any potential net benefit from a wine-tasting "education" aside).[18]

A more everyday sort of case would perhaps be that of means, which a person does not know how to use. Even an easy-to-operate device might be of no value without the necessary instructions for its use. Of course, I might well want the device for my current task in hand if I did have the requisite know-how, that is, if I had sufficient information as to what the potential effects were of using the device effectively. But it does not follow that in my present ignorance having the device would in any way advance my objective interest, for, even if informed, I might not *particularly* prefer possession of the device without the knowledge of how to use it (or any prospect of getting that knowledge) over the possession on my part of neither the device nor the requisite knowledge.[19]

In the case of the wine-tasting savvy necessary to discriminate the flavors of *premier cru* clarets, we stopped to notice that acquiring it might or might not be worth the trouble. Not only is the acquisition of knowledge not necessarily in all cases advantageous at any cost, but there are some cases where coming to know the truth (no matter how easily) may in fact be a positively bad thing for the person concerned. A Marxist intellectual's Catholic mother lay dying. "Do you now understand that God and the after-life are real, after all?" she asked, hoping against hope for some reassurance. "Yes, Mother, I think I can see it now," he replied, lying excusably. It is evident that to "humor" people in this sort of way does and does not show respect for them. It shows concern for their feelings, but not concern for their actual desires, for in this case, they do not have any desire as such to be told lies, nor even any desire as such to be given pleasant answers irrespective of the truth. To treat people in this way is certainly paternalistic. Sometimes, no doubt, it is justifiable. Whatever the necessary conditions are for its justifiability, one of them undoubtedly is this, that the individual in question, if sufficiently informed about potential effects, would probably on balance prefer such paternalistic treatment in the existing circumstances, that is, would probably on balance be truly sorry to know the truth.

After this discussion of how people's interests and their actual desires can conflict, it is time to see how it is that what a person predominantly desires, on balance, and what is in a person's long-term objective interests, on balance, cannot really in the last resort conflict. Not really in the last resort, that is. In view of our earlier account of what it is to desire something, and our later account of what it is for something to be in somebody's objective interests, it is clear that each of us has an actual desire right now (at least a desire in the abstract) to bring to pass anything that is in our objective interests—only, we do not always know how; for, when it comes to something that is in our interests, we do not always know what it is. The point is that anything that is in our objective interests is something that we would desire if sufficiently informed about its potential effects. Accordingly, the possession of sufficient information about something to enable us to know that its realization would be a means of furthering our interests must necessarily make it something to which we would be inclined to take means if we knew of possible means that seemed to us available and necessary and effective and not-too-onerous. But, in view of what it means to have a desire, anything like that is something that we already do desire, although perhaps we do so only in the abstract. When we do not know what our interests are specifically, we do not have any desire for the actual ends in question under their own specific descriptions, but only—whether articulated or not—under the general description of things that are in our interests. Not only do we in each case have a desire, at least in the abstract, for that which is objectively in our interests; it also may be said that on balance we desire the realization of this, whatever it might be, predominantly. For, if we were sufficiently informed of its potential effects as well as the potential effects of any competing or conflicting ends, we would then prefer, on balance, the realization of it. That follows directly from what it means for something to be objectively in our interests.

The point is certainly worth repeating and stressing that it is no valid conclusion from this that people already have a concrete desire for anything that is in their interests. And it is likewise worth repeating and stressing that there is no automatic justification here for trying to force upon people whatever is seen as being in their interests objectively, on the grounds that "they do really desire it, after all." In the first place, such coercion may block a valuable learning process of trial-and-error, which it is by no means in their interests to miss. Secondly, coercion, even necessary coercion, always blocks people to some extent from liberty, something for which human beings tend to have a desire, very often a desire immune to being extinguished by any acquisition of causal information; that is to say, liberty as such is very often objectively in people's interests.

I began by remarking that Marxists are concerned with people's interests normatively and also in our sociological class analysis. But why should Marxist (or any) social science concern itself with people's interests as opposed to their desires (their "perceived" subjective interests), given that the only kind of desire people can have for what is in their objective but not their subjective interests is necessarily a purely abstract kind of desire? Are not all the motivations effectively responsible for people's actions specific concrete desires for different things? To this objection there are two answers. In the first place, knowing what is in a group of people's objective interests is not, indeed, the same as knowing what actual concrete desires are currently motivating them, but to know their objective interests is to know by what desires they will tend to be motivated, insofar as accurate cause-and-effect knowledge does come their way. To unearth an ever-present tendency in the events of the world, imperfectly realized though it may be, is without doubt to make an authentic contribution to science. In the second place, even the unspecific desire for the advancing of their interests in the abstract does practically motivate people in one definite way: it motivates them to seek out new knowledge of the world so as to learn better how to proceed and thus how to live.

Knowledge and theory, says Marxism, primarily exist for the sake of practice. I hope this paper will have helped to clarify our picture of the roles of these things within social life.[20]

Notes

1. In *The Poverty of Philosophy*, Karl Marx and Frederick Engels, *Collected Works*, volume 6 (London: Lawrence and Wishart, 1976), p. 211.

2. V. I. Lenin, *Collected Works*, volume 4 (Moscow: Progress Publishers, 1972), p. 236.

3. Marx and Engels in *The German Ideology* (1846): "The tireless propaganda carried on by these [communist] proletarians, their daily discussions among themselves, sufficiently prove how little they themselves want to remain 'as of old,' and how little they want people to remain 'as of old'.... They know too well that only under changed circumstances will they cease to be 'as of old,' and therefore they are determined to change these circumstances at the first opportunity. In revolutionary activity the changing of oneself coincides with the changing of circumstances" (Marx and Engels, *Collected Works*, volume 5, p. 214). Cf. Marx's third Thesis on Feuerbach (original version, 1845): "The coincidence of the changing of circumstances and of human activity or self-change can be conceived and rationally understood only as *revolutionary practice*" (*Collected Works*, volume 5, p. 4).

4. *Anti-Dühring* (Moscow: Foreign Languages Publishing House, 1962), Part III, chapter 2, second to last paragraph.

5. More formally: to say an individual I is "inclined" to take means to an end E is to say that either I does take, or at least tried to take, means to E, or else I *would* take, or at least try to take, means to E but for the fact that none seems to I available or none seems to I effective or none seems to I necessary, or but for the fact that either I is taking, or at least trying to take, means to something other than E, or else I would take, or at least try to take, such means but for the fact that none seems to I available or none seems to I effective or none seems to I necessary.

6. In his paper, "Freedom and Action," R. M. Chisholm cites a case in which somebody does something because he believes it will increase the chances of realizing a desire of his though *not* as a means to such realization.

Suppose, for example: (i) a certain man desires to inherit a fortune; (ii) he believes that, if he kills his uncle, then he will inherit a fortune; and (iii) this belief and this desire agitate him so severely that he drives excessively fast, with the result that he accidentally runs over and kills a pedestrian who, unknown to the nephew, was none other than the uncle. In *Freedom and Determinism*, Keith Lehrer, ed. (New York: Random House, 1966), p. 30.

In the case imagined, the nephew certainly does not kill his uncle to inherit a fortune even though he does kill him as a result of a belief that killing him will in fact bring it about that he inherits a fortune. Nor is it even essential to the example, for our purposes, that the nephew should actually desire to inherit a fortune. He might, indeed, really desire not to inherit a fortune (because that would oblige him to pay off some old debts to creditors whom he detests), and it might be that he then becomes agitated as a result of this upon realizing that one of the pedestrians he keeps almost hitting in the fog could well be his rich uncle. Or again, it might be that he is completely indifferent to whether he inherits a fortune or not, but so abhors the act of murder as to become extremely agitated when made to realize that killing the uncle would bring him more wealth than would be necessary to motivate many others to do as much. In all of these cases, the killing does take place as a result of a belief on the killer's part that it will bring him the legacy, and yet the legacy has not motivated the killing; the killing was not done as a means to securing it. The point, however, is that in none of these cases does the nephew take means (or even try to take means) to the killing, and that in none of these cases is this merely because no means are regarded as being available and effective and necessary and not-too-onerous.

7. This last proviso is added to exclude the sort of mere "by-product" result exemplified by the cases discussed in note 6. The five sentences given in the text here do not purport to provide a noncircular analysis of the concept of "desire." For our purposes it is quite enough if they correctly set out (even though not altogether in noncircular terms) a genuine necessary and sufficient condition of somebody's desiring something. In one respect, however, it is necessary to note that the sense of "desire" that is involved here does deviate from the ordinary sense of the term in English. In the ordinary sense of the English verb, one is not said to "desire" anything that with full certitude one considers completely impossible of attainment, such as (for most of us) a change in the past, say. Ordinarily, one is said only to "wish" for such things, not to "desire" them. But here the word "desire" is being used deliberately in a broad sense, inclusive of all such "wishes."

8. Howard R. Smith, of the University of Georgia College of Business Administration, penned a classic *reductio ad absurdum* of this (presumedly unconsciously) in his monograph, *Democracy and the Public Interest* (Athens: University of Georgia, 1960):

> Because it is so fundamentally undemocratic to tell people what they want before they have been asked, *no analysis of what is in the public interest that does not rely heavily on a democratic decision-making process can be taken seriously* (p. 27);

Here again an important summary statement can be abstracted—although it is actually only another way of saying that a definition of the public interest, to be taken seriously, must rely heavily on a democratic decision-making process: *no analysis of public interest in terms of concrete policies as such is entitled to be taken seriously as a definition of THE public interest.* Either the analyst is bringing in Absolutes from outside the democratic process, in which case he is no democrat; or he is endeavoring to tilt the balance of the governmental process in favor of his own policy preferences, thereby becoming simply another party in interest (pp. 20–30). [Presumedly by an "Absolute" here Smith means any normative idea other than a procedural one.]

Here, then, is the paradox of democracy. Because there is no set of policies equally in their interest of all the people, and because the ideological dilemma requiring that power be shared by individuals and groups who do not desire to share it makes it necessary that preferred policies nevertheless be supported in the name of the entire community, the idea of a common good as an element in the myth of democracy performs the function of disguising the fact that the decisions made are ultimately sanctioned by power. In short, the concept of public interest is insisted upon precisely because (as applied to particular public policies) there is no such thing (p. 25).

9. See "A Paradox in the Theory of Democracy" by Richard Wollheim, in *Philosophy, Politics and Society* (2nd series), Peter Laslett and W. G. Runciman, eds. (Oxford: Basil Blackwell, 1962), pp. 71–87; and "An Alleged Paradox in the Theory of Democracy" by D. Goldstick, *Philosophy and Public Affairs* 2, no. 2 (Winter 1973): 181–89.

10. Nor have Marxists been willing to accept that lack of technical expertise would have to permanently exclude mass participation in even the relative details of governmental decision-making. For instance, Lenin on the eve of the October Revolution:

We are not utopians. We know that an unskilled labourer or a cook cannot immediately get on with the job of state administration.... We demand that *training* in the work of state administration be conducted by class-conscious workers and soldiers and that this training be begun at once, i.e., that a *beginning* be made at once in training all the working people, all the poor, for this work. ("Can the Bolsheviks Retain State Power?", V. I. Lenin, *Collected Works*, volume 26, p. 113).

11. In at least the following paragraph from Bernard Mandeville's famous eighteenth-century attack on mass education in Britain ("An Essay on Charity and Charity Schools") the hypocrisy is winningly transparent:

It being granted then, that abundance of Work is to be done, the next thing which I think to be likewise undeniable is, that the more cheerfully it is done the better, as well for those that perform it as for the rest of the society. To be happy is to be pleas'd, and the less Notion a Man has of a better way of Living, the more content he'll be with his own; and on the other hand, the greater a Man's Knowledge and Experience is in the World, the more exquisite the Delicacy of his Taste, and the more consummate judge he is of things in general, certainly the more difficult it will be to please him. I would not advance any thing that is Barbarous or Inhuman: but when a Man enjoys himself, Laughs and Sings, and in his Gesture and Behaviour shows me all the tokens of Content and Satisfaction, I Pronounce him happy, and have nothing to do with his Wit or Capacity. I never enter into the Reasonableness of his Mirth, at least I ought not to judge of it by my own Standard, and argue from the Effect which the thing that makes him merry would have upon me. At that rate a Man that hates Cheese must call me a Fool for loving blue Mold. *De gustibus non est disputandum* is as true in a Metaphorical as it is in the Literal Sense, and the greater the distance is between People as to their Condition, their Circumstances and manner of Living, the less capable they are of judging of one anothers Troubles or Pleasures." (*The Fable of the Bees: or, Private Vices, Public Benefits*, by Bernard Mandeville, volume I (Oxford: Clarendon Press, 1924), pp. 314–15.

12. See Karl Marx, *The Eighteenth Brumaire of Louis Bonaparte*. At the time this paragraph was first written, bureaucratic oligarchies of Marxists were a prominent form of working-class rule in a number of countries—and in some of them this still holds good today (July 4, 1990). In others, the Marxist political oligarchies collapsed in short order with the withdrawal of popular support and have been replaced with governments bent on restoring capitalism. But turning the historical clock back like that will guessably prove to be easier said than done—present wishes and intentions (widespread as they are) aside—when it really comes down to moving massively against working people's basic economic interests, and for the moment what we actually have in a number of countries are procapitalist governments in practice administering socialism. Similarly in England before 1688 and France before 1830 there were (initially supported or at least tolerated) ideologically pro-feudal governments administering capitalism. They too exhibit the phenomenon of political "stewardship" discussed in this paragraph. No wonder Marxists combine their claim that a country's state fundamentally reflects the interests and will of its ruling class with an insistence also upon the greater or lesser "relative autonomy" of state politics in relation to the underlying economic reality.

13. Cf. "Assessing Utilities," by D. Goldstick, *Mind* 80 N.S., no. 320 (October 1971):535; and *A Theory of the Good and the Right*, by Richard B. Brandt (Oxford: Oxford University Press, 1979). The purpose of Brandt's book differs from our purposes here, because it is not people's interests with which Brandt is primarily concerned, but rather "what a 'rational' person might want and choose to do" and "how to criticize our basic motivations" (preface, page v; the book does, however, devote pages 328–31 to exploring inconclusively the concept of "self-interest"). Brandt, in accordance with the primary focus of his inquiry, is prepared to stigmatize a prejudice against something, caused by a conditioned psychological association of it with something else, as being an "irrational" aversion if it would be curable by sufficiently intense and prolonged attention to factual information contradicting any notion of a real connection existing between the two, even though there had not actually been any belief in the existence of such a connection (pp. 11–12). But, from the interests standpoint of this essay, while it may be in people's interests to be cured of such an aversion if this should readily be possible, it

does not follow that in the meanwhile they have an interest in acting, or being treated, as if they were cured already. (Brandt himself makes a point like this, in effect, on page 161.) Secondly, unlike the first cited reference, Brandt restricts himself for his purposes to "all available information," understood as "the propositions accepted by the science of the agent's day, plus factual propositions justified by publicly accessible evidence ... and the principles of logic" (p. 13), in contrast "with the beliefs an omniscient being might have, beliefs in all true propositions, since we do not know the identity of such beliefs and can hardly use them as a tool of criticism" (p. 12). From the interests standpoint pertinent to our purposes here, the case is different. On the one hand, something can hardly be in our true interests merely because current science erroneously considers it also to have a certain effect. On the other hand, very often a scientific inquiry is at least partly motivated by the aim of finding out certain things precisely in order to be able to determine what is and what is not in fact in our interests. (By contrast with what is in our interests, however, what probably is in our interests does depend upon the actually available evidence only.)

14. *An Essay Concerning Human Understanding*, book 2, chapter 1, section 6.

15. There is no intention here to suggest that what an individual would desire if apprised of some particular information is necessarily any different from what that individual does desire currently. Secondly, just as what any persons are said to "desire," in the extended sense used here (see note 7), can be something that they are utterly convinced is absolutely unattainable, note should be taken of the consequence that such a supposed—or, for that matter, a genuine—impossibility can be described accordingly as something in their "objective interests," in the sense defined here.

16. "Modern Utilitarianism," *Revue internationale de philosophie*, no. 141, 1982, fasc. 3, pp. 334–5.

17. We here have an instance of "iterated counter-factuality," so to speak. Regarding an individual who happens to possess certain information, the question can be put: Would this person rather be without that information and in situation S or without that information and in situation S'? Concerning such an individual who actually does not possess the information, it is possible to ask: If this person did possess that information what would the answer to the first question be?

18. Reminiscent of the strawberries-and-cream example for its contrast of personal preferences before and after a process of psychological transformation is Griffin's sensible discussion in an earlier paper of the following case: "My son now hates piano practice but someday will want to play well. Is he better off irked now and pleased later, or irked later and pleased now?... But the intra-personal case of two rankings, mine now and mine later, is formally similar to an interpersonal case of two rankings, mine and yours." "On Life's Being Valuable," *Dialectics and Humanism* 8, no. 2 (Spring 1981): 55.

19. The desire for X-under-conditions-C in preference to Y-under-conditions-C, where conditions C are plainly unattainable, at least in the short run, is more aptly called a "wish" than a "desire," in the ordinary English senses of these words; but, as noted above (note 7), the term "desire" is being used consciously here in a wider sense than the ordinary one.

20. Twenty friends and colleagues were good enough to offer comments and criticisms in response to earlier versions of this paper. Where I have not followed their suggestions, that cannot be their fault! But may our ongoing debates continue to be fruitful. On the other hand, I am indebted for particular improvements incorporated in the present text to Derek Allen, Jerry Cohen, Jay Drydyk, Oliver Iwuchukwu, David Leadbeater and (especially) András Gedö—none of whom, of course, are responsible for the result, or even necessarily in general agreement with it.

Index

About the Contributors

John P. Burke has taught philosophy at the University of Washington and the University of Puget Sound. Coeditor of *Marxism and the Good Society* (1981), he has also published on topics in social and political philosophy. He is a Senior Research Associate at the William O. Douglas Institute. His research interests are in ethics, Marxist theory, and political philosophy.

Arthur DiQuattro has taught political theory at Texas A & M University, Indiana University, Reed College, and University of Washington. He is a Senior Research Associate at the William O. Douglas Institute. He has published on topics in political philosophy and is writing a book on liberal and Marxist theories of justice.

Iring Fetscher is professor emeritus of political science and social philosophy at the J. W. Goethe University Frankfurt/Main. Recent publications include *Utopien, Illusionen, Hoffnungen–zur politischen Kultur in Deutschland* (1990), *Toleranz–von der Unentbehrlichkeit seiner kleinen Tugend für die Demokratie* (1990), and *Überlebensbedingungen der Menschheit–ist der Fortschritt noch zu retten?* (1991). His research interests include the history of political theory, democratic theory and totalitarian ideologies, and moral philosophy.

Danny Goldstick is professor of philosophy at the University of Toronto. His research interests include Marxism and ethics. He is currently working on a philosophical study provisionally entitled *Reason, Truth, and Reality.*

Timothy Kaufman-Osborn is professor of politics at Whitman College. He is the author of *Politics/Sense/Experience: A Pragmatic Inquiry into the Promise of Democracy* (1991). He is working on a book tentatively entitled *Political Artifacts* that enlists feminist and neopragmatist perspectives to explore the political import of diverse fabricated objects.

Lyman H. Legters is professor emeritus at the University of Washington and Senior Fellow at the William O. Douglas Institute. Coeditor of *Marxism and the Good Society* (1981), among his more recent publications is *Eastern Europe: Transformation and Revolution, 1945-1991* (1992).

Mihailo Marković is a member of the Serbian Academy of Sciences and Arts and maintains research interests in the philosophy of the social sciences, political philosophy, ethics, and East European studies. He is the author of several books including *From Affluence to Praxis: Philosophy and Social Criticism* (1974), *Democratic Socialism: Theory and Practice* (1982), and *Dialectical Theory of Meaning* (1984).

Ron Perrin is professor of political theory at the University of Montana. He is the author of *Max Scheler's Concept of the Person: An Ethics of Humanism* (1991), and several essays on the role of the humanities in public policy. He is writing a book on a theory of democratic pluralism.

Philip Resnick is professor of political science at the University of British Columbia. His two most recent books are *The Masks of Proteus: Canadian Reflections on the State* (1990), and *Toward a Canada-Quebec Union* (1991). His current research interest lies in democratic theory.

Joseph M. Schwartz teaches political science at Temple University. His book, *The Permanence of the Political* (forthcoming, 1994) advances a democratic critique of the radical tradition's desire to transcend the need for politics in a good society. He is working on a second book dealing with the problem of social solidarity in fragmented, inegalitarian Western polities.

The **William O. Douglas Institute** engages in research and publications concerned with contemporary social problems.